THE KOCH PAPERS

My Fight Against Anti-Semitism

Edward I. Koch

with

Rafael Medoff

First published in 2008 by
PALGRAVE MACMILLAN™
175 Fifth Avenue, New York, N.Y. 10010 and
Houndmills, Basingstoke, Hampshire, England RG21 6XS.
Companies and representatives throughout the world.

PALGRAVE MACMILLAN is the global academic imprint of the
Palgrave Macmillan division of St. Martin's Press, LLC and of Palgrave
Macmillan Ltd. Macmillan® is a registered trademark in the United States,
United Kingdom and other countries. Palgrave is a registered trademark in
the European Union and other countries.

ISBN-13: 978-0-230-60102-4
ISBN-10: 0-230-60102-2

Library of Congress Cataloging-in-Publication Data

Koch, Ed, 1924–
 The Koch papers : my fight against anti-Semitism / Edward I. Koch ; with
Rafael Medoff.
  p. cm.
 Includes bibliographical references and index.
 ISBN 0–230–60102–2
 1. Antisemitism—History—20th century. 2. Antisemitism—New York
(State)—New York. 3. New York (N.Y.)—Politics and government—20th
century. 4. Holocaust, Jewish (1939–1945)—Influence. I. Medoff, Rafael,
1959– II. Title.
 DS145.K54 2008
 305.892′4073092—dc22

                                                              2007027285

A catalogue record of the book is available from the British Library.

Design by Letra Libre

First edition: March 2008

10 9 8 7 6 5 4 3 2 1

Printed in the United States of America.

CONTENTS

ACKNOWLEDGMENTS

Rafael Medoff and I are grateful to Richard Lieberman, president, and Douglas Di Carlo, archivist, of the La Guardia and Wagner Archives at La Guardia Community College, and Martin Zimmerman, reference librarian at the La Guardia Community College Library, for their invaluable assistance in locating documents in the Edward I. Koch Collection that were used in this book. We are equally thankful to Benyamin "Buddy" Korn for his assistance.

When I was mayor, I had a speechwriting team that included Clark Whelton, Kevin McAuliffe, and Atra Baer. Atra, my top assistant, was the daughter of the famous Hearst columnist and humorist Bugs Baer. Terrific. Mary Jo Shapiro, sister of Paul Crotty, also worked in our office. A fine writer. Also, Diane Fisher, former assistant editor of the *Village Voice*. And Michael Smith, another *Voice* writer, who also worked in our press office. This team was brilliant. My speeches included material that I brought to the attention of the speechwriters and material that I included as a result of what I like to believe was inspiration at the time of the event, which permitted me to speak extemporaneously. My speechwriters' work was seamless with mine. I am very grateful to them.

My assistants Jody Getman and Mary Garrigan were invaluable in their patient assistance with all stages of the process leading to the publication of this book.

Wendy Schmalz, our agent, was indefatigable in shepherding this book from drawing board to reality. We are grateful, as well, to the editorial staff of Palgrave Macmillan for their assistance.

Edward I. Koch
New York City, September 2007

PREFACE

Learning the lessons of the Holocaust, including the need to confront and combat anti-Semitism, is one of the greatest moral challenges facing the civilized world today. This is not merely because anti-Jewish bigotry, like all racism, is immoral and should be fought as a matter of principle. Rather it has become a matter of special urgency because the war against the Jews is an inseparable part of the broader war against Western civilization. The Islamist terror onslaught against the West is being waged simultaneously on numerous fronts, and Jews, both in Israel and the Diaspora, are among its targets. The hijacked planes that crashed into the World Trade Center and the bombs that ripped through the Madrid train station are ultimately no different in their purpose from the rockets that Hezbollah fired at Haifa or the shooting attack on the Jewish Federation in Seattle.

Not that contemporary anti-Semitism is some recent creation of Muslim extremists. Until its collapse in 1991, it was the Soviet Union that was the world's worst post–World War II persecutor of Jews and exporter of anti-Semitic propaganda. Here in the United States, by contrast, we have always faced a different kind of anti-Semitism, one that has been mostly rhetorical and that has only rarely turned violent. But in recent decades, it has emerged from new and unexpected sources, such as the extreme radical wing of the African American community, and that has posed its own particular challenges.

Those challenges are explored in the essays, speeches, and memoranda that comprise this collection. We have brought together a broad sampling of what I have said or written in recent decades about anti-Semitism, both at home and abroad, and about the Holocaust. My appointment in 2004 to the U.S. Holocaust Memorial Council, the agency that governs the U.S. Holocaust Memorial Museum, stimulated me to more fully explore the links between the experience of the Holocaust and the ongoing struggle against the anti-Semitic individuals as well as regimes that dream of perpetrating a second Holocaust.

Neither my principles nor my fighting spirit has wavered over the years, as the battle against anti-Semitism has taken new forms and spread to new fronts. My hope is that the lessons to be learned from the Holocaust, and from past battles against anti-Semites around the world and against those who intentionally or unintentionally assist them will enable people of goodwill to more effectively combat and deter the haters of today and tomorrow.

Edward I. Koch
New York City, September 2007

INTRODUCTION

Pete Hamill

A SOLDIER OF MEMORY

On May 8, 1945, the city of New York erupted in tears and joy. On my street in Brooklyn, people danced to a crazy mixture of Glenn Miller, a million church bells and a baritone growl of fog horns from the harbor. Women beat huge spoons against metal pots from the fire escapes and behind some of them, you could see the gold stars in their windows. A spontaneous block party erupted and all the bars rolled beer kegs into the street and set up tables. The beer was free. I saw my father coming across the street—not looking, for there was no traffic. He was swinging his wooden left leg, the one that had kept him out of the war. And, pumping a fist, he said: "We beat that son of a bitch Hitler. We beat him. We beat him."

I was six weeks short of turning ten, and I had never seen anything like that day in my entire life. The war had been there—in the streets, in my head—for a very long time. We heard about it every morning and evening on the radio. We could read about it in the *Daily News* and the *Brooklyn Eagle*, and most of us learned geography at school by studying the daily war maps in the papers. The war was in the comics too, in *Terry and the Pirates* and *Gasoline Alley* in the *News*, and in the comic books about Batman and Captain America fighting saboteurs, and in the movies we watched in the dark of the Sanders, the RKO Prospect and the Minerva.

Now it was over. All the young men from our neighborhood (we called them "the big guys") would be coming home. At least from Europe. There were still some big guys in the Pacific, and that wasn't over yet. But "we" were winning. Soon it would all be over. And when the big guys were back, they would include the ballplayers. Reese and Reiser would be back in Ebbets Field. DiMaggio would stroll out to center field in Yankee Stadium. My father said so. It must be true. The war was in the bottom of the eighth inning, and we only had to play the ninth, out there, at the far end of the Pacific.

Then, about a month after that great roaring day, I went to the movies with some of my friends. I think we went to the RKO Prospect. I don't remember exactly, nor do I remember the movies that played in the double feature. I do remember the newsreel. It showed me, for the first time, the true nature of that son of a bitch Hitler and his Nazis. For there on the screen, in stark black and white, were the first newsreels from Buchenwald. I saw the gaunt faces and the hollow eyes. I saw the emaciated bodies. I saw the tattoos on arms and wrists. I saw the piled corpses, too, arms extended at odd angles, the shoveled corpses of dead humans who resembled those who still lived.

I awoke twice that night because the gray bony dead were staring in anger at me from the graves. My mother comforted me. I was filled with questions: who *did* this and *why?* And my mother talked about bigotry (as a Catholic immigrant from Belfast she knew the subject well) and its deadly evil but I still could not understand. On the walls of our tenement kitchen, there were two pictures: the Sacred Heart of Jesus, and Franklin D. Roosevelt. When I was about eight, I was convinced that if God could talk to us, He would sound like President Roosevelt. But the footage from Buchenwald made me think other things, none of them spoken, all of them creating doubts that would last a lifetime. Later I would know that my unspoken questions were shared by millions of others. Where was Roosevelt? Where was God? How could either have let this horror take place?

Among the many people who asked such questions was a young American soldier in Europe.

He was born in the Bronx in 1924, the son of Jewish immigrants from Poland, the middle child of three kids. His father was a furrier, and when the Depression arrived, not many New

Yorkers were buying furs. Some could not buy food. The family moved to Newark, and moved in with relatives. The young man would graduate from South Side High School in 1941. That year he enrolled in City College in New York City, where there was no tuition and academic standards were very high. But he could not avoid the news on the radios or in the newspapers. Some of it had been there in the years before Pearl Harbor. He was, after all, a Jew. And there were people in his country who hated Jews.

A sick Catholic priest named Coughlin was broadcasting his rants from a church studio in Detroit. In nearby Dearborn, Henry Ford, who had made so much money peddling motor cars, was also peddling the vile forgeries of *The Protocols of the Elders of Zion,* while his own book, *The International Jew,* was becoming a favorite of a certain mustached, strutting Jew-hater in Berlin. American bundists were packing Madison Square Garden and waving swastikas. Gerald L.K. Smith was a voice in the chorus, and so, in a milder way, was Charles Lindberg and his fellow members of America First. All in their separate ways spoke about "the Jew."

The young man we speak about here knew that there were many ways to be a Jew in America. All he had to do was look around and stay alert. In Newark, as in the Lower East Side or in Brownsville, out in Brooklyn, there were religious Jews and secular Jews. There were Jews who worked with their minds and others who employed their hands and their backs (when they could get work at all). There were communist Jews and socialist Jews. There were Zionists and anti-Zionists. There were Jews who had pledged their loyalty to Tammany Hall, and its big city Democratic Party equivalents, and Jews who resisted the corruptions of the machines and enlisted as partisans of the Republican Party. There were Jewish gangsters, too, ranging from former bootleggers to the hired killers of Murder Inc. There were Jewish cops. There were Jewish ballplayers and Jewish prizefighters, along with young Jewish writers and scholars who were emerging from the City College of New York. There were great American musicians and composers, too, ranging from the Gershwin brothers to Benny Goodman, and many, many others.

There were Jewish comedians, Jewish movie directors, Jewish actors who had come out of the glorious Yiddish theater along New York's Second Avenue or the Group Theater, and new Jewish playwrights such as Clifford Odets. And there were Jews, many of them, who went off to Spain in the Lincoln Brigade to fight the fascists of General Franco, who were supported by Hitler and Mussolini. Other people talked a good fight. The Jews in the Lincoln Brigade picked up rifles. Many of them did not come back. So who, exactly, was "the Jew" that the radio ravers were speaking about? Who exactly did Henry Ford and Father Coughlin have in mind?

In 1943, when he was 19, the young man enrolled in a different school: the United States Army. By September 1944, as a member of the 104th Infantry Division, he was in France as a combat soldier. Like most soldiers, he seldom discusses this part of his life. But he would stay on when the war ended, after being awarded two Battle Stars, and was discharged in 1946.

That young soldier was, of course, Edward Irving Koch. Many years later he would become the 105th mayor of the greatest city in the United States.

———

Combat changes almost every man, but sometimes the true horror begins after the shooting has stopped. In this book Koch remembers his own version of what I saw in the RKO Prospect: those first films from Buchenwald and Auschwitz. There was a major difference. I saw them as a Catholic school boy. Ed Koch saw them through the eyes of a tough proud Jew, the knowing eyes of a New Yorker, the eyes of an infantryman at whom bullets had been fired with intent to kill. And he, too, was shocked.

"Many people had suspected what the Nazis were doing," he wrote in 1985. "Some evidence had reached the outside world. But the full horror wasn't known until the photographs and eyewitness testimony began to appear in the papers. Only by then it was too late for six million Jews and millions of others." (p. 73)

Too late. Those words appear over and over in these dispatches from the war that didn't completely end in 1945. Many young men who fought their way into the ruins of Hitler's Berlin found that their triumphant sense of hope would quickly be tempered by other events.

"When the world saw at last the full scope on what the Nazis had done," he writes, "we had every right to expect that a wave of revulsions would sweep every last trace of Nazi ideology from the face of the earth. We had every right to expect that the deadly infection of Nazi hatred would perish in its own funeral pyre." The deadly virus of anti-Semitism, one that has been around for more than twenty centuries, did not perish. It ebbs, flows, rises, retreats: it never goes away. And much of this collection is driven by the lesson that Koch has carried throughout his life:

"Never take for granted that the evils of the past will remain in the past. Always be alert to opportunities for progress, but never ignore the warming signs of bigotry and hate, no matter how distant they may seem."

So in these pieces Koch is not speaking as a former mayor of New York. He speaks, over and over again, a Jew, and as a rememberer. He tells us that he is not a religious Jew; as stated, there are many, many ways to be a Jew. But he has never forgotten one terrible lesson from Hitler and his Final Solution: differences don't matter. A Jew is a Jew. And so we shall kill them. Koch says: no you won't.

Over and over again, he defends Israel, driven by the belief that if it had only existed in the 1930s, those six million might have lived. He makes distinctions: those who criticize individual governments of Israel are not mindless anti-Semites. Such criticism is common to many Israelis. But the existence of Israel itself is no longer up for discussion. Hitler settled that argument long ago.

"Is it wrong for American Jews to be critical of Israel?" he asks at one point. "Of course not. Criticism is warranted, and I have criticized Israel. But there are Jews who carry the guilt of the world on their shoulders, which requires them to regularly excoriate Israel and blame themselves and Israel for the ills of the world."

He is fully aware of the occasional anti-Semitic accusations of Jewish "dual loyalty," a canard that also plagued the Irish during the nineteenth-century heyday of the Know Nothings. The accusation then was that Irish Catholics were loyal first to the Church of Rome, not to the United States, and thus were a conspiratorial threat to our democracy. Bigots always look for a noble-sounding excuse for their bigotry. Koch once addressed this nasty accusation in a way that could now serve all the new immigrants from Latin America and China:

"We are all Americans. That does not mean that we should ever turn our backs on our roots or our traditions. The marvel of America is that we can take pride in our origins and nevertheless continue to be first-class citizens." And he got more specific at a breakfast meeting when he was a Congressman: "If Israel ever invades the United States, I would stand with the United States." (p. 24)

It should have been unnecessary to even state it that baldly. Or even for me to say that Ed Koch is absolutely American in every fiber of his mind and body. In the years when I was a newspaper columnist and he was Mayor I wrote about him occasionally with the point of my pen (as Jonathan Swift urged), not the feather. He answered in kind. But I always saw him then (and now) as the very best kind of American: a free man, who says what he believes should be said, directly, without fear. He is also, in this time of pervasive national amnesia, an American with memory.

He remembers the luxury liner called the St. Louis that sailed from Germany in May 1939, crowded with 930 Jews on board, all in flight from the Nazis. The ship was turned away from Cuba, and hovered off the coast of Florida, able to see the lights of Miami. The passengers hoped that Roosevelt would find a way to let them land. But there was so much anti-Semitism in the country that Roosevelt never found the courage to save these people, these Jews. The ship returned to Germany. Most of the passengers ended up in Nazi ovens.

He remembers how Hitler, on the eve of full-scale war, once offered to send Jews to any country that would take them, and no country would do so, even the home of the free and the land of the brave. He remembers that the Americans never found a way to bomb the rail lines into Auschwitz, the lines that carried so many Jews crammed into boxcars, soon to breathe Zyklon X. He remembers the righteous gentiles, too, because not all human beings colluded in what came to be known as the Holocaust. And he remembers those pictures from the death camps that I have remembered all my life too. He remembers. He remembers.

"And what we remember, the world will remember, whether it wants to or not," he writes in this book "Because remembering is a personal obligation. A moral obligation. A national and international obligation. And we must not only remember how it ended but also how it began." (p. 158)

We must.

CHAPTER ONE

CONFRONTING ANTI-SEMITISM IN NEW YORK CITY

The election of Ed Koch as mayor of New York City, in the autumn of 1977, came during a lull in the tensions between the city's Jews and African Americans. Nine years earlier, the eruption of black anti-Semitism during the Ocean Hill–Brownsville teachers' strike had caused long-lasting fissures in the black-Jewish relationship. Liberal Jewish activists such as Koch, who had traveled to Mississippi to help blacks register to vote and mount legal challenges to racial discrimination, were stunned by the anti-Jewish hostility expressed by radical black civil rights activists in New York and nationally. Now Koch, as mayor of the city with the nation's largest Jewish and black communities, faced the task of trying to keep the varying interests and attitudes of Jews and blacks from flaring into outright conflict.

This chapter begins with an early document, a previously unpublished private memo written by Koch as a U.S. Congressman in 1972, that offers insights into his views on black-Jewish relations. Among its striking aspects is Koch's unhappiness over black leaders criticizing Israel while ignoring Arab persecution of black Africans in Sudan. Reading Koch's admonitions regarding Sudan, written fully thirty-five years ago, is a sobering reminder of how long the international community has turned a blind eye to the brutal oppression in that country.

We then proceed to Koch's first term as mayor and his experiences with black anti-Semitism in the city. As mayor, and as a Jew, Koch grappled with serious racial issues and tried to navigate a steady course through rough waters, as the writings and statements in this section amply reflect. It was no mean feat.

THE PROBLEM OF BLACK ANTI-SEMITISM

Memorandum from Box 080057, Folder 1, Edward I. Koch Papers (hereafter EIK), La Guardia Community College, Long Island City, NY.

June 1, 1972

MEMORANDUM
to: Matt Nimetz
from: Ed Koch

RE: Anti-Israel and Anti-Semitic References Made by Black Leadership

Enclosed are various publications received from the ADL [Anti-Defamation League] which relate to Anti-Israel and Anti-Semitic references made by the Black leadership as well as some good things by Roy Wilkins, Bayard Rustin and the Black Congressional Caucus.

Let me at this point put down some random thoughts for your consideration. My feelings at this point vis-à-vis the black community are not simply distress but anger. The leaders in the white community overwhelmingly in support of the rights of full citizenship for blacks have been Jews, for whatever reasons, and I happen to think that those reasons, for the most part, have been on the highest moral plane. It has been the Jewish community which has put itself on the line.

I am not a Talmudic student but I have always been imbued with one concept which I learned in my days at Hebrew school in the study of "The Ethics of Our Fathers." In that small volume there is one phrase which means a lot to me and it is, "Justice, justice, shalt thou render." And the explanation of the Talmudic scholars for that admonition is that we are, as Jews, required not only to seek justice for fellow Jews but equally for the stranger and that is the reason for the repetition, say the scholars, of the word "justice."

In 1964 when Chaney, Schwerner and Goodman were missing in Mississippi, I was one of a number of lawyers who went to Mississippi in August of that year, the very week that the bodies were found, to assist black and white COFO[1] workers registering blacks. And in Laurel, Mi., then a hotbed of the KKK, I appeared in court for white and black youngsters who had been arrested as a result of their civil rights activities.

And one of the proud recollections that I have of my law career, which spanned 22 years before my election to Congress, is that I demanded of the court that it allow the black defendants and spectators to sit in all parts of the courtroom and not be relegated to an all black section. And the judge granted my request.

It wasn't a new request. It had been done many other times and in many other courtrooms and was the law of the land. But with, perhaps immodesty, I must say, I was proud to be making that demand under the tense and threatening circumstances in and around that courtroom and I did it for two reasons. One, because I was so taken with the strengths of the white college students who had come from outside the South and of the black youngsters, all of whom were living daily lives subject to intimidation and maybe death, surely assault, and were willing to fight the constant fight because it was right. And secondly, because I believed then and now in the mandate, "Justice, justice, shalt thou render"—no matter what the cost.

Parenthetically, I should add that I was, in fact, during my stay in Laurel, not only subject to verbal abuse but threatened by a mob at the time.

I give this by way of background because it is so distressing to me to see black leaders and black groups striving to elevate their own people by standing on the necks of the Jews. I will not sit back and tolerate that so long as there is a breath in my body.

What do I mean? Jewish teachers and principals, good and bad alike, in their professional duties, find in too many cases that they are not judged on their professionalism in the school system located in black communities but rather on their color and religion. They have strived over the years to have a merit system instead of a patronage system applied to the school system. Today they find not only are they insulted, taunted and threatened so many times, but their positions in the school system are under attack and they are judged not on the merits but on quotas. I will not defend [individual tests] because I don't have the expertise in any of the tests now given insofar as their fairness is concerned, but I do defend a system which uses testing to determine ability to teach and I deplore a system which assigns quotas. . . .

[T]here are two standards today and by permitting two standards, one applying to blacks engaging in intemperate, vile remarks and excusing them, as opposed to higher standards applying to whites in similar positions, we are really pandering to the worst in people and in effect saying that they are second class citizens requiring specific rules. . . .

Let me talk about Shirley Chisholm[2] for a moment. Here is a woman running for President. The Black Convention passes a scurrilous anti-Israel resolution calling for the dismantling of that state. The Black Congressional Caucus, in response, issues its statement denouncing that resolution (copy enclosed) and Shirley Chisholm, whose name appears on the Black Caucus statement, sent a letter to the leading Arab apologist, Dr. Mehdi,[3] in which she clearly says that she would have voted against the statement even if the procedural requirements, which she makes much of, had been observed. Her follow-up letter of April 18 to Dr. Mehdi, while it reiterates that her repudiation of the Black Caucus statement was based on the "undemocratic way in which the position was arrived at and released, not the content," does not square with her original letter to him which I suspect is her real position.

My feeling in this matter is reinforced by the fact that she felt obliged to disassociate herself from the Black Caucus by writing a letter to Dr. Mehdi, instead of, if she wished to do so, issuing a statement for release to the press or a statement on the Floor of the House in which she could have set forth her position on the issue.

Then I look at the statement of her position on "The Middle East Crisis," which in her letter to Dr. Mehdi she says she stands on her official position paper on the Middle East and I see that while there is nothing that one should denounce in terms of her concerns, although I surely could argue with her priorities, the tenor of her whole statement relates basically to the rights of Palestinian refugees. She doesn't give comparable billing to the plight of the Jews in Syria and Iraq who are the subject of torture and death, or to the terroristic activities of Arab groups against Israel and its civilians.

In other words what I am saying is, her concerns are not my concerns and while I appreciate that she will have a different attitude toward Jews in Israel than I as a Jew would have, I would have hoped for greater understanding on her part for the concerns of Jews in this country vis-à-vis their brothers and sisters in Israel than she has exhibited.

Then to get to LeRoi Jones (Imamu Baraka).[4] He is a man who has denounced Jews in the vilest terms and has been elevated to two positions of great authority by the black community. It is well known that he is, if not the most important person in Newark, at least the second most from a political point of view and he was the chairman of the Black Convention in Gary. Just think of that. Assume for a moment that whites or Jews were to hold a convention and have as their chairman Mr. Imperiale of Newark.[5] With his point of view being so well-known, does anyone doubt that an overwhelming number of whites and Jews would have denounced such a choice?

Then what did they do? They passed a resolution for the dismantling of Israel and when they found that it didn't serve their purpose to have it as scurrilous as it was, they sought to temper it by having it conform with the U.N. and African States resolution which, to most impartial observers on the scene and certainly to those who support the State of Israel, is thought of as being outrageously prejudicial and the product of Arab-Soviet alignment. I was so angry with what had occurred that I wrote to Richard Hatcher,[6] who I believe was the overall Convention Chairman, and copies of my correspondence are enclosed. To date, no answer has been received.

Just assume for a moment that a Member of Congress had participated in some anti-black convention and the Mayor of Gary, Indiana, had written and requested clarification along the lines of my letter and no response had been received, what the feelings would be on the part of that Mayor vis-à-vis the Congressman and his confreres.

Did the Black Convention concern itself with the Sudan, where millions of blacks and animists have been slaughtered over the years by their Arab overlords? Did that same convention take any position that there is not, to the best of my knowledge, a single African state which hasn't succumbed either to one party rule or rule under a military junta? No, it chose to single out Israel as the object of its concern.

I have also included comments which I made on the Floor relating to support of blacks in South Africa. I think you will have to look long and hard in the Congressional Record to find many statements from blacks supporting matters of concern to Jews. . . .

As Mayor Koch soon discovered, ordinary neighborhood or community conflicts could be easily transformed by demagogues into episodes of full-blown ethnic tension. In this exchange of letters from 1983, a black religious leader resorts to extreme, threatening, and anti-Semitic rhetoric to make his points.

BLACK–JEWISH TENSIONS IN BROOKLYN:
REVEREND SAM'S OUTBURST

Letters from Box 080065, Folder 4, EIK.

Each spring, traditional Jews celebrate a minor Jewish holiday called Lag B'Omer. It marks the conclusion of a period of semi-mourning and is celebrated with outdoor festivities, typically including athletic events, picnics, and small parades. None of which would normally concern anyone outside the Jewish community—anyone, that is, except for those looking to stir up the embers of ethnic conflict.

In the spring of 1983, I received a vitriolic letter from the Rev. Heron Sam, of Brooklyn's Church of St. Mark, complaining bitterly that the recent Lag B'Omer celebration by Hasidic Jews in the Crown Heights (Brooklyn, NY) had caused various inconveniences to the area's non-Jewish residents. Unfortunately, Rev. Sam attempted to turn a routine neighborhood dispute into something much more, claiming that the Lag B'Omer event, which took place on a Sunday, had resulted in "preventing Christians from attending their Church on their Sabbath. . . . This obstruction of people and discommoding [*sic*] of worshippers on the Christian Sabbath is unconscionable. . . ."

Sam then proceeded to denounce me in what appeared to be a comparison to the Nazis: "Mayor Koch, you are demonstrating more and more a most alarming trait, a trait which was responsible for one of the greatest holocausts this world has ever known, a blatant and benign disregard for a significant 'minority' of your constituents."

Apparently hoping to pre-empt the charge of anti-Semitism, Rev. Sam added: "[P]lease again don't waste your time and mine to honor me with the title of 'anti-semitic.' I am the only black leader in Crown Heights who risked his reputation among his people, and initiated a coalition with the Hassidic Community . . . [but] the dialogic relationship was never intended by them to accomplish anything more than . . . to further their own political and material development." Needless to say, Rev. Sam's disavowal of anti-Semitism was less than convincing.

Rev. Sam sent copies of the letter to various political figures and newspaper editors. In view of his extremist rhetoric, I doubt they took his letter very seriously, but as a mayor with a special interest in improving black-Jewish relations, I felt he deserved a reply. Here's what I wrote:

May 31, 1983

Reverend Dr. Heron A. Sam, Rector
The Church of St. Mark
Brooklyn Avenue & Union
Brooklyn, New York 11213

Dear Rev. Sam:
I received your letter of May 2, 1983 and I must tell you that I was shocked by its tenor and the misrepresentations it contains. This is particularly true because in the past, you and I have met privately in my office, in order to discuss problems impacting on the residents of Crown Heights. Now without any effort to contact me personally, you deliver a vitriolic missive with overtones

of anti-Semitism, to myself and the press, which seems deliberately aimed at fanning the flames of racial and religious intolerance. I think such an action ill-befits a religious leader.

I realize from the tone of your letter that you have made up your mind and do not really want a response. Nonetheless, I think it is important to "set the record straight." Until receipt of your letter commenting on the celebration of the "Lag Bomer" festival by the Hasidic community in Crown Heights, I was completely unaware of the event. The Mayor, as you are aware, does not pass upon individual parade or street fair permits. Such decisions are made by the City's Community Assistance Unit, which bases its decision almost entirely on approvals from the local community planning board. And, you should also know, that the Mayor appoints no one to that community planning board. Those appointments are made by the Borough Presidents and members of the City Council. I am informed by my staff that Community Board 9 gave this street fair its approval.

The same regulations apply to the festival that you objected to, as well as to the enormous West Indian Day Parade which takes place on Labor Day and fills Eastern Parkway with more than one million Brooklyn residents. I approve of both of these festivals and support them as well as others. Obviously, there has to be an accommodation made to make certain that those not participating in the festival have an opportunity to use appropriate streets to get to and from their homes, their places of business and, most importantly, their places of worship. If that was not done, it should have been. I have always been available to you and your parishioners to rectify legitimate complaints and I stand ready to do so now. But to turn what at most was an innocent administrative judgment by governmental instrumentalities based on the recommendation of the community board, into a racist conspiracy, does not serve the interests of your parishioners, the residents of Crown Heights or the people of this City.

One final point, in your letter you imply that you would be honored by the title of "Anti-Semitic," for a minister of the gospel to make such statement must offend every decent person in this City, Christian and Jew alike.

Sincerely,

Edward I. Koch
Mayor

Although Koch's frank criticism of black anti-Semitism received widespread support in the Jewish community and Jewish organizational leadership, there were some Jewish leaders who feared his statements might exacerbate Jewish-black tensions. In this unpublished essay, Koch recounts an episode in which the New York–based leader of the Union of American Hebrew Congregations—Reform Judaism's national network of synagogues—publicly chastised the mayor for saying that Jesse Jackson, Louis Farrakhan, and Albert Vann, three prominent black leaders, had made anti-Semitic remarks.

TAKING BLACK ANTI-SEMITISM SERIOUSLY
Draft of an unpublished column, 1984, from Box 080065, Folder 12, EIK.

I am an activist mayor who believes I should take public positions on controversial matters. I also must be prepared, as I am, to defend my positions against the criticisms that sometimes result.

Over the last seven years, I've often been criticized for my comments on anti-Semitism among many black leaders I know. There are many advisers, editorial writers, and good citizens who've cautioned against my making any statements on racial issues. I don't agree. If I refuse to speak out against apartheid in South Africa or quotas at home are those who suffer under apartheid or quotas served by my silence? I don't think so.

As with my comments on other matters, in commenting on racial controversy I've always said what I thought was correct and factual. Particularly since I'm interviewed so many times and speak extemporaneously, on occasion I may have made errors or not articulated my views as fully as I should have. By and large, however, what I've said has been consistent and factual.

This matter recently came up again when, as is usual at the end of the year, I was interviewed by reporters who cover City Hall. On the first day I was interviewed by the print

press, on the second by the radio media, and on the third by
the television media. The format on each day was that I
would not release a prepared statement, but would respond
to any questions asked by reporters. Without my raising the
issue, on each of the three days reporters asked me very
pointed questions related to the state of racial relations, particularly between blacks and Jews.

On the first day of the interviews I was asked whether I believed that all blacks were anti-Semitic. I said no and added that
I have never believed that. What I do believe and what I said in
response to questions is that many black leaders have used anti-
Semitism. When asked to substantiate my claim, I cited a 1978
poll commissioned by the National Conference of Christians
and Jews and conducted by Lou Harris which found a significantly higher degree of anti-Jewish prejudice among black leaders than among leaders of any other group.

Later, I was asked by a reporter to name some black leaders
who fit this category. In response to the reporter's question, I
cited Reverend Jesse Jackson, Minister Louis Farrakhan, and Assemblyman Al Vann as having made anti-Semitic comments.

On January 31, I was told that Albert Vorspan had issued a
statement on behalf of the Union of American Hebrew Congregations describing my comments as "generalizations" and asking
"by what report card" black leaders had been rated. It said "it is re-
grettable that the Mayor, in a year-end statement, should make a
wholesale condemnation of black leadership as anti-Semitic." My
comments, the statement said, are "harmful and inflammatory."

They were intended to harm no one and to inflame no situation. They were merely honest answers made only in response to
reporters' questions. If my comments are condemned by Mr.
Vorspan, would he also condemn the reporters whose questions
elicited my comments?

Moreover, in making my comments, I indicated what my "report card" was—the Lou Harris poll. Finally, my comments were
not intended as a "wholesale condemnation" of black leadership,
but only of those black leaders who have used anti-Semitism.

I thought to myself, who's more denigrating in their comments, Vorspan or I? I'd stated a simple fact, offered substantiation for it, and provided specific examples. Is there anyone who doubts that each of these three leaders have made anti-Semitic statements? I doubt it. I will not repeat their statements here, but simply rely on the memories of people because the comments of Reverend Jackson and Minister Farrakhan have been made within the last year. Assemblyman Vann's statements were much earlier but never recanted.

While I take the statements of these leaders seriously, Mr. Vorspan does not. He says that citing Reverend Jackson or Minister Farrakhan as representative black leaders "would be like identifying a couple of flakes in the Jewish community and saying that's what the Jewish leadership thinks." Jesse Jackson a "flake"? I don't think so, Mr. Vorspan. Reverend Jackson is perceived by the black community as a major black leader. In the May 1984 issue of *Ebony* magazine, for example, its editors selected him as one of the 100 most influential black Americans. That's probably been reinforced as a result of his run in the 1984 presidential election.

Minister Farrakhan is also perceived favorably by the black community. How do I know? A poll taken by the *Los Angeles Times* and reported in *The National Journal* found that 47 percent of all black delegates and 69 percent of the Jackson delegates at the Democratic National Convention held a favorable opinion of the minister. And he received a standing ovation at the convention of the National Conference of Black Mayors. Though he may not be as popular as Reverend Jackson, Minister Farrakhan clearly has significant support in the black community.

My comments on certain black leaders have gotten even more attention because, as most New Yorkers know, I've recently said I won't approve a City Council resolution giving city employees a twelfth holiday in honor of Dr. King. Some people may view my decision as an insult to Dr. King.

No insult was intended. I admire Dr. King. In fact, he's one of the reasons I went to Mississippi to do voter registration in the 1960s.

I'm not supporting the Council's resolution for another reason. Earlier this year city unions proposed that as part of the contract they and the city are now negotiating, the number of holidays for city employees be increased from eleven to twelve in honor of Dr. King. It's an appropriate issue to be discussed in collective bargaining and, since it is, shouldn't be subject to the Council's action.

Why? Right now city employees enjoy eleven holidays a year. By comparison, nationally employees in the private sector enjoy only 9.8 holidays. To give city employees a twelfth holiday would cost $17 million in overtime and pensions and $6 million in lost productivity. Since it directly benefits only city employees, shouldn't a twelfth holiday be considered part of the overall cost of the labor settlement?

In the event that unions do not want to charge the cost of a twelfth holiday against the final settlement we reach, I've proposed as an alternative that city employees could begin celebrating Martin Luther King Day right away if their union representatives agreed to trade-in one of their other holidays—Veterans Day or Election Day, for example—and celebrate King Day in its place. Though my proposal has been on the bargaining table since March, union representatives have given it only minimal consideration.

If I wanted to win a popularity contest, I could agree with the Council, ignore the collective bargaining talks currently taking place, and by Executive Order take the millions required from other essential city services to establish a twelfth holiday in honor of Dr. King. However, that would be like using the city treasury as a campaign fund. I don't think the overwhelming majority of New Yorkers would assent to that. I know I can't.

As the debate over the King holiday has heated up, what's bothered me in particular was a *New York Times* editorial last week which agreed with my decision to keep it as part of collective bargaining, but said I had "erred by making that point in defiant language." I've since reviewed my comments on the subject and have found not one "defiant" word in what I've said.

So, I wonder why the *Times* said I've been defiant. My concern is that the *Times'* reaction may mean that there's still a fear of discussing publicly any controversies involving blacks. If you're not on what appears at first glance to be the right side of an issue involving blacks, those who obey this fear believe, then you should keep your lips zipped. I believe that blacks are equal to whites—no better, no worse.

I also believe that I should and do treat any matters involving a black in the same way I would treat those involving a white. Isn't that what non-discrimination is all about?

And yet, regrettably, it appears that many people cannot do that and believe that discussion of black/white or black/Jewish controversies should not be held in an open public discourse. If we cannot discuss these matters publicly, then aren't we in effect saying that blacks should not be discussed and, thus, treating them differently than whites? If so, we'll be guilty of practicing discrimination of the highest order.

FACING THE REALITY OF BLACK ANTI-SEMITISM

Remarks at the Bellerose Jewish Center, Queens, February 10, 1985, from Box 080078, Folder 5, EIK.

Last week, a columnist for *Newsday* named Les Payne wrote an article in which he attacked my administration, and me personally, for creating a "deadly atmosphere" in New York City. Mr. Payne, who happens to be black, said that I was polarizing the city by saying that anti-Semitism is a problem in the black community just as racism remains a problem in the white community. I'm sure Mr. Payne would agree with the second half of that statement, but he resents the idea that blacks could be considered anti-Semitic.

No individual of good will, and no group of such individuals, like to think of themselves as prejudiced; nevertheless, we have to face certain facts, even if those facts are unpleasant. Prejudice, bigotry, and racism have plagued humanity for thousands of years. I am not aware of any segment of human society that has been immune to these evils in the past. I am not aware of any segment of our society today that is immune to them now. I believe that racism, anti-Semitism, and other forms of prejudice can be eliminated, but only if decent people work together in an atmosphere of honesty.

The fact is that anti-black racism still exists in our society. It is also a fact that anti-Semitism still exists. I can understand that some people might wish to believe that anti-Semitism is not a problem in the black community. However, I also believe the evidence indicates that it is. In the February 4th issue of *New York* magazine, Michael Kramer reported some of the findings that have been made in this area. A 1978 poll by Louis Harris, for example, found that while anti-Semitism was declining slightly in America, "blacks tend to be more anti-Jewish than any other group." Harris also found a higher degree of anti-Jewish prejudice among black leaders than among leaders of any other group.

Other, more recent studies have confirmed Harris's findings and have uncovered a higher incidence of anti-Semitism among younger, educated blacks than among younger, educated whites. We shouldn't make too much of this, but we shouldn't ignore it, either. Eliminating prejudice is like stopping the arms race. The trick is to get everyone to lay down their weapons at the same time, including the weapons of hate and bigotry. I think it can be done; it must be done. The first step, however, is for everyone to face the facts honestly and to work together from there.

THE "BLACK-JEWISH COALITION"

Draft of an unpublished column, April 19, 1985, from Box 080078, Folder 5, EIK.

Recently, I saw and then read the transcript of a *Firing Line* show hosted by William F. Buckley, Jr. His guests were Dr. Mary Frances Berry, Rabbi Balfour Brickner and Dr. Nathan Glazer. The subject was the "Black-Jewish Coalition."

A major item of discussion related to affirmative action and what it means to different people. To Dr. Berry it means racial quotas, with the quotas being filled only by qualified blacks. Dr.

Berry, who is a member of the Federal Civil Rights Commission, believes that those who oppose racial quotas are setting up a straw man. The straw man is that the positions to be filled would not require the persons filling them to be qualified. I believe that it is Dr. Berry who has created a straw man. The issue is not whether the minorities who are selected for positions on the basis of affirmative action programs requiring numerical goals, timetables and sanctions are qualified, but whether they are less qualified than other contenders for the job. Let me explain.

Every lawyer who has passed the bar is qualified to try a case, but most people agree that some lawyers are better than others. In selecting a lawyer, you would want to pick the best of those available. Similarly, every medical doctor who has a license to practice medicine can, under the law in many states, perform any medical act, including surgery, even if he is not a surgeon. And yet no one would go under the knife of a doctor who was qualified but not considered to be the best of those available to the patient. I use these two professions because they so easily make the case, but the same principle applies to every occupation and profession.

Those of us who are against racial quotas say that special efforts should be made to encourage people to apply for jobs, but, when a selection is made, it should be on the basis of who is best, whether it be by civil service tests or an evaluation of the individual that goes beyond a simple written test. Obviously, the test, written or oral, has to be job-related and fair. And if persons administering tests and making selections are not color blind, they should be removed, disciplined and punished where intentional discrimination has occurred. Where it is not intentional, they should be required to change their ways and become conscious of the need to be fair.

We must make everyone aware that this country does not permit racial, religious or sexual discrimination. But I also believe that we have to acknowledge that such discrimination exists and then root it out. There are those who believe it can only be rooted out by creating group rights. Most Americans, both black and white, oppose group rights. Some Americans, however, support group rights. I would like to tell you why I oppose them.

If we accept the concept of reparations to particular groups in this country, where do we stop? Do we provide reparations to the Irish who suffered when they came here as laborers during the Great Irish Famine and were discriminated against for such a long period of time? At one time, there were signs throughout this country which read, "No Irish Need Apply." Jews, Italians and Catholics of many ethnic backgrounds also suffered discrimination in this country. Nevertheless, the idea of group rights to rectify past discrimination is not acceptable to most groups in this country. As a result of the endeavor to provide group rights and because of what is known, quite correctly, as reverse discrimination, many programs intended to help the poor have been allowed to languish and, in many cases, have been terminated.

On *Firing Line,* Dr. Glazer talked about affirmative action in education and the problems that he has seen at Harvard. It was a shock to learn that, at Harvard, black students are declining in number. "I'll give you one reason they're declining," Dr. Glazer said. "Fifty percent of the blacks offered positions at Harvard don't accept them, and ninety percent of the Asians do." It is a pity that this decline is occurring since there are many who are turned away from Harvard who would jump at the chance to go.

I was interested in what Dr. Berry said about Jews and why they became involved in civil rights. Dr. Berry said: ". . . If Jews—some of them—got involved in the civil rights movement because they thought civil rights would help them, if that is the case, then people who got into it only for that reason would obviously have to consider now whether it would help them."

I suspect that Jews, such as myself, got involved in civil rights and went to Mississippi (in my case in 1964) not because of some special alliance with blacks, but because it was the right thing to do. I didn't go to Mississippi because it was helpful to me, but because I wanted to help end segregation.

Rabbi Balfour Brickner said: "We have a tendency to have a mythic memory about black-Jewish relations in this country, and it is more myth than reality." I agree. I do not believe there is any historic relationship that brought a special closeness between blacks and Jews. I have asked a number of Jews my age—both friends and acquaintances—whether their fathers and mothers had any special relationship with blacks. The response was generally negative. Relations between blacks and Jews were no better than between blacks and other whites. There are black and white leaders today who talk about the friction between blacks and Jews as though it were worse than the problems between blacks and Hispanics, blacks and Irish, or blacks and Italians. In comparison, black-Jewish relations are better.

I have no personal objection to seeking to make black-Jewish relationships even better than they are, although it is the least troubled relationship when you consider how much worse things are between blacks and other white groups.

I was distressed to hear Rabbi Brickner denounce the Vice-President of the United States because he (George Bush) "suggests that the Democratic Party is soft on anti-Semitism because it didn't condemn Jesse Jackson sufficiently with a firm plank condemning anti-Semitism. . . . That is, in my judgment, an attempt to drive a wedge between blacks and Jews."

I was at the Democratic Convention and I was just as distressed as George Bush that the Democrats could not adopt a platform plank denouncing anti-Semitism because of the opposition of black leaders, who believed it would be perceived as an attack on Jackson or Farrakhan.

I was even more distressed by some of the statistics as they relate to the feeling of blacks vis-à-vis Jewish delegates at the convention. (A poll taken by the *Los Angeles Times* and reported in *The National Journal* found that 47 percent of all black delegates and 69 percent of the Jackson delegates at the Democratic National Convention held a favorable opinion of Louis Farrakhan.)

Rabbi Brickner went on to say that: "My friend, Roscoe Brown, who sits on the Black-Jewish Coalition and is president of the Bronx Community College, is very, very much involved. I've learned a ton from this man just by listening to him outline the problem. My head and eyes have been opened in a way which I never was aware of before because I haven't followed the intricacies of the public school system."

Roscoe Brown believes absolutely in racial quotas. He has told me so. Rabbi Brickner agreed with that position. Let me say a word about Rabbi Brickner. I was shocked by what Rabbi Brickner said in an interview with the *Jewish World*. I now quote directly from that article: "Brickner was asked whether the fact that the coalition is composed of a small group of one hundred prominent blacks and Jews which one can join by invitation only might not leave the group open to criticism that it is merely a select contingent of elitist Jews and blacks engaged mainly in talking to each other. He replied forcefully: "I prefer to use the word 'leaders' rather than elitists. The fact of the matter is that intellectual and cultural leadership can shape the attitudes of the masses. We certainly cannot make decisions based on the bigoted attitudes of the masses or on the ideas of taxi-drivers from Queens."

Asked if there was not an element of irony in a spokesman for progressive causes speaking disparagingly of the "masses," Brickner remarked: "All of us are elitists. You are an elitist as a journalist because you shape the ideas of others. Should we shape our relationship with the black community on the basis of the pain of semi-literate and semi-educated Jews in Queens whose hatred (of blacks) predicates all they do?" Brickner added: "The attitude of such people is 'Instead of being grateful for all we have done for them, the blacks come and rape my daughter and rip off my son.' What these people don't understand is that that element (of the black community) will only cease to prey on them when we as a society can provide jobs for the jobless and homes for the homeless, better public education, and increased safety in the streets." According to Brickner, "Too many Jews see this problem in terms of race rather than of class. We are not going to solve the problem by responding on the level of their complaint."

Now it is true—undoubtedly after he was deluged with complaints about his language—that Rabbi Brickner did apologize. In a letter to the Long Island *Jewish World,* he wrote: "I would like to apologize to your readers for any derogatory references to residents of the Borough of Queens which I may have made during a press interview with one of your reporters. . . ." Brickner acknowledged that the Jewish community of Queens includes individuals who are interested in improving Black-Jewish relations. By way of explanation, he said that after the creation of the Black–Jewish Coalition, he had received harassing letters, and telephone calls, much of which came "from persons, identifying themselves as Queens residents." Rabbi Brickner conceded that those harassers did not represent most of the Jews in Queens and he expressed sorrow that he "momentarily lost my perspective" and had "allowed myself to have said what was quoted by your reporter." He added that he regretted the words he had spoken, and "would retract them if I could."

To me, however, Brickner's letter did not constitute a withdrawal of his earlier comments. I believe he simply regretted saying what he said, but not the substance.

How do I come to that conclusion? Aside from a simple reading of his letter, I point to his latest comments on the *Firing Line* show, where he said the following:

> No, here's where it begins to come up. "Jesse Jackson is an anti-Semite." That's what they'll tell you. It doesn't take more than ten seconds into these kinds of calls. Now they're not all old folks. Believe me, they're not. They're not all old people who are, you know, fat, fifty and fascist. That's not the case. There are some young, lean fascists out there in the Jewish community and they will say to me in no uncertain terms that "You have, as a rabbi, no right to be supportive of blacks when blacks are basically anti-Semitic, i.e., Jesse Jackson and Louis Farrakhan." As though the whole Black-Jewish Coalition has to be held hostage for remarks of one or two black spokesmen who may not even be leaders of the black community, as if everything else that has ever been said by anybody else in the black society was never said and doesn't count.

Now it happens that Rabbi Brickner is really disparaging Jesse Jackson and Louis Farrakhan when he says that they may not even be leaders of the black community. Does he really mean that, and isn't that an affront to the black community, which perceives Jesse Jackson as one of its major leaders? Was Rabbi Brickner being honest with us?

Toward the end of *Firing Line,* Dr. Berry said: "I see the Israel issue for Jews as I see the affirmative action issue for blacks. And if Jews will not try to get us to define our interests in a way that will be counterproductive and recognize that we are emotional about affirmative action [just as] they are about Israel, because if I were Jewish I would feel just as strongly about Israel. . . . But you cannot measure things by two yardsticks. They can't expect us to be that supportive all the time of Israel and then trash— the same people turn right around and trash—the things that we think are in our best interests and tell us that we must not believe that they really are in our best interest." Dr. Berry then went on to say: "If you want to join in an alliance, don't expect me to abandon what I am emotionally committed to while you adhere to yours and say, 'Understand me. Understand me. Understand me.'"

Dr. Berry confuses the two litmus tests that should apply here. It is perfectly appropriate to talk about Israel and South Africa and what the former means to the Jews and the latter to the blacks. It is perfectly appropriate to say that if Jews do not support the aspirations of black freedom in South Africa, then they would have no right to expect blacks to support the concept of security for the State of Israel. But should Jews have to give up a fundamentally held principle in order to secure black support for Israel? I would say that, with most Jews, there is no possibility of such a trade.

The vast majority of white Congressmen support the security of Israel because it is in the national interest of the United States to do so. It is accepted by both the administration and the members of Congress who are overwhelmingly white and not Jewish that Israel is the only ally in the Mideast that we can count on.

Black Congressmen, I assume, also vote in support of Israel for the same reasons as their white counterparts and not because they simply want to support American Jews. I assume they are not voting against their own conscience in supporting Israel. Because, if the latter is the case, they should stop. We are all Americans first. That does not mean that we should ever turn our backs on our roots or our traditions. The marvel of America is that we can take pride in our origins and nevertheless continue to be first-class citizens.

I once summed it up when, as a member of Congress, I suggested to those attending a breakfast meeting that one question they might want to put to me was, "Do Jews have dual loyalty?" I said, "No one ever asks that question of blacks or those who are of Italian, Hispanic or Irish extraction. Nevertheless, I want to answer it forcefully and fully." I raised my right hand and said to those assembled: "If Israel ever invades the United States, I would stand with the United States." I know that what I was saying applies to every single group in America which reveres its own traditional ties with other lands. We will all stand with the United States and are not required to give up fundamental principles to satisfy one another.

I am not suggesting that blacks ever give up the demand for racial quotas if that is what they feel they need.

However, a plurality of blacks polled on the subject do not believe that is what they need. Whites overwhelmingly believe racial quotas are wrong and so do I. I believe that blacks and whites will eventually reach a consensus that equal opportunity and an end to discrimination are our best hope.

The destruction of Torah scrolls in an arson attack on a Brooklyn synagogue by teenagers in 1988 was a brutal reminder that anti-Semitism comes in many forms. In accordance with ancient Jewish tradition, the holy scrolls were given a formal burial. In these remarks at the funeral, Mayor Koch takes issue with the legal prohibition against publicizing the names of the attackers because they were minors. Making anti-Semitism "a social disgrace" by shining a harsh spotlight on such vandals was precisely the point, he argues.

MAKING ANTI-SEMITISM A SOCIAL DISGRACE

Remarks made at a funeral for Torah scrolls, September 18, 1988, from the private files of Edward I. Koch.

What an extraordinary people the Jews are. They've been called the People of the Book, the People of the Law, the People of the Torah, and why is that? When a rabbi was being martyred and burned and the Torah was being burned at the same time, because he was wrapped in it, the most important thing to be recalled was that the Torah did not burn. The paper burned, but the words lived on forever. That's an extraordinary story and it speaks of what it is that we're doing today. Is there anywhere else to be found, in any situation, where the destruction of the Book, the Law, the Torah, would be treated with the same reverence and respect as we would treat the death of a great sage in Israel?

Perhaps there are others who do it. We have to be proud knowing that we do it, that within the casket lies something that we revere as much as, or more than, a human being, that has kept us for 5,000 years, that that Torah is the same Torah that existed 5,000 years ago, that is depicted on the Dead Sea Scrolls, the same Torah. It lives on forever.

We have seen in the last twenty-four hours two actions, human in nature, one bestial and the other sublime. The bestial

act is reminiscent of Kristallnacht, which we will be commemorating on November 9th, the fiftieth anniversary of that bestial
act in Nazi Germany where they destroyed the Torah in synagogue after synagogue and burned them and also destroyed
human beings. Some were killed, others assaulted. Here in our
city, we saw that even though this act was done by two adoles-
cents, and the quality and the quantity of an adolescent act cannot be equated with that of an adult, nevertheless it has to be
assailed and they have to be punished and there has to be a message that you cannot engage in discrimination and assault. You
cannot do it. We will not permit it.

The law, the Holy Law, now encased in that casket, and the
civil and criminal law will not allow it, and we will not allow the
social engineers to dismiss it as a childish prank. It is not a childish prank. And when we, because of what the social engineers
have done, have said that we will not permit their names to be
made known, so that they can be held up for contempt in their
own community, we make a mistake.

Community pressure, community denunciation, is important—in the case of juveniles more important than other sanctions because we don't give other sanctions. We have removed
the community sanction of social disgrace and it's a disgrace that
we have done that.

This crowd is probably about 10,000 in size now. It's an extraordinary outpouring of anguish, but also of faith, and so I say
to the distinguished rabbis and to the public officials that there
are few events that any of us will ever go to, including funerals of
human beings, as important and overwhelming as they can be
and have been, that will rival the anguish that people are suffering today as a result of the destruction of this Torah. But the
people of Israel live.

*No African American leader outraged the Jewish community, and indeed the
general public, in the 1980s more than the black Muslim clergyman Louis Farrakhan. His string of extremist statements attacking Jews and Judaism, and even
praising Adolf Hitler, ignited controversy after controversy. When 25,000 of
Farrakhan's followers filled Madison Square Garden in October 1985 to cheer
his speech railing against Jews, Koch compared it to the Nazi rallies in 1920s
Germany. In the correspondence that follows, Koch takes to task a black clergyman in Philadelphia who had invited Farrakhan to address his church.*

INVITING FARRAKHAN

Portions of this article previously appeared in *The Jewish Press*, November 4, 1988.

In the spring of 1988, Minister Louis Farrakhan was invited by
Reverend Leon Sullivan to speak at Reverend Sullivan's Zion
Baptist Church in Philadelphia.

On May 20, Barry Morrison, the Anti-Defamation League's
Regional Director there, wrote to Rev. Sullivan that Farrakhan
"is a symbol of hate; he has sown seeds of division and is, at best
highly insensitive, and, at worst, blatantly anti-Semitic. . . . Farrakhan's supporters may maintain that his message is one of self-
help and economic advancement and that these features
outweigh and dilute the negative characteristics ascribed to him.
In our view, the opposite is true. In fact, Farrakhan's anti-
Semitic, racist, and violent language cannot be separated from
his message or his being."

In a similar vein, Murray Friedman, the regional director of
the American Jewish Committee, wrote to Rev. Sullivan: "I am
deeply troubled by the legitimacy provided for his anti-Jewish
views by his association with a mainstream church such as your
own. I know that he along with all of us have the right of freedom of expression, but we are not required by this to make our
platform available to a person who utters racial or religious bigotry. Let him hire his own hall."

Rev. Sullivan's response was unequivocal: "I have known Mr. Louis Farrakhan for a number of years. I have very high regards [*sic*] for him. His message of self-help, strengthening the Black male, uniting the Black family, and fighting drugs is very, very much needed in Philadelphia today. Mr. Farrakhan has spoken at Zion before, and he is welcome to speak at Zion again."

After reading the correspondence between Mr. Friedman, Mr. Morrison and Reverend Sullivan, I wrote to Reverend Sullivan, expressing my own concerns as follows:

Dear Reverend Sullivan:
We have met on a number of occasions. I have [supported] and continue to support your position on South Africa and apartheid. Because of the admiration and respect I have for your views, I was shocked when I read your explanation for inviting Reverend Louis Farrakhan to your church.

You say you have "very high regards" for Mr. Farrakhan. Reverend Sullivan, I appeal to your sense of fairness. If someone referred to the Baptist faith as a "gutter religion"—a term Mr. Farrakhan used to describe Judaism—and that person was invited by a nationally respected religious leader to speak in church, wouldn't you be distressed by that leader's decision? Wouldn't you be even more distressed if the invitee had described Adolf Hitler, the very incarnation of racist evil—as "a great man"? What makes the situation even worse is that Mr. Farrakhan puts out surreptitiously anti-Semitic material, including the tape recordings of Mr. Cokely in Chicago, who alleged that Jewish doctors injected the AIDS virus into black children. I fail to understand how you, who have worked so hard to build a coalition against racism and bigotry, can have a high regard for Mr. Farrakhan, who deliberately seeks to encourage fear and suspicion among different groups of Americans.

It is not enough to say that you're sorry we don't agree on this particular matter. You would not accept such an explanation from a leader who supported Prime Minister Botha or the evil of apartheid, which uses fear and suspicion to separate different groups of South Africans. I assume you would, quite correctly, think such a person should be rebuked.

"I hope to hear from you," I said in closing, and on October 12 I did.

Rev. Sullivan began by invoking the issue of racism, emphasizing that "all my life I have worked hard to build a coalition against racism and bigotry," and that "Poverty and continuing racial discrimination have increased the social, economic and psychological deterioration among our people."

As for Farrakhan, he insisted that "I did not invite Mr. Farrakhan to speak, but when his representative requested the use of our Church for him to speak, I consented, because our Church historically has been open to different points of view. . . ."

But then he went further and, alluding to Farrakhan's message of self-help, argued that "we are reaching for strengths in our community." In other words, Farrakhan's message was a way to make the black community stronger.

He concluded by recalling "our marching together in Washington against apartheid in South Africa."

On October 24, I sent the following reply to Reverend Sullivan:

I appreciate your history of working so hard through the years "to build a coalition against racism and bigotry." I also appreciate the fact that you are concerned with the "Poverty and continuing racial discrimination [which] have increased the social, economic and psychological deterioration among [your] people." Indeed, helping to build self-pride and self-sufficiency is a necessity. However, should it be done with someone who is particularly famous in white and Jewish communities for his anti-white and anti-Semitic comments?

Assume for a moment that a Southern minister invites the leader of the Ku Klux Klan to speak from the pulpit. Let us also assume that the minister invited this man because the Ku Klux Klan has taken a strong stand in favor of law and order, something the minister feels should be impressed on his parishioners. Wouldn't you agree that though the message has some value, the source from which it comes is polluted by bigotry and outrageous racism? Should such a person be given the authority of a pulpit, or should he be shunned?

You say "[you] consented [to his appearance at your church] because [your] Church historically has been open to different points of view." Would you suggest that the point of view of the Ku Klux Klan or a Professor Shockley[1] be given opportunity for discussion at the churches and synagogues of this country? I doubt it.

When you say "we are reaching for strengths in our community," I can only conclude that it is erroneous to perceive Minister Farrakhan as such a strength. He is to the black community what Adolf Hitler was to the German community, no less, except less effective—thank God.

I do "remember . . . our march together in Washington against apartheid in South Africa," and I want us to march again in opposition to apartheid and in opposition to religious bigotry. Supporting Minister Farrakhan's appearances at your church create[s] huge obstacles for me in joining with you—shoulder to shoulder—to achieve our common goals of fairness and justice for all.

All the best.
Sincerely,

Edward I. Koch
Mayor

After leaving office in 1989, Koch continued to speak out against anti-Semitism, especially the refusal of mainstream African American leaders to condemn anti-Semitic extremists in their community. In the letter that follows, Koch confronted NAACP director Benjamin Hooks for failing to challenge an anti-Semitic speaker at an NAACP convention.

THE NAACP AND THE PROBLEM OF BLACK ANTI-SEMITISM
Letter from Box 080087, Folder 6, EIK.

July 24, 1990

Mr. Benjamin Hooks
Executive Director, NAACP
4805 Mount Hope Drive
Baltimore, Maryland 21215–3297

Dear Ben:

Do you know the old aphorism, "Everything that goes around comes around"? After recent events I am convinced it is true. Let me tell you why.

I read in the July 13 edition of the *New York Times* that Legrand Clegg, President of the Coalition Against Black Exploitation who, according to the Anti-Defamation League, has a history of anti-Semitism, spoke at a workshop at the annual NAACP convention. Mr. Clegg charged that there was collective "Jewish racism" and excessive Jewish influence in Hollywood. And according to the *Los Angeles Times,* he was engaging in "familiar anti-Semitic calumnies and conspiratorial innuendos." I was outraged that the NAACP felt no responsibility to repudiate him.

Of course, other Jewish leaders were also outraged and expected that you, in your capacity as NAACP's Executive Director, would do two things: First, apologize for the NAACP having invited a well-known anti-Semite to participate at the convention; secondly, publicly, directly and meaningfully repudiate his racist views. Instead, you responded in a less than forthcoming manner, saying, "We have 29 workshops with 125 panelists, and we do not take responsibility for their statements. We neither agree nor disagree with what they say. . . . We don't have a position because we haven't done a study on it, but we do know there is racism in Hollywood." Ben, aren't you and the NAACP responsible for the people invited to speak at your convention, particularly when you know of their racist and anti-Semitic views? Can you, in good conscience, keep such an artful distance from this noted anti-Semite as your statement would indicate?

You also said, "We do not agree with the statement, but we do not exercise thought control. I would not invite a panelist here and then say you cannot say this or that." So my question is should you have invited the panelist knowing his anti-Semitic views? Can you, at this point in our history honestly say that you are unaware of what Jews have done in a whole host of areas, including Hollywood, to eliminate racism and help black employment?

Subsequently, you announced, "Some of our friends in the Jewish community have suggested a meeting, we respond in the affirmative. To that end, the chairman and the executive director are appointing a committee to meet and discuss this matter."

Ben, all of these statements are not worthy of you. If they were made by others on matters which affect you and blacks, you would find it unacceptable. Let me cite chapter and verse, which is why I think the aphorism "Everything that goes around comes around" is apropos.

An aide to Senator Jesse Helms, James Meredith—
heretofore for most of us a renowned and respected civil
rights hero who integrated, at great personal danger to
himself, the University of Mississippi—recently made
pejorative statements about other blacks and, in particular, members of the NAACP. You demanded that Senator Helms repudiate his statement. If we apply your
logic, why should he? Doesn't Mr. Meredith, a civil rights
hero, have just as much right as Mr. Clegg to make his
comments?

Abraham Foxman of the ADL said it correctly
when it came to Clegg: "There's nothing to talk about
as it relates to slanderous charges of 'Jewish racism' by
an anti-Semite under the auspices of the NAACP. It is
incumbent upon the NAACP, particularly when asked,
to repudiate the charges." Do you propose a dialogue
with Senator Helms to discuss the accuracy of Mr.
Meredith's charges?

I think you have a greater moral obligation to repudiate the remarks of Legrand Clegg than does Senator
Jesse Helms to denounce the views of Mr. Meredith, because Helms probably agrees with Mr. Meredith. Surely,
philosophically your friends can expect you not to align
yourself through silence with the comments of an anti-
Semite. Quite correctly, you did not like the fact that
James Meredith said that a majority of the NAACP delegates were involved in "criminal or immoral activity." In
your letter to Senator Helms you say that Meredith's as-
sertions "irresponsibly impugned the integrity and
honor" of the NAACP delegates, and you challenged
the Senator to have Meredith produce any evidence of
criminal wrongdoings. You go on to say that you expect
"Senator Helms will have the courage and respect for
probity and fair play to take appropriate disciplinary action against Mr. Meredith." But let's put the shoe on
your foot. Are you going to take appropriate disciplinary

action against those who invited Legrand Clegg to speak at the NAACP convention? If not, why not?

You later said at a news conference that "One must ask the question whether this is all a part of a sinister, devious and unholy plot that Mr. Meredith used to advance the political career of his employer." Couldn't the same question be asked by Jews of you and the NAACP, to wit, that you, if not others, are using Mr. Clegg to sow the seeds of anti-Semitism?

I must say, Ben, when we were recently together on *Face the Nation,* discussing the black boycott of Koreans in Flatbush, you took a hands-off attitude and would not denounce that racist black boycott. You said, in effect, that you didn't know anything that would allow you to take a position, this after the boycott has been in effect for many months, received nationwide attention in the media, and the Mayor of New York City, David Dinkins, has himself said it is a racial boycott which should end. Have you lost your moral compass?

There is a danger in all of this that you, and others like you, are causing others like myself to conclude that supporting the NAACP and its objectives is becoming a one-way street.

Sincerely,
Edward I. Koch

Spike Lee, the outspoken African American filmmaker, resurrected the old ca-
nard about Jewish control of Hollywood in a 1990 interview. Mainstream Jew-
ish leaders generally refrained from commenting. Koch, by contrast, pulled no
punches in addressing Lee's bigotry.

SPIKE LEE AND THE JEWS

Originally published in the *New York Post*, August 10, 1990.

I recently saw an interview with Spike Lee, the filmmaker, by
ABC-TV's Chris Wallace. Here's the heart of the exchange:

> WALLACE: Do the studios care what the message is, or
>   do they just care how much money it makes?
>
> LEE: It depends what the message is. Now, if I did some
>   anti-Semitic thing, like . . .
>
> WALLACE: That wouldn't go down in Hollywood?
>
> LEE: Not at all.
>
> WALLACE: Why not?
>
> LEE: Because a large part of the people that run Holly-
>   wood are Jewish. I mean, that's a basic fact.
>
> WALLACE: So is that wrong for them to object to hav-
>   ing an anti-Semitic movie?
>
> LEE: No, it's not wrong for them to object. I mean if it's
>   your business, you can do what you want. And when
>   black people start owning our own businesses, run-
>   ning our schools, making our own movies, then we
>   can do what the hell we want to do.

The obvious question for Chris Wallace to have asked was
"Well, when you start making your own movies financed by
black bankers so that you can do what you want to do, do you
want to make anti-Semitic movies?"

We know his answer. According to *New York Post* film critic David Edelstein, in his new movie *Mo' Better Blues,* "Lee makes the Jewish (jazz) club owners Transylvanian ghouls, drooling over black-generated profits as over a batch of necks." The *Village Voice* reviewer, Gary Giddins, says that this part of the movie "undoubtedly is anti-Semitic." The Anti-Defamation League (ADL) says it is "offensive and stereotypically anti-Semitic." I haven't seen the movie, but I think we can depend on these critics for a realistic judgment on this issue.

Can you imagine a similar interview with a white director? Say, for example, that Francis Ford Coppola said on national TV that he'd like to do an anti-black movie. Does anyone think he'd get any money to do films of any kind, from white, black and especially Jewish bankers? What would the NAACP be saying?

Banks don't finance anti-Semitic or anti-black movies because of moral conscience and because—more importantly—such movies wouldn't be profitable. They would be rejected by a great majority of people in this country, and denounced by every reviewer and every editorial writer.

Why am I so concerned about Spike Lee? His comments are part of a larger picture. In July, the NAACP invited Legrand Clegg, who according to the ADL has a history of anti-Semitism, to speak at a workshop. At the workshop, Mr. Clegg charged that there was collective "Jewish racism" and excessive Jewish influence in Hollywood. According to the *Los Angeles Times,* he engaged in "familiar anti-Semitic calumnies and conspiratorial innuendos."

You would think that Ben Hooks, executive director of the NAACP, would apologize for having invited this well-known anti-Semite to participate, and repudiate his racist views. Instead, Mr. Hooks said, "We have 29 workshops with 125 panelists and we do not take responsibility for their statements. We neither agree nor disagree with what they say. . . . We don't have a position because we haven't done a study on it, but we do know there is racism in Hollywood."

As for Mr. Clegg's comments, Ben Hooks said, "We do not agree with the statement but we do not exercise thought control. I would not invite a panelist here and then say you cannot say this or that."

The allegation by Spike Lee and Legrand Clegg that Hollywood is "owned" by Jews is intended to encourage anti-Semitism. But let's assume that the Jews who helped start the film industry seventy-five years ago continue to play a large role in acting, directing, producing, and financing. Do they have to apologize for that? Is it possible it occurs because of individual talent and investment opportunities?

In that light, I wrote to Ben Hooks: "There is a danger in all of this that you, and others like you, are causing others like myself to conclude that supporting the NAACP, and its objectives, is becoming a one-way street."

I have yet to hear from him.

In 2007, Congressman Charles Rangel became chairman of the powerful House Ways and Means Committee. One of the most prominent black political leaders in New York City since the 1960s, Rangel was often Koch's ally, but the two sparred on occasion, sometimes bitterly. In early 1991, Koch criticized Rangel for endorsing an anti-Semitic black congressman from Chicago. Here Koch describes the firestorm that ensued.

CHARLES RANGEL AND THE JEWS

Remarks from Box 080092, Folder 3, EIK.

In a discussion on the New York City–area television program *Sunday Edition,* on January 20, 1991, I said this about U.S. Congressman Charles Rangel, according to an official transcript of the show:

> I wanted to ask him, I only regret I didn't have the time. If he was so concerned about Israel and he has made that issue, why did he support Congressman Gus Savage, who is not only anti-Israel, but anti-Semitic and he went out of his way to campaign actively for this anti-Semite. When you compare what the Republicans did with respect to David Duke, who was running for a major political office, they denounced him and said he wasn't a Republican. And here you had Charlie Rangel supporting a well known anti-Semite. Now he can't say he didn't know it, because everybody knows that Gus Savage is anti-Semitic, anti-Israel and Charlie Rangel supported him— actively.

A few days later, I received a heated letter from Congressman Rangel. He characterized my remarks as "slanderous" and "malicious," and as "demagoguery," "hatred," and "prejudice," among other choice terms. He even claimed that I was "insinuating" that he—Rangel—"was an anti-Semite and an enemy of Israel." His only response to my point about his endorsement of

Gus Savage—which of course was the real issue at stake—was to charge that I "attacked [him] with race-baiting innuendo for [his] political endorsement of a fellow member of Congress." He also urged me to publicly apologize.

Here was my response:

January 29, 1991

The Hon. Charles B. Rangel
U.S. House of Representatives
2252 Rayburn House Office Building
Washington, DC 20515–3216

Dear Charlie:
I have your letter to me issued on January 29 as a press release.

I received the release from a reporter who requested my response. My response appeared in the *New York Post* and *New York Newsday.*

I don't believe my remarks were slanderous at all. I never insinuated or called you anti-Semitic or an enemy of Israel. Enclosed is a transcript of my comments. I wouldn't withdraw a single word. It is all accurate.

I was told by a reporter that when he asked you whether you thought that Congressman Gus Savage was anti-Semitic or anti-Israel you declined to so characterize him. You and I know, as does every member of Congress, that Gus Savage is one of the worst on both of these subjects.

I found it very offensive that you would campaign actively for him as you did. You knew of his anti-Semitic and anti-Israel remarks and yet they apparently did not stop your campaigning for him. Yes, of course, you have campaigned for many people, but I would hope never for someone who was anti-Semitic, racist or anti-Catholic.

It seems to me that what you should have done is what many people in the Republican party did when that well-known racist and anti-Semite David Duke, who was running for the United States Senate in Louisiana, called for support from his party. President George Bush, former President Ronald Reagan, Senator Bob Dole and then Republican Party Chairman Lee Atwater all denounced David Duke. The Republican Party and its leadership asked Republicans in Louisiana to reject David Duke because of his views and to vote for the Democratic Senator Bennett Johnston. You should have done the same rather than allow your party loyalty, or whatever else motivated you at the time, to support the re-election of Congressman Gus Savage. This is particularly true when his opponent, Mel Reynolds, an outstanding black leader and Rhodes scholar, came so close to winning. Perhaps if you had done "the right thing" as they say and campaigned for him, he might have won.

I suspect your anger stems from your distress that some of your constituents who may have been watching my program may not have known of your behavior. I am certain that the vast majority would have found your behavior irresponsible at the very least.

Aren't you prepared yet to acknowledge that Congressman Gus Savage is anti-Semitic and anti-Israel? To refresh your memory I am enclosing a *New York Post* editorial and major *New York Times* article, just two of the numerous articles on the subject. If you now are willing to stand up and call Gus Savage by his rightful name, I would be happy to acknowledge that on Channel 2, WNEW or in the *New York Post*, indeed, in all three of these channels of information.

All the best and love to Alma.

Sincerely,
Edward I. Koch

In the summer of 1991, the New York press reported that the chairman of City College's Department of African American Studies, Leonard Jeffries, had been teaching his students that blacks were genetically superior to whites. His remarks about Jews were equally reprehensible. Koch urged the City College authorities to take immediate action.

WHEN PROMINENT BLACKS ENGAGE IN OVERT RACISM

Originally published in the *New York Post*, August 16, 1991.

When is racism not called by its rightful name? Apparently when it is practiced by blacks against whites.

An extraordinary story is now unfolding involving Prof. Leonard Jeffries, chairman of City College's African-American Studies Department. According to the *New York Times*, Prof. Jeffries has lectured in his classes that people of European ancestry, whom he calls the "ice people," are fundamentally materialistic, greedy and intent on domination. He has said that people of African descent, whom he calls the "sun people," are essentially humanistic and communal. In addition, he says the skin pigment melanin makes blacks physically and mentally superior to whites.

Last month, Dr. Jeffries gave a speech at the 1991 Empire State Black Arts and Cultural Festival—a speech broadcast over state-run radio facilities, all at taxpayers' expense. He said, among other things:

> There was a conspiracy, planned and plotted and programmed out of Hollywood by people named Greenberg and Weisberg and Trigliani . . . aimed at blacks.
>
> Russian Jewry had a particular control over the movies, and their financial partners, the Mafia, put together a financial system of destruction of black people. It was by design, it was calculated.

> The white boy can't be trusted . . . these white folks, even the
> good ones, you can't trust. There's a devilishness out there when it
> comes to this African thing.

This speech caused a furor, but CUNY has known about Dr. Jeffries and his racist views for years. Last year, a City College faculty committee rebuked him for his comments about racial superiority, but recommended no disciplinary action.

Apparently, once you have tenure, you can teach that the world is flat, Nazism, racism or whatever. How bizarre.

Tenure, however, does not extend to his departmental chairmanship. CCNY President Bernard Harleston can remove him as department chairman—and he should.

I met Prof. Jeffries about a year ago. I'm told he mentioned our meeting in his July 20 speech. I asked him to have breakfast with me after reading about his "ice people/sun people" antiwhite views. He did agree to meet with me, but said he would not eat because white people were trying to poison him. When he arrived, I offered him coffee and danish, but he refused it. I then offered to be his food taster, but he still declined.

He spoke in a nonconfrontational, affable manner, primarily about his "ice people/sun people" views. He also said he had evidence that originally the Statue of Liberty was to have the face of an African woman, but the sculptor, Frederic Bartholdi, was compelled to change it. No doubt that would have come as a shock to Bartholdi's mother, who is widely believed to have been his model. In any event, I had the sense that I was in the presence of a bizarre individual.

Prof. Jeffries' bigotry is distressing, but even more disturbing is the reaction of some black leaders. Assemblyman Al Vann, head of the Black and Puerto Rican Legislative Caucus, proposed a study to examine whether Jeffries' anti-Semitic, antiwhite comments were valid.

What if a white state legislator were to suggest that we examine the validity of anti-black, racist statements made by CUNY Prof. Michael Levin or the late Nobel Laureate William Shockley, who held that blacks are genetically inferior to whites? Would Al Vann support a study on the validity of such obvious racism?

Gov. Cuomo, Mayor Dinkins, Sen. Al D'Amato, Assembly-man Oliver Koppell and others have excoriated Jeffries. But Al Vann and other black members of the Assembly—fifteen in all—and those other members of the state Assembly who re-fused to join their colleagues in signing a letter Koppell circu-lated denouncing Jeffries, deserve our scorn and a vote for their opponents.

All year long our legislators prattle about confronting bias: racial, ethnic, religious and gender. But when they are given an opportunity to stand up and be counted, they retreat into silence.

A BIGOT IS A BIGOT, NO MATTER WHAT THE COLOR OF HIS SKIN

Originally published in the *New York Post*, August 23, 1991.

The violence and anti-Semitism in Crown Heights has pushed CUNY Prof. Leonard Jeffries out of the headlines. But his anti-white, anti-Semitic rhetoric can't be ignored, especially because some well-known and respected people are continuing to de-fend him.

Daily News columnist Juan Gonzalez defended Jeffries in a recent column, saying anti-Semitic and anti-Italian remarks taken from Jeffries's July speech were just "a few snippets from a speech." Gonzalez added that people should not be "calling for his academic scalp without talking to the man or examining his theories."

What are some of those theories? That "rich Jews" were re-sponsible for the slave trade; that the African "sun people" are humane and the European "ice people" are not, and that the skin pigment melanin makes blacks mentally superior to whites.

Gonzalez wrote, "You may disagree with Jeffries after listen-ing to him, but the man has done extensive scholarship on world and African history. In fact, throughout the speech, Jeffries held up book after book by other scholars, many of them white, to buttress his arguments."

Does Gonzalez feel that we should also seriously examine the racial theories of the Ku Klux Klan for nuggets of truth? Should we study the doctrine of David Duke, the former imperial wizard of the Ku Klux Klan, because he is well read and can produce literature supporting his racist views?

Gonzalez went on to say that Jeffries occasionally may generalize "and say things that can be construed as anti-Semitic and anti-white," but that "Malcolm X, much admired in the grave . . . also voiced anti-white views in his early years. But Malcolm's thought evolved." Malcolm X did refute his earlier anti-white statements and is now deservedly venerated. Jeffries cannot be so admired, because he continues to spew his racism with enthusiasm.

There is an amazing difference between the reaction of white leaders and the reaction of many black leaders in this matter. Of course, there are white racists like CUNY Prof. Michael Levin, but they are overwhelmingly denounced by both whites and blacks. That's not the case when a black individual like Jeffries engages in comparable racial rhetoric. In Jeffries's case, what's missing are denunciations from most black leaders. Too often there is leaden silence or support for his views.

Applying special rules to black bigots was demonstrated this week by the New York state chapter of the NAACP. In an apparent reference to Jeffries's racial pronouncements, it passed a bland and banal resolution which said, "It is our belief that no useful purpose can be served by launching assaults on any one racial, religious, or ethnic group." But the resolution did not say that those "assaults" were perpetrated by Jeffries on whites, nor did it condemn him by name. Why not? Was the NAACP's condemnation of David Duke treated the same way?

Gonzalez pointed out that Jeffries's speech was almost two hours long. Undoubtedly, some non-racist facts crept in. He is not being attacked for those statements, but rather for his overall racist point of view. Even Hitler—and Jeffries should not be equated with Hitler—spoke some words of truth. He said that the Versailles Treaty imposed on Germany after World War I was unfair—and that was true. Does that true statement sanitize his volumes of vitriol?

On Sunday, I watched *Sunday Edition,* the show I once co-hosted on Channel 2. (They fired me because they said I was too controversial; I am now a commentator on Channel 5.) Jim Jensen and Ernest Tollerson, editorial page editor at *New York Newsday,* two people who usually show intelligence and good judgment, disgraced themselves by trying to excuse Jeffries's racism and anti-Semitism. They sought to convey that the balance of his message on multiculturalism was more important than his views on race and that we should not be diverted by the occasional lapses in his rhetoric—in effect, Gonzalez's "snippets" reference.

Paraphrasing Gertrude Stein: A bigot is a bigot is a bigot, no matter what the color of their skin.

In a series of letters to City College officials and faculty in the autumn of 1991, Koch continued to press for removal of Jeffries as department chair.

THE LEONARD JEFFRIES CASE: TWO EXCHANGES
Letters from Box 080096, Folder 6, EIK.

9/25/91

Mr. Edward Koch
Robinson, Silverman & Associates
1290 Ave. of the Americas
New York, NY 10104

Dear Ed:

As a CCNY alumnus and ex-Mayor, I appreciate your concerns related to the issues that have been raised by the racist and anti-semitic views of M. Levin and L. Jeffries in your letter to me of 8/28/91. What I find particularly disturbing is the media hyp[e] that has been given to the views of two faculty that are shared by a tiny handful of the 700 faculty on this campus. The enclosed article by Martha Weisman, a leading leftist faculty member who is now emeritus, is representative of the general opinion of the vast majority of our faculty. The huge press coverage has made a mountain of a truly minor speech.

I think the Jeffries issue is a poor investment of your time. There are 200,000 students in CUNY and they are treated like second-class citizens compared to SUNY. Faculty and students have finally gotten angry enough to file a class action suit against the Governor and State Legislature. I think your energy and help in this matter would be far more rewarding. The enclosed news clippings and summary describe the essence of the suit.

Sincerely,

Sheldon Weinbaum
CUNY Distinguished Prof.
The City College of The City University of New York1

———

October 3, 1991

Sheldon Weinbaum
School of Engineering
The City College of The City University of New York
138th Street & Convent Avenue
New York, New York 10031

Dear Professor Weinbaum:
I received your letter of September 25.

I am in total disagreement with you regarding the anti-Semitic views of Professor Jeffries and the anti-black views of Professor Levin. I do not believe that either one of them has the right to teach racism or anti-Semitism in the classroom.

As I understand it, Professor Levin does not teach his racist views in the classroom but does write about them independently. While his views are obnoxious, he has a right to them.

On the other hand, Professor Jeffries teaches anti-white and anti-Semitic views in his classroom. As far as I'm concerned, this is unacceptable even under the widest interpretation of academic freedom.

On a number of occasions, the editors of the student newspaper, *Campus,* have published pieces expressing their anti-Semitic views. This is unacceptable. *Campus* is published with student fees including those contributed involuntarily by Jewish students. The president of CCNY should put a stop to this as a publisher of any other newspaper would when an editor engages in anti-Semitism or racism.

I don't think that press coverage has made a mountain out of a mole hill in this matter. Indeed, not enough has been said about the rising tide of anti-Semitism and racism—black and white—in this city. You should be denouncing what is taking place on your campus instead of foolishly thinking it is unimportant.

All the best.
Sincerely,
Edward I. Koch

———

On November 4, CUNY Chancellor W. Ann Reynolds wrote to inform me that in view of "the irresponsible and inflammatory statements made by Professor Jeffries during the summer at the forum in Albany," Jeffries would be reappointed as chair of the City College Black Studies Department for one year (until June 1992) "rather than the usual three-year term."

Here is my reply.

November 8, 1991

Chancellor W. Ann Reynolds
The City University of New York
535 East Eightieth Street
New York, New York 10021

Dear Chancellor:

I received your letter of November 4 and the memo enclosed with it.

I believe that you as Chancellor and Dr. Bernard Harleston as President of City College failed in your responsibilities to the people of the State of New York by recommending that Dr. Jeffries continue as chair of the City College African-American Studies Department through June 1992.

I find that that recommendation is particularly offensive not only because of what the public knew before the vote was taken but also because of what we all now know. In an interview with the *New York Times,* reported on November 5, Dr. Harleston said he believes Dr. Jeffries is guilty of racism and anti-Semitism. How in the world can you and he justify reappointing someone who has no tenure in the position under discussion and who by admission of the president of the university is guilty of such outrageous behavior?

I believe the matter has not ended. The State Legislature should take appropriate action, including reducing funding for CUNY. If the people of this state—whites and blacks, Jews and Christians—are having their tax dollars used to promote anti-white and anti-Jewish sentiments at an institution of higher learning and the State Legislature takes no action, then it too will bear the same responsibility that you and your colleagues at the Board of Trustees who voted to support your recommendation must bear.

All the best.
Sincerely,
Edward I. Koch

———

On December 2, Chancellor Reynolds responded with a lengthy defense of the action taken regarding Jeffries. The essence of her argument was that Jeffries' statements were not made on the job site nor as a representative of the university. She wrote: "The issue which was before the Board of Trustees is the extent to which the University, as a public sector employer, could take action against an employee of the University for comments made in his capacity as a private citizen, during his summer vacation at an event unrelated to the University." The decision to extend his term for one year instead of three "attempted to balance his First Amendment rights and the President's desire to continue his ongoing review of the impact of Dr. Jeffries' statements on his ability to perform his duties as chair as well as the impact of his statements on the City College's relationship with the academic, business, and government communities."

Below is my reply.

December 20, 1991

Chancellor W. Ann Reynolds
The City University of New York
535 East Eightieth Street
New York, New York 10021

Dear Chancellor:
I am responding to your letter of December 2, 1991.

I read your review of the issues which you, President Harleston and the Board of Trustees considered in determining whether to reappoint Dr. Leonard Jeffries as Chairperson of the Black Studies Department of City College.

While the extensive nature of your reply is welcome, I believe your focusing solely on Professor Jeffries' July 20, 1991, speech is a mistake. The parameters of President Harleston's review seem artificially narrow, leaving the distinct impression that they were framed to elicit a predetermined outcome.

The most glaring problem is the time frame used to review the activities of Dr. Jeffries. By limiting the scope of the inquiry solely to the period following Dr. Jeffries' Albany speech (p. 4, synopsis memorandum: "The newspaper accounts of Dr. Jeffries' July, 1991 speech led the President of City College to review whether Dr. Jeffries' statements had affected his ability to carry out his duties and responsibilities as chairperson of the Black Studies Department. . . ."), the review failed to take into account the serious questions raised by Professor Jeffries' pattern of behavior as chairman of Black Studies at City College extending back several years.

Shouldn't you investigate, or have you, other allegations that have been made concerning Professor Jeffries which include the following: That at a November, 26, 1984, luncheon of City College department chairs and administrators, Dr. Jeffries made a series of anti-Semitic and racist remarks to Professor Mitchell Seligson, then a candidate for the post of Director of International Studies. Information provided to me by the Anti-Defamation League alleges that the remarks of Dr. Jeffries were corroborated by the other professors present at the luncheon and Dr. Jeffries attended the luncheon in his capacity as Chairperson of the Black Studies Department. I believe Professor Seligson subsequently asked that his name be removed from further consideration for the post and apparently indicated that Professor Jeffries' remarks were the reason for his decision.

At the time of this incident, as now, questions were raised as to whether Professor Jeffries should continue to serve as chairperson of his department. According to documents supplied to me by the Anti-Defamation League, President Harleston was reminded of his prerogative under the Bylaws of the Board of Trustees (Sect. 9.1.c) to remove a department chairperson if he or she has acted in a way detrimental to the best interests of the college. President Harleston, however, decided not to make use of this power and, instead, issued what amounted to a reprimand to Jeffries, the gist of which was contained in two memoranda—one to the professors and administrators concerned with the original incident, dated March 8, 1985, and a second, to the entire college community, dated March 15, 1985.

According to President Harleston's memorandum of March 8, 1985:

> I have told Professor Jeffries—and take this opportunity to affirm these views anew to the College community—that such comments and remarks (as made by Jeffries to Seligson), whether intended or not, are intolerable and indefensible for individuals charged with officially representing the College, or for individuals functioning in a role such as Department Chair, which makes them representative of the College. . . .
>
> I want to state unequivocally for the future that The City College will not accept in a leadership role any individual whose official actions or statements create the perception that this College supports racial or ethnic bigotry.

There is also the question of Dr. Jeffries' alleged intimidating behavior towards faculty and students both before and after July 20, 1991.

Dr. Jeffries' being accompanied on and off campus by his so-called "bodyguards" does not befit his leadership role as a department chair at City College. Their presence at the recent Faculty Senate meeting, which adopted a resolution critical of Jeffries was[,] I'm advised, considered intimidating by some as it has been at previous Senate meetings. I'm told that these "guards" have accompanied him to meetings with other faculty members or outside visitors and have had a chilling effect on the City College campus.

I am also advised that Fred Rueckher, a white City College student, wrote a series of articles on Black Studies critical of Dr. Jeffries in *Campus* in March/April 1985, and then refused to appear before a Special Fact Finding Committee established to review the allegations contained in the articles. Is it possible and shouldn't it be a subject of an inquiry as to whether or not he had been intimidated by Professor Jeffries? Ought there not be an inquiry to determine the purpose of Dr. Jeffries in having one such "bodyguard," "Brother Larry," present at his widely reported recent interview with another student reporter, Eliot Morgan of the *Harvard Crimson*?

It is also alleged that on October 31 of this year, Professor Jeffries appeared at a City College Economics Faculty Student Luncheon and issued veiled threats to Professor Morris Silver, chair of the Economics Department.

Rather than being conducive to an atmosphere of racial and ethnic understanding, Dr. Jeffries' behavior has engendered a climate of fear and intimidation on campus which seems to have seriously impaired the functioning of his Department as well as the College as a whole.

The question raised in all these instances is the one your memorandum clearly recognized. Can Professor Jeffries ". . . continue to act effectively as departmental administrator and as a participant in the formation, development, and interpretation of college-side interests and policy"?

Dr. Jeffries' behavior discredits the entire City University community. It is time to act decisively. The overwhelming majority of hardworking students and faculty cry out for you to exercise true leadership in putting an end to this intolerable situation.

Ought there not be new hearings based on the issues raised in this letter and other actions on his part bringing the University into disrepute?

All the best.
Sincerely,
Edward I. Koch

In the midst of the debate over anti-Semitic rhetoric—the Jeffries case—New York City was suddenly engulfed in anti-Semitic violence. For three days, black mobs in Brooklyn attacked Jewish homes, stores, and passersby in the worst outbreak of anti-Semitic violence in the city's history. The reluctance of Mayor David Dinkins to order the police to forcefully intervene soon became the focus of public controversy, and would ultimately play a role in his defeat by Rudy Giuliani in the subsequent mayoral election.

SILENCE IN THE FACE OF A POGROM

Originally published in the *New York Post*, August 30, 1991.

In May 1990, the French public was enraged by a wave of anti-Semitic attacks, including the desecration of several Jewish cemeteries.

French President Francois Mitterand, Prime Minister M. Michel Rocard, the Roman Catholic primate of France, Albert Cardinal Decourtray, and the mayor of Paris, Jacques Chirac, led over 100,000 marchers through the streets of Paris in protest. It was the first time that a French president had joined in such a public demonstration since World War II.

In Crown Heights over the last two weeks there have not simply been displays of anti-Semitism, but a modern-day pogrom. Or, if you don't like that word, call it a lynching. Last week, gangs of young blacks rushed through the streets yelling, "Jews, Jews" and hunted down one young Jew, Yankel Rosenbaum, a visitor from Australia. They stabbed him to death in revenge for an automobile accident three hours earlier which, regrettably, took the life of a young black boy, Gavin Cato—an accident which Rosenbaum had nothing to do with. Where in this city do you see outrage against this anti-Semitism comparable to that of the French being expressed?

Not since the last pogrom in Poland in 1946 has the Western world witnessed such an event. Dozens of Jews were injured and hundreds suffered property damage during the rioting. How did our religious, civic and political leaders, and many in the media, react? In most cases, there was no public reaction or, when there was a response, the accidental death by automobile was equated with the intentional-bias murder.

Why haven't our civic leaders and clergy denounced this pogrom? One would think they would be at City Hall demanding that the mayor denounce not only the violence of the mob, but also the demagogues who were and are inciting further violence. When Yusef Hawkins and Michael Griffith were murdered because they were black, the clergy and public officials responded. Why don't they denounce this violence, committed against Jews because they were Jews?

Instead the traveling salesmen of hate (Sharpton, Mason, Maddox, Carson, Moore, Daughtry to name a few) have brought their racial road show to Crown Heights. At Gavin Cato's funeral the pulpit seemed less an altar than a place from which to issue calls for further violence.

The black demagogues defended black anger and the recent violence by saying the Lubavitchers in Crown Heights receive preferential treatment from the police. Even if this were true, does that excuse the pogrom? We currently have a black mayor, David Dinkins, and a black police commissioner, Lee Brown (and before Brown, Ben Ward). Are they providing preferential treatment to the Jewish community? Hardly likely. And neither did I as mayor.

While there may be no official preferential treatment, many cops—black, Hispanic, and white—feel hostility directed at them from sections of the black community which has no counterpart in the Jewish community. Cops may find the Lubavitchers odd and perhaps difficult to like, but they know they will not be in any danger from them. While many blacks see the police as an occupying army, the Jews welcome the cops, and the cops know it.

When the police come to the defense of citizens in both black and white communities, or protect themselves from physical attack and the perpetrator is black, they fear that they may themselves become the subject of false charges of police brutality.

Many cops now believe that at City Hall, in the media and in the eyes of too many citizens, they are presumed guilty until they prove their innocence.

There are those who criticize the Lubavitchers because they are a closed community. The Lubavitchers do have their own religious customs and beliefs. But odd or not, clannish or not, they are entitled to be free from violence and pogroms.

It appears that the only people willing to march in outrage against anti-Semitism are the French. What's happened to the rest of us?

DINKINS SHOULD TAKE RESPONSIBILITY FOR HIS CROWN HEIGHTS FAILURES

Originally published in the *New York Post*, November 27, 1992.

Most of those who voted for Mayor David Dinkins did so because they believed a black mayor would be able to reduce racial antagonism and bring racial peace. He said his election would change race relations.

I had hoped that in his speech on Wednesday he would accept responsibility for matters within his control, such as the police response to the Crown Heights riot. He did not.

Many of those on the left as well as on the right point to the following sins of omission on the part of the mayor: He stubbornly refused to post a $10,000 reward immediately following Yankel Rosenbaum's murder; he initially failed to support a federal probe after Lemrick Nelson's acquittal; he failed to convey the same degree of anger at the Nelson acquittal that he expressed about the Rodney King verdict 3,000 miles away. Instead he wrapped himself in the mantle of the court system.

No responsible—or even irresponsible—Jewish leader has accused the mayor of the murder of Yankel Rosenbaum. Nor accused the mayor of anti-Semitism. Nor in the mayor's words "blame[d] [him] for the verdict reached by the jury in the Rosenbaum cause." By continuing to defend himself against these spurious, indeed, self-generated attacks, he seems to be trying to make himself the victim.

Many believe the mayor's worst omission was his inexplicable refusal to apologize to the city and the Lubavitcher community in particular for his failure to order the police to take action immediately when black mobs were assaulting Jews and vandalizing Jewish-owned property. Does anyone believe that if a comparable white mob was running through the streets of Bed-Stuy after having murdered a black, the police would not have moved in immediately?

It is not enough to point to the failure of the Police Department. David Dinkins acknowledges that at a certain point he substituted his own judgment for that of the police—but that was three days too late. He must take direct responsibility for not intervening earlier. His acceptance of general responsibility—without reference to specifics—is meaningless.

The mayor referred to "race baiters and rabble rousers." Did he mean Rabbi Avi Weiss, whom he has publicly singled out as the villain? The mayor's concern with Rabbi Weiss seems absurd while he himself embraces such figures as Bill Tatum of the *Amsterdam News,* Rev. Al Sharpton, Rev. Herbert Daughtry, Rev. Timothy Mitchell, and hangers-on like Jitu Weusi and Sonny Carson. These individuals have fomented racial unrest by their rhetoric on many occasions. Avi Weiss has never to my knowledge used racist language or urged physical assault on any community.

If I had been mayor and not denounced the Rodney King verdict for what it was—a travesty and a failure of the judicial system—would I have had the backing of editorial writers who now support the mayor when he refuses to denounce the Lemrick Nelson acquittal? I doubt it. The mayor in his speech Wednesday still could not bring himself to denounce Nelson's acquittal, although he has in the past protested verdicts in the Rodney King and St. John's University cases, as well as the conviction of Winnie Mandela for the kidnapping of a black child.

The mayor himself missed an opportunity. Had he accepted personal responsibility for his sins of omission, he would have been applauded by the overwhelming majority of citizens in this town—black and white. Instead, he brought to mind the lyrics from *My Fair Lady*—"words, words, words. I am so sick of words." I believe only Mayor Dinkins's coterie of black and Jewish leaders, limousine liberals and editorial writers—those who want to paper the matter over—will applaud his speech.

There are some matters that will never be brought to a conclusion unless and until justice is done. If justice cannot be done, then those in charge, such as the mayor, must admit their failures and ask forgiveness. Otherwise, the voices from the grave will haunt our days and mar his.

THE CROWN HEIGHTS POGROM: TEN YEARS AFTER

Originally published in *Newsday*, August 31, 2001.

On August 16, 1991, a pogrom started in Brooklyn.

David Dinkins was mayor. For three days following the accidental death of seven-year-old Gavin Cato, mobs of black New Yorkers roamed the streets of Crown Heights attacking Jews. Young Gavin's tragic death was an accident involving the motorcade of the Lubavitcher grand rebbe, Menachem Schneerson, as he returned from a visit to his wife's grave.

The pogrom that followed was not an accident. During the three days of violence, mobs deliberately targeted Jews. Yankel Rosenbaum, a yeshiva student, was stabbed to death by Lemrick Nelson as the crowd chanted, "Jew, Jew, kill the Jew!" Some have called the actions of the mob a riot, and David Dinkins called it both a riot and a "lynching."

On June 22 [2001], WNBC-TV aired a documentary on Dinkins' legacy. The reporter asked me how history would view Dinkins. Should I do what was expected, I thought, heap encomiums on David, whom I like, or tell the truth as I see the truth? I said David Dinkins' place in history will always be marked by the memory of the Crown Heights pogrom.

In an interview with *Jewish Week* commemorating the tenth anniversary of the Crown Heights riots, Dinkins said he was distressed by the use of the word pogrom. "I don't think that it is useful, and it certainly is inaccurate for continued characterization of that tragedy as a pogrom, which I define as state-sponsored activity. It was not state-sponsored or directed, and the courts have so held to this day."

Of course, Dinkins and his police commissioner, Lee Brown, now the mayor of Houston, Texas, did not sponsor or condone the mob actions. But they did not take the necessary police measures to protect the Jewish community or other innocent civilians. At least eighty assaults and countless acts of vandalism went unabated for three days.

Dinkins has a superb record of supporting the Jewish community. He demonstrated his courage by denouncing Louis Farrakhan when he came to Madison Square Garden in 1985. "In light of Minister Farrakhan's visit to New York, I must say that I find his blatantly anti-Semitic remarks offensive and I condemn them," he said. As mayor, I made the decision to assign police protection to Dinkins.

The WNBC reporter who interviewed me recently said there were two ways to handle a riot: one, to use whatever force was needed, or, alternatively, to allow a riot to "peter out." The next time there is a riot in her neighborhood, I responded, the authorities should allow it to peter out and we will see how she feels.

On midnight of the third day of rioting, Dinkins finally gave the order for the NYPD to take the necessary forceful action to stop the riot. Gov. Mario Cuomo appointed prosecutor Richard Girgenti to a special commission to investigate the actions of law enforcement. The report held Dinkins responsible. "The Mayor, as the City's Chief Executive, did not act in a timely and decisive manner in requiring the Police Department to meet his own stated objectives: to protect the lives, safety, and property of the residents of Crown Heights, and to quickly restore peace and order to the community." It is a classic example of government inaction fueling the fire of a pogrom.

Dinkins' definition of a pogrom as only "state-sponsored" rioting is wrong, but he is not alone. Nobel Prize—winning author Elie Wiesel and *New York Times* writer Joyce Purnick objected to the use of the word. Historically, many pogroms were initiated by parish priests who referred to Jews as "Christ Killers" or invoked the blood libel, falsely accusing Jews of using the blood of Christian children to bake Passover matzos. One of the deadliest pogroms, the Kishinev massacre in 1903, was fueled by the wild agitation of a local newspaper. Civil and military authorities remained neutral. "Pogrom" is defined as "an organized and often officially encouraged massacre or persecution of a minority group, especially one conducted against the Jew," according to the American Heritage dictionary.

History shows pogroms are not always initiated by government. The impact of a pogrom depends on the response of law enforcement. In Eastern Europe, authorities stood aside and allowed mobs to wreak havoc unchallenged. On Eastern Parkway in Brooklyn, the NYPD did not protect the victims while mobs ran amok for three days. Yes, it was a pogrom. Using the rightful name and recognizing what happened can only help heal the wounds.

BLACK–JEWISH RELATIONS: LOOKING AHEAD
Written in January 2007.

I have had my ups and downs with the African American community.

Through it all, both before I became mayor and when I was mayor, I never lost my sense of justice or my feeling that the black community has suffered greater injustices perpetrated against it than any of the many communities that live in the city of New York—including Hispanics, Jews, Catholics, Irish, Italians, and so many others.

Former assemblyman and Bronx county leader Roberto Ramirez has said to me on several occasions that I endeared myself to him because of a remark I once made to him. That remark was, "If I were born black and had suffered the discrimination which, while undoubtedly less today, still exists in the United States—and I am not referring to slavery which was the absolute worst of inhumane treatment in human affairs—I would have become a revolutionary or at least a Communist, and if I had lived during slavery, I would have been a bomb thrower."

I first saw Jesse Jackson on the shuttle traveling from New York to Washington, D.C., in 1968 when I was elected to Congress. Jackson was someone who stood out immediately upon entering a public space. He was attired in a leather vest, and sported an Afro and a commanding presence. My recollection is that I did not go over and introduce myself (I was much more shy then than I am today). But we had a lot of contact over the years.

One such occasion was when I was mayor and he was in charge of a meeting of supporters of boycotts of then-apartheid South Africa. As I recall, I was one of the very few white public figures—and the only white mayor—in the entire crowd of public figures holding a press conference in Washington, D.C. The press conference was held in the House of Representatives office building. In those days, much of the press was very hostile to Israel, as were many liberals (or progressives, as many called themselves), and I was asked by a reporter, "Will you urge the government of Israel to stop sending arms to South Africa?"

I replied: "It is the United States and Great Britain that are sending arms to South Africa. It is Israel that is boycotted by all of the black African states, and it should be understandable that Israel, surrounded by Arab states that want to destroy it, will continue to have economic relations with South Africa, since its government supports the state of Israel."

I went on to say that the United States and Great Britain should stop doing business, military and economic, with South Africa, and the black African states who are boycotting Israel at the demand of the Arab states, should open up relations with

Israel and then I will urge Israel to end its relationship with South Africa. Jesse come over to me later in the day and said, "You are some piece of work." He understood my feelings, as I understood his.

During the 1988 presidential election, I did everything I could to help Al Gore, then running for president, and to prevent Jesse, who was very popular in some parts of New York City, from winning New York state. Gore's support for Israel was very important to me, as was the hostility of Jesse to Israel and to the Jewish community, as he had expressed it in his infamous "Hymie town" remark and other aspects of his campaign.

Governor Mario Cuomo sought to bring us together during the election, and while he did not accomplish his purpose, he did establish what became a truce. Jesse and I actually met later on at a television studio, and while not scheduled to be jointly interviewed by Sam Roberts, a *New York Times* reporter, we were persuaded by Roberts to submit to a joint interview. We communicated on that show and I think we both changed our respective attitudes. For the first time—and it has continued—we understood that while at times we might be at cross purposes, we actually liked one another. And that is still true for me and I hope for him.

Al Sharpton and I have become good friends. He often tells people, "He [Koch] made me famous, by having me arrested." Then he goes on to say, "Even after he had me arrested in 1978, he never stopped talking to me." Indeed, after Sharpton was imprisoned in the Brooklyn federal prison after being arrested and convicted in Puerto Rico for trespassing on the island of Vieques in 1999, I visited him.

Sharpton and I have worked together on legislation—the Second Chance bill—for nonviolent drug offenders who have served their time in prison. As a result of our working together, some other public figures came to regard him as someone whose endorsement should be solicited. When Bill Bradley, U.S. Senator from New Jersey, ran for president, he asked me to introduce him to Al Sharpton. When Hillary Clinton was running for senator from New York State, she asked me to do the same, and I accommodated both of them.

American society sets certain boundaries for what is acceptable in public life. When Jesse Jackson's "Hymie town" remark became known, he quickly understood that he needed to publicly apologize, and he did so. Likewise, Al Sharpton recognized that there were things he had said or done in the past that crossed that boundary, and that he has come to regret.

The past cannot be changed, and my feelings about things that Jesse and Al have said and done in the past have not changed. But those who accept the rules of American political culture, refrain from repeating irresponsible words or actions, and genuinely regret their past mistakes, put themselves back on the playing field.

I have had my share of run-ins with both Jesse and Al. Yet no one can deny that they are smart and talented, and both are significant leaders in the African American community. Indeed, to some extent they can be regarded as crossover leaders, considering the large numbers of citizens outside of the black community who support them and in many cases voted for them. Their achievements demonstrate how far this country has come in the fight against racism. No doubt there will be many more battles against racism, and against anti-Semitism, in the years ahead. I hope we will have the opportunity to join those fights as allies.

CHAPTER TWO

CONFRONTING
ANTI-SEMITISM
IN THE
UNITED STATES
AND ABROAD

While working to combat anti-Semitism in New York City, Mayor Koch si-multaneously played an active role in protesting the persecution of Soviet Jewry, the most severe manifestation of state-sponsored anti-Semitism since the Nazis. This chapter begins with Koch's writings and remarks pertaining to the plight of the Jews in the Soviet Union and then moves into other, more recent incarna-tions of anti-Jewish bigotry. These include the rise of anti-Semitism in post-communist Russia, electoral gains by right-wing extremists in Germany, "dual loyalty" accusations against Jews who supported U.S. military action against Iraq, and anti-Israel hostility in France. This section includes a discussion about what action can, or should, be taken in response to the publication of a cartoon mocking the Holocaust in a student newspaper at Rutgers University. The dis-cussion takes the form of a correspondence between Koch and a range of promi-nent scholars, university presidents, and legal experts, in which they grapple with an array of moral and legal questions concerning free speech, civic responsi-bility, and anti-Semitism.

In this chapter, Koch also revisits one of the most controversial episodes in his public career, his exposé of then–Secretary of State James Baker's obscenity-laced verbal attack on American Jews. Koch's revelation was front-page news around the world and continued to reverberate for years in the American Jewish community and beyond. Although senior U.S. government officials have privately made anti-Jewish remarks in the past, typically evidence has surfaced only long after the official has departed from public service. For example, Franklin Roosevelt remarked at the 1943 Casablanca Conference that "over fifty percent of the lawyers, doctors, school teachers, college professors, etc, in Germany were Jews," which, he said, caused the "understandable complaints which the Germans bore towards the Jews in Germany." However, this did not become public knowledge until the proceedings of the conference were published in 1973. Harry Truman's 1947 diary entry asserting that "the Jews are very, very selfish" did not become public knowledge until the discovery, in 2003, of the heretofore unknown diary. Richard Nixon's 1971 tirades about "rich Jews" and the "Jewish cabal" he thought was out to get him were not known until the National Archives released tapes of his conversations twenty-five years later.

Such revelations therefore affected only the individual's posthumous reputation. By contrast, Koch's revelation about James Baker was significant because Baker was still secretary of state and the controversy therefore could have affected the administration's domestic standing, not to mention U.S.-Israel relations and the role of the United States in Middle East peace negotiations.

Despite vehement denials by both Baker and President Bush, Koch insisted on the accuracy of his column and was supported by prominent journalists. In this chapter, Koch presents, for the first time, his private correspondence with President Bush about the issue—and reveals the identity of his source for the Baker statement.

———

Shortly after taking power in 1918, the government of the Soviet Union began persecuting its Jewish citizens. Motivated partly by Communist ideology and partly by traditional Russian anti-Semitism, the authorities were determined to stamp out Jewish religious life and ethnic attachments, and forcibly assimilate the country's three million Jews into the new Soviet culture. Synagogues and other

Jewish institutions were shut down, Jewish religious education was forbidden, the teaching of Hebrew was outlawed, and emigration was prohibited. Many Jews were jailed or executed during the Stalinist show trials of the 1930s.

American Jews' awareness of the plight of Soviet Jewry during the 1920s and 1930s was dulled by their relief at the overthrow of the anti-Semitic czar, a lack of information about the situation in the U.S.S.R., and the Soviet authorities' publicly declared opposition to anti-Semitism. The persecution of German Jews by the Nazis in the 1930s and, later, the Soviet Union's participation in the war against Hitler further distracted attention from the treatment of Jews in the U.S.S.R.

By the mid-1960s, the American Jewish community's perception of Soviet Jewry began to change, in part because of the Soviet government's publication of blatantly anti-Semitic literature, its active support of the Arab war against Israel, and its harsh response to attempts by small numbers of Soviet Jews to assert their Jewish identity or seek permission to emigrate to Israel. Through demonstrations, lobbying in Washington, and other activities, American Jews increasingly made the plight of Soviet Jewry a top communal priority and sought to rouse U.S. and international pressure on the U.S.S.R. to permit Jewish emigration.

The Kremlin regarded emigration as a repudiation of the Soviet system, and only a few hundred Jews had been permitted to leave each year as part of family reunification arrangements. But in response to international criticism, and especially the U.S.S.R.'s concern that its trade relations with the United States were at risk, the U.S.S.R. allowed more than 13,000 Jews to emigrate in 1971 and similar or greater numbers in the years to follow, reaching a peak of over 51,000 in 1979 before beginning a long downward trend. In 1983, the year that Ed Koch made the following remarks, only about 1,300 Jews were permitted to leave the U.S.S.R.

LET MY PEOPLE GO

Remarks at the twelfth annual "Solidarity Sunday" rally, sponsored by the
Greater New York Conference on Soviet Jewry, May 22, 1983, from Box 080065,
Folder 4, EIK.

I am very pleased to be here today to take part in this tremendous show of solidarity with the Jews in the Soviet Union. Each one of us stands up today for the three million of our brothers and sisters who cannot. Three million who suffer Soviet persecution simply because they are Jews. Very few Americans have any idea what it's like to live under a tyrannical regime. But it doesn't take long for those who visit Russia to understand what it means to be in a land where life itself is subject to sudden cancellation. I went to the Soviet Union in 1971. There was a distinct sense of oppression in the air, but it wasn't until I boarded my flight home—and many other visitors to Russia have reported the same feeling—that I really began to worry. Human rights as we know them don't exist in the Soviet Union. Suppose they didn't let my plane leave? Suppose they decide to hold me captive, the way so many other Jews are being held captive behind the Iron Curtain? Finally, the plane took off, but the feeling of anxiety remained until I heard the voice of the pilot. He said: "Ladies and gentlemen, we have just left Soviet air space." And the entire plane burst into applause.

Now, I have been to other countries with authoritarian governments, such as the People's Republic of China. But I didn't feel afraid in China. I didn't have that terrible fear of being held captive. People didn't applaud when the plane left Chinese air space. No, there is something special about the Soviet system, something that sets it apart even among governments that rule by terror. A look at the history books will tell us why.

In 1917, the Russian Revolution overthrew a corrupt monarchy and briefly offered hope to the people of that beleaguered country. But very quickly the hope was replaced by despair as a new form of corrupt government took hold. Fifty million—fifty million!—of its own citizens disappeared into slave labor camps or fell before firing squads. A secret police apparatus—worse than anything imagined by the czar—kept the people in constant fear.

We must never forget that the Soviet Union made peace with Adolf Hitler—may his name be forever damned—in the hope of dividing the spoils of war, of feeding together on the innocent lives wasted in the madness of World War II. Today, I firmly believe that Stalin and Hitler are rotting in hell together! The advent of Soviet Communism was a tragic betrayal of the cause of human rights. The millions who died knew what we know—that the red flag of the Soviet Union does not represent revolution. It represents blood—the blood of its own people.

Today, the Soviet system still maintains a stranglehold on the lives of its citizens. But nowhere does the hand of oppression grip tighter than at the throats of Soviet Jews. Unfortunately, the situation has deteriorated considerably since Solidarity Sunday last year. Jews are being imprisoned for trying to assert fundamental rights granted to them under international law. Trials are coming up on a weekly basis, trials that are intended to strike even greater fear into the hearts of those wishing to emigrate or practice their religion freely. And most ominous is the declining rate of emigration. Since 1979, there has been a 90 percent decline. In the early days of our people, we had heroic men and women who were successful in their fight for freedom. Today, there are brave men and women behind the Iron Curtain who fight against Soviet tyranny.

As Americans and Jews, we point with pride and admiration to the courageous Jewish activists—the refuseniks of the Soviet Union—who dare to oppose one of the most powerful military machines of all time. We hear their voices crying out for justice, for freedom, for the right to speak their own language, to study their own culture and religion.

Sometimes I wonder where they get their strength. How did young Yosef Mendelevich survive for years in the Soviet gulag, living on bread and water, bereft of family and friends? And yet he not only lived to tell the tale, he came away from his long struggle as a pillar of faith—a living torch of liberty burning to set his people free. How can we find words to express our admiration for the incredible moral strength of those who have sacrificed security, brilliant careers and the praise of their countrymen in order to tell the truth about the horrors of Soviet Communism?

The rulers of the Soviet Union are attempting to cover up the truth about their government. They play on public opinion around the world, and right here in America, like master violinists. When they needed our trade and our grain to strengthen their war machine and satisfy their hungry people, they permitted first 20,000, then 30,000, and then over 50,000 Jews to leave the Soviet Union. They also relaxed enforcement of regulations against Jewish religion and culture.

Then, suddenly, the gates of emigration slammed shut. Those who had applied for exit visas found themselves fired from jobs, hounded by authorities, and forced out of schools and factories and drafted into the army. In some cases, exit visas were granted, but with a sadistic twist. Families were purposely divided. Two victims of this senseless cruelty are with us today, Tzvi Essas and Avital Scharansky.

Perhaps worst of all is the feeling of uncertainty, not knowing for years what will happen next. And now we see the recent unleashing of anti-Semitism, with the revival of the hateful word "zhid" to describe Jews. High school students in Leningrad are playing a new game called "concentration camp," where Jewish classmates are no longer identified by name, but by assigned numbers by their non-Jewish classmates. How dare these propagandists of hate and inhumanity attempt to reenact the infamy of the Holocaust on innocent Jewish children! What can we, as Americans, as freedom-loving people, and as Jews do about it?

The first thing we can do is to let our government in Washington know how we view these latest developments. We want the United States to put the rights of the oppressed and beleaguered Jews of the Soviet Union at the top of the negotiating list, along with the MX and Pershing missiles, grain shipments and technological exchanges.

We can demand specific conditions and restrictions to be placed upon trade with the Soviet Union, not just rhetoric.

We must raise our voices together in outrage. No opportunity must pass, no gathering in the Jewish community must take place where the participants are not asked and exhorted to speak out in defense of Soviet Jewry.

We must flood Soviet embassies and consulates, and indeed the Kremlin itself, with letters and telegrams. We must let both the Communist rulers and the Jews of the Soviet Union know that the world is watching, and caring, and recording what is taking place today.

Over one quarter of a million Jews—250,000 of our co-religionists—have already gotten out of the Soviet Union in the last decade. All because people like you came to demonstrations like this. Let us unite in a common resolve that we shall not rest until every voice has been raised in protest. Let us commit ourselves to the idea that part of us can never be free as long as the Jews of the Soviet Union are enslaved under the yoke of tyranny.

If Anatoly Scharansky, Yosef Begun and countless others can find the strength to endure, to grow and not to lose hope, we can certainly find it within ourselves to draw attention to their plight.

Today, New York is taking the lead. We are showing the nation and the world where we stand. We must all work together until others follow our lead, until they hear our voices. And so I ask you now to join with me in saying three times, "Let my people go!" Like the trumpeters at the walls of Jericho in an earlier day, may our voices cause the walls that incarcerate our brothers and sisters in the Soviet Union to come tumbling down. So let's say it loud enough to be heard in that den of iniquity across the street. Are you ready?

Let my people go!

Let my people go!

Let my people go!

Will the next generation be ready to confront the menace of anti-Semitism?
Concerned that the comforts of American life in the 1980s would dull the
community's vigilant instincts, Mayor Koch spoke frankly to a convention of
young Reform Jewish activists—some of them future communal leaders—
about the ever-present dangers posed by anti-Semitism in old forms and new,
from Third World regimes wrapping their Jew hatred in attacks on Israel, to
homegrown extremists of the more familiar variety. "It's not a good idea to be
an alarmist," Koch told them. "But it's a worse idea to keep your head in the
sand."

MAKE A DIFFERENCE

Remarks to the North American Federation of Temple Youth, Arlington, VA, February
18, 1985, from Box 080078, Folder 5, EIK.

I note that the theme of this year's convention is "making a difference." I could give you a hundred reasons why this is a
tremendously important theme for a convention of young people, especially those who are committed to both the civic and
spiritual values that make our nation great. However, I will spare
you the one hundred reasons and instead will tell you this. One
day, about twenty-five years from now, you're going to look
around and realize that America is being run by people you went
to high school with. Your senior class president is now the president of IBM. Your student council representative is now your
U.S. senator.

And that guy in the back row of your class picture, that guy
who was already beginning to go a little bald, is now the mayor
of New York City.

What you do now, what you learn now, the habits and skills
are all helping to determine where you'll be in twenty-five years.
They are helping to determine the ways in which you will be able
to make a difference.

I know that when you're young the problems and pleasures of the moment take precedence. It's not easy to think ahead twenty-five, thirty, or forty years, or to remember what took place twenty-five, thirty, or forty years in the past.

Sooner or later, however, the past and the future will meet. This year, 1985, is an example of what I mean. Forty years ago today, Allied armies were sweeping across Nazi-occupied Europe and into Germany itself. I know, because for me the past is very real. Forty years ago today, I was a twenty-year-old soldier in the 104th infantry division. We fought our way into Germany. As the days and weeks passed, as the Nazi regime collapsed, shocking news began to reach the outside world of the death camps at Auschwitz, Dachau, Buchenwald and other places.

Many people had suspected what the Nazis were doing. Some evidence had reached the outside world. But the full horror wasn't known until the photographs and eyewitness testimony began to appear in the papers. And by then it was too late for six million Jews and millions of others. Forty years ago, 1985 was the future for me. If anyone had suggested in 1945 that I would some day be mayor of New York City, I would have complimented that person's judgment, but I don't think I would have believed it. And, if someone had told me in 1945 that, forty years later, one of the worst of the Nazi murderers would be living in South America, I don't think I would have believed that either. It would have seemed too incredible. And yet the infamous Dr. Josef Mengele, a sadistic killer, is today living in Paraguay, apparently under the protection of the government of that country. Forty years ago, if someone had told me that a Nazi SS butcher would be apprehended in Bolivia, returned to France where he committed his worst atrocities, and not be brought to trial, I don't think I would have believed such a thing possible.

And yet Klaus Barbie, who was responsible for the torture, mutilation and murder of countless French men and women, today languishes in a French prison. What are the French afraid of? When will Klaus Barbie be brought to trial? I say the time is now! The time should have been forty years ago. Very few people survived the Nazi death camps. The bodies of the dead were burned in ovens, forty years ago. When the world saw at last the full scope of what the Nazis had done, we had every right to expect that a wave of revulsion would sweep every last trace of Nazi ideology from the face of the earth. We had every right to expect that the deadly infection of Nazi hatred would perish in its own funeral pyre.

Forty years later, however, we find ourselves facing an ugly and troubling truth. Anti-Semitism not only survived the destruction of Nazi Germany, it has spread to other parts of the world. Sometimes the new anti-Semites are careful to phrase their hatred in new ways. We see this phenomenon in the United Nations, where Israel is regularly subjected to vicious attacks and is made the target of despicable falsehoods.

Right here in the United States we see the ancient evil of anti-Semitism taking root among extremist groups. It is shocking to contemplate but we must face the facts. Right here in America there are organizations of people who would like to see every single person in this room dead. They hate Jews. They spout all the old lies about Judaism. They are out there right now, and they believe in using guns to get what they want.

It's not a good idea to be an alarmist. But it's a worse idea to keep your head in the sand, the anti-Semitic hate groups in America are sometimes called "the lunatic fringe," or "the far right," or various other names. It is well to remember, however, that Hitler was once the leader of a lunatic fringe. He served time in jail for his political activities. He was dismissed by many as a crackpot. Some people laughed at the thought that Hitler might be able to take over Germany, but they didn't laugh long.

Never take for granted that the evils of the past will remain in the past. Always be alert to opportunities for progress, but never ignore the warning signs of bigotry and hate, no matter how distant they may seem. Some scholars have said that without Hitler there would have been no Holocaust. We know from history that it is indeed possible for one person to have a tremendous influence on the world, for good or evil.

Let us hope that the people who will be running the world with you in twenty-five years will be good. But don't be surprised if a few of them are evil. Don't be surprised if you have to struggle to make the good prevail. My generation fought against Hitler. Your generation may one day be called on to continue the struggle for freedom and democracy. You may be called upon to "make a difference." In closing, I want to say that the best way to eliminate the need for conflict and war is to eliminate the things that make them possible. The challenge that faces all generations is to do away with bigotry, racism and prejudice in all its forms. Part of this challenge is to ensure that the old evils do not become accepted under new names. Always be ready to support programs such as affirmative action, which reach out and encourage people to apply for jobs, which give them a chance to succeed on their merits. Beware of programs that call for quotas. Quotas are invariably based on ethnic, racial or religious discrimination. The way to get rid of bigotry is not to bring it back under a new name. Your presence here today shows that you're getting a good start in the right direction, a bright future awaits you. Never be afraid to stand up for what's right, never be afraid to make a difference.

In 1985, the Jewish community's annual Solidarity Sunday rally in New York City for Soviet Jewry coincided with President Ronald Reagan's controversial visit to a cemetery in Bitburg, Germany, where a number of SS veterans are buried. In his remarks, Mayor Koch emphasized the inseparable nature of the horrors perpetrated by the SS, the brutality of the Soviet regime, and the obligation of American Jews to learn from the former in order to combat the latter.

WATCH WHAT THE SOVIETS DO, NOT WHAT THEY SAY

Remarks at the fourteenth annual Solidarity Sunday rally, sponsored by the Greater New York Conference on Soviet Jewry, May 5, 1985, from Box 080078, Folder 6, EIK.

Today is Solidarity Sunday. It is also "Bitburg Day." Both have very great meaning for us. We know what Solidarity Sunday means, because for fourteen years we gathered here to let the Soviet Union and the entire world know that we will never— never!—forget the Jews who are detained and oppressed in the Soviet Union. Some people, however, are never quite convinced that we mean what we say; they think—and perhaps they even wish—that we will let our memory grow dim. They think that the horror of the Holocaust and the reality of anti-Semitism today will fade into silence. They are wrong! We will not stand silent. We will speak out whenever the occasion calls for it. And we will speak to whomever needs to hear what we say, even to the president of the United States.

The meaning of Bitburg is in the outcry that Bitburg provoked. We will be heard, we will remind the world again and again that the Holocaust did not happen in some distant time or place. It happened to us, it happened to our families, it happened to the six million, but it also happened to generations that would have followed them, generations unborn. Fortunately, we can make our voices and our message heard in the

United States and in other free countries. We can appeal to the moral fiber of decent people and we can see them respond.

In the Soviet Union, however, free speech is feared and censored. That nation is controlled by a system of government that actually believes it can bury the truth and replace it with propaganda. It is a system of government that talks about religious freedom and human rights for its citizens, but practices oppression of its minorities. The Soviet government tries hard to snuff out the voices of dissent, the voices that cry for freedom. This oppression is directed with particular severity against Soviet Jews. In recent months, there have been numerous arrests, searches and threats, anti-Semitic propaganda is increasing, the flow of immigration has dwindled and almost died.

We who can speak freely bear special responsibility. We must not only speak our own consciences, we must speak for those inside the Soviet Union who cannot make themselves heard. We must raise our voices together and say "Let my people go!" We have fought long and hard to seek justice for Soviet Jews. We have had our victories. Hundreds of thousands now live in freedom who might otherwise still be in bondage. But the job isn't over. I know we sometimes wonder how long the struggle will continue. There can be only one answer. The struggle will continue for as long as necessary. There is a new leader in the Soviet Union. Mikhail Gorbachev has tried to make a good impression on world opinion and, in some areas, he has succeeded. That is, he has succeeded in making a good impression. But impressions can be deceptive. What can we expect from Gorbachev in the months and years ahead?

We can expect soft words and diplomatic maneuvering. What we must demand, however, are results. We must watch what the Soviets do, not what they say. I wish I could say our job is nearly done. But the facts tell a different story. A major in the United States army, Arthur Nicholson, was shot down in cold blood in an area where he had the right to be. It might be possible that this shooting was an accident. But the Soviet reaction since the shooting is no accident. They refuse to apologize. They refuse to offer compensation to Major Nicholson's family. They refuse to conform to the standards of decent behavior. If they take such a disgraceful stance toward the shooting of an American officer, how can we expect them to treat Jewish citizens inside Russia?

Yes, we face a hard road. But today we come together to give each other strength, to reaffirm our commitment to the work that remains to be done. Thank you for lending your voice and your conscience to the cause. Together, we will seek justice. Together, we will prevail.

Speaking in Israel three days later, Koch turned his attention to the miracle of the Jewish state. Rising from the ashes of Auschwitz, it stands as a haven for the oppressed and a symbol of Jewish determination, providing the only real answer to the timeless peril of anti-Semitism.

FROM THE ASHES OF THE HOLOCAUST

Remarks at a Holocaust Memorial Ceremony, Israel, May 8, 1985, from Box 080078, Folder 6, EIK.

As mayor of New York, I am pleased and honored to bring the greetings of my city to the people of Israel. In recent days and weeks, we have seen extensive news coverage of the fortieth anniversary of the end of World War II. Some events were recalled in triumph, others in sorrow. Some, such as President Reagan's visit to Bitburg, aroused a storm of controversy. Others, such as ceremonies marking the liberation of the concentration camps, brought back bitter memories of the Holocaust.

But in virtually every observance of this fortieth anniversary year, there has been a hidden presence, because the end of World War II also marked a new and vital phase in Israel's successful struggle for independence and nationhood. The sacrifice, courage and hardships of the pioneers in this land were finally rewarded in 1948 with the foundation of the State of Israel. This modern democracy arose from the very ashes of the Holocaust. By the thousands, and the tens of thousands, the survivors of Hitler's death camps and the desperate refugees known as displaced persons came to Israel and found a home.

Rejected by the world, they were accepted by Israel. They were strong people, dedicated to the principles of Israeli society and to denying Hitler his victory, not only in this generation but for all generations to come. Because the survival of Israel is the negation of everything the Nazis stood for. Each day that Israel lives, the Nazis sink deeper into their graves. Israel's willingness to live as tested by fire—the fire of the Holocaust and the fire that was aimed this way in 1948, in 1967 and 1973. Israel survived those tests, and also has prevailed against the terrorists who do not hesitate to murder children and innocent civilians. Israel's enemies failed on the field of battle. They failed in their terror campaigns.

They failed to separate Israel from her friends and allies. Their armies no longer dare to test Israel's borders. Their terrorist nests in Lebanon have been disrupted. Their terror ships are intercepted off the coast. But still they persist in their efforts to destroy Israel. They are focusing their attention more strongly than ever on undermining Israel's legitimacy, by employing the crude lies and propaganda of ancient anti-Semitism. Sometimes they attempt to manipulate votes in the United Nations or other international groups. And, sometimes, incredibly, they seek to make others believe that the Holocaust never happened.

Such attempts to deny history have been seen in publications appearing in Canada, France, Sweden, the United States, and other locations. There is no mystery about this apparent lapse of sanity. Those who say the Holocaust never happened are trying to deny history so they can rewrite the history of Israel. If they can make the world forget what happened at Buchenwald, Auschwitz and Dachau, they will be one step closer to making it happen again.

But we will not forget. We will not let others forget. We will not let them weaken Israel at the negotiating table, on the field of battle, or in the pages of history. We will remember the Holocaust, now and forever. We will honor those who died, and be grateful for the courage of those who survived. And we will never, never let it happen again.

By late 1985, it was becoming painfully clear that it would be one of the worst years ever for Jewish emigration from the U.S.S.R. The total would eventually reach only about 1,100. At this Soviet Jewry rally, Mayor Koch referred to his recent remarks at the United Nations against South African apartheid and called on critics of South Africa to be equally outspoken against the Kremlin's human rights abuses. The evil of Soweto—the black township in Johannesburg where the white authorities killed hundreds of protesters in 1976—and the evil persecution of Soviet Jews made both regimes "moral pariahs," he contended.

WHETHER SOWETO OR SIBERIA

Remarks at a rally for Soviet Jewry, New York City, September 23, 1985, from Box 080078, Folder 6, EIK.

Thank you, Howard Kronish, Rabbi Saul Berman, Avital Scha-ransky, and good afternoon, fellow lovers of freedom. A few months ago, I stood here to plead publicly with the president of the United States not to go to Bitburg. We did not win that fight. But it was a fight worth making. We spoke truth to power that day—and we said what had to be said. Today, we are here once again to speak truth to power. We are here to confront the hypocrisy and the brutality of the Soviet Union.

Last week, I was inside the United Nations, bearing witness to the evil nature of the regime in South Africa. On that point, what I had to say was welcome. But when I spoke my mind, when I spoke truth to power, and said that the oppression in the Soviet Union is just as bad as the oppression in South Africa, some people didn't like it.

Because some people don't like the truth. They never have, and they never will. But today, whether they like it or not, they are going to hear it. And they had better listen—because the truth about the Soviet Union is not going to go away, and nei-ther are we. Once before, the world stood silent while an evil dictatorship had its way with the Jewish people. Today, another totalitarian empire thinks that the world can be manipulated—can be intimidated—into being silent again. But they are wrong. For now we know the high price of silence. And never will the outside world be silent again.

Today, whether it be in Soweto or in Siberia, we must confront evil everywhere—the evil of apartheid and the evil of the Gulag Archipelago. For what they are doing every day to their own citizens, let us hold both South Africa and the Soviet Union in contempt. Let us treat them both as the moral pariahs they are. Let us condemn them both equally. Let us place sanctions on them both. Today, if you are a Jew in the Soviet Union—as 2.5 million human beings are—you are considered disloyal. You are automatically suspect. You are a second-class citizen. You are always subject to harassment, intimidation, and arrest. Yet, if you want to leave, you can't. In 1975, the Soviet Union signed the Helsinki Accords. They made promises—and they have broken their promises.

Under the Helsinki Accords, all people have the right to emigrate. Families have the right to be reunited. People have the right to be repatriated to their homelands. Religious freedom and human rights are supposed to be guaranteed. But every day that goes by, the Soviet Union breaks the Helsinki Accords. Six years ago, the Soviets let 51,000 Jews leave. Last year, they let less than 1,000 leave. They have clamped the gates shut. They have decided that the Jewish community of the Soviet Union must no longer be allowed to escape their oppression. Instead, I believe, they have decided that community must be destroyed. We must not let that happen. There is a new leader in the Soviet Union, with a new foreign minister who will come here to speak tomorrow. His name is Mr. Shevardnadze, and he will try to tell us that things are changing in the Soviet Union, that the Soviet Union only wants peace.

To this we say: Mr. Gorbachev, Mr. Shevardnadze, if you want our trust, you're going to have to earn our trust. If you want agreements on arms control, you're going to have to live up to the agreements you've already made. If you want the borders of your country and your empire to be respected, then you must show us that you know how to respect the human dignity of all those who live behind your borders—or, in the name of God, let them go!

Ladies and gentlemen, the Soviet Union despises public opinion, as it despises all freedom. But, no matter what they say, they listen to it—especially when it is pressed, day after day, on something that embarrasses them, on what they know is their weak point—their miserable record on human rights.

So let us not despair. They hear us. We do make them nervous. And, because we live in America and not Russia, they cannot shut us up. So we will not shut up. We will go on talking and speaking and shouting and demanding, until every last prisoner of conscience and every last refusenik is free. If Anatoly Scharansky cannot be here to say, "Next year in Jerusalem!" then we must say it for him and, on behalf of all the Soviet oppressed, we will say again and again: "Let my people go!"

A MESSAGE FOR ALL TIME

Remarks at a celebration of Israel's thirty-eighth anniversary, Forest Hills Jewish Center, Queens, New York, May 14, 1986, from Box 080078, Folder 3, EIK.

Last weekend, during the Solidarity Sunday rally, and later at Gracie Mansion when I presented Natan (Anatoly) Scharansky with the Eleanor Roosevelt human rights award, Natan graciously thanked us. But he said that the important thing, the only thing to remember, is that Americans should not be "deceived by the mere cosmetic improvements" that the Soviets are trying to pass off as a genuine human rights program.

"The Soviets won't open the door for 400,000 Jews to leave," he said. "This is most important for American Jews to remember." Natan Scharansky put his life on the line every day of every year of his long imprisonment. He would not bow down. He would not keep silent. With simple words that will live long after we are gone, he said: "I knew I was never alone. My wife and all of you were with me. They tried their best to find a place where I was isolated. But all the resources of a superpower cannot isolate a man who hears the voice of freedom, a voice I heard from the very chamber of my soul." And then he added, "I never sold them my soul."

The selling of one's soul is a leitmotif running through literature, legends and religions of the ages. And who is always the buyer of souls? Throughout the centuries, evil has answered to many names. The greatest heroes of all times are heroes because they have stood up to evil. In the indomitable goodness of a Scharansky lies the immortality of the human race.

There are two sides of the human coin. The obverse of Natan Scharansky is Kurt Waldheim.[1] The question now remains, was Kurt Waldheim's diplomatic career merely one long cover-up of a secret life as a Nazi barbarian? In a visit to Vienna, I met with members of the Jewish community. A small community, but one that has been growing steadily since the end of World War II. The war vanquished Hitler and the Nazis. But was that the end of Nazism? The Waldheim affair makes this more than a rhetorical question. Under his leadership, what would become of Vienna's Jews?

Democracies like Israel and America are in the minority. But Israel is subjected to conditions and threats such as no other nation endures. Surrounded by enemies sworn to its destruction, Israel nonetheless preserves its democratic government and keeps its humanity and its faith. And in Israel today, there are people ready and willing to sponsor every one of the 400,000 Jews who are waiting to leave the Soviet Union.

These hopeful émigrés have had the courage—it may not be Shcharansky-like courage, but it is great courage nonetheless—to sign their names for applications indicating that they want to leave. Without such proven sponsorship, they would never even be considered as candidates for emigration. This is how we know how many remain behind the Iron Curtain. Natan Scharansky came here to speak for those who cannot speak in freedom for themselves. Wherever they may be, whatever their religion, let us not forget this great man's message. Because it is a message for all time.

In 1986, Jewish emigration from the Soviet Union dropped even lower—to less than 1,000. At Soviet Jewry rallies in early 1987, Mayor Koch recalled his recent visit to Auschwitz, warning that the "weakness and indifference" of the free world, which helped pave the road to Auschwitz, could have similarly disastrous results for Jews in the USSR. He urged intensification of international pressure, to send a message to the Kremlin that its image abroad, and its relations with the West, would suffer if Soviet Jews continued to suffer.

LET'S GIVE THEM SOME BAD PRESS

Remarks at a rally for Soviet Jewry on the steps of City Hall, New York City, February 26, 1987, from Box 080078, Folder 8, EIK.

Recently I returned from a trip to Eastern Europe, where I visited Auschwitz. Three million Jews, including some of my own relatives, were murdered there during the Holocaust. I am still filled with anger and horror over what I saw.

While those innocent millions were being butchered, the world stood by and did nothing. Outsiders did not want to concern themselves with what was happening in Germany until it was too late. And so an evil dictatorship thought it could get away with the ultimate crime. Today, will we send that same message of weakness and indifference to another totalitarian empire?

I don't think so. For we have learned the high price of standing by, and we will not be silent. We must raise our voices together and say, "Let my people go!" until every last one is free.

Mr. Gorbachev says he wants to reform things in the Soviet Union. Indeed, he told a delegation of visiting Americans only last week that the changes he has begun to make in Soviet life are permanent and irreversible.

But, almost at the moment he was saying that, goons from the KGB were beating up demonstrators in the street because they were publicly demanding the release of a prisoner of conscience named Yosef Begun.

Mikhail Gorbachev subsequently released Yosef Begun from prison. Did he do so because he knew Begun's imprisonment was wrong? Because he sincerely wants to end such human rights abuses in the U.S.S.R.? Perhaps, but we cannot count on that. What we do know is that the Soviet Union was getting bad press for the actions of its state-security apparatus, and the Soviet Union—for all its contempt toward such democratic institutions as public opinion—respects public opinion. It doesn't like to get bad press.

Very well, then. Let's give them bad press until every refusenik is allowed to leave, until every internal exile is ended, until every gulag is closed. Let's tell them they can never have the relaxation of international tensions they want until they relax the controls of their own repression. Now more than ever, let's keep the pressure on.

LET THEM BE, OR LET THEM GO

Based on remarks at the sixteenth annual Solidarity Sunday rally for Soviet Jews, New York City, May 3, 1987, from Box 080078, Folder 8, EIK.

I am proud to be here with you once again on behalf of three million of our brothers and sisters still trapped in the Soviet Union, still living behind barbed-wire frontiers, still suffering under a system that calls our nation's barring of Kurt Waldheim "an unfriendly act," inspired by "Zionist circles."

A few months ago, I visited the site of the Auschwitz death camp, in Poland. I am still filled with anger and horror at the unspeakable things I saw there—and at the world's silence. It was a domestic matter, they said at first. Germany is a powerful nation and will feel criticism is intervention in its internal affairs, they said. Not making an issue out of what Germany is doing to the Jews will help keep world peace, they said.

Will we repeat the mistake of apathy and appeasement to another totalitarian regime? To another bureaucratic dictatorship that has oppressed Jews, and lied to the world about that oppression? Once before, we saw the tragic price of silence. This time, we will not be silent. We are winning, but our mission is far from accomplished. We will raise our voices together and demand their release from oppression.

I hope Mr. Gorbachev means it when he claims to favor reform. I hope he can succeed. Andrei Sakharov, released by him from internal exile, says we should encourage his campaign of glasnost. But who can forget Dr. Sakharov's wife, the courageous Yelena Bonner, bearing her witness here with us last year on this platform, yet not daring to speak publicly for fear of her husband's life back in Russia? Even if Mr. Gorbachev is totally sincere, he and his system have a long way to go. And who will ever forget Natan Scharansky, joining us in triumph here last year on this platform? Natan knows, his wife Avital knows, and we know that his Soviet captors did not release him out of the goodness of their hearts.

They finally released him because he wouldn't give up—and neither would we. His will could not be broken. And the Soviets were being criticized around the world. The Soviet Union is a monolith, but the monolith is cracking. After all these years of claiming not to care what the rest of the world says, it is finally revealing that it does respond to pressure, that it is feeling the pressure. Let's help Mr. Gorbachev and his glasnost. Let's help him by protesting without letup until Soviet Jews are granted the freedom to emigrate, until every internal exile is ended, until every gulag is closed. Let's tell him he can have all the arms-control treaties he wants—when he and his country show they are truly ready for peace by living up to the Helsinki Accords.

Let's continue to raise our voices until not just a few, not even just a few hundred, but every one of the 400,000 Soviet Jews waiting for emigration, for liberation, are free, free to practice their faith without harassment, or free to leave. Mr. Gorbachev, let our people be, or let our people go!

Amid the collapse of the Soviet Union in 1990 and the ensuing torrent of Jewish emigration, there also emerged a new wave of old-fashioned Russian anti-Semitism. Some things, it seems, never change.

RUSSIAN JEWS FACE NEW WAVE OF HATRED

Originally published in the *New York Post*, February 23, 1990.

Here we are, more than seventy years after the Russian Revolution, and communism—in Eastern Europe and in the Soviet Union itself—is disintegrating before our very eyes.

I participated in a service on New Year's Eve to celebrate the resurgence of freedom in Eastern Europe. When I spoke, I said, "Communism has failed and God has prevailed."

There was a smattering of applause for God, but the truth is that these events take your breath away. It is right that we extoll the virtues of Latvians, Lithuanians, Estonians, Ukrainians, Poles, Czechs, East Germans—all of whom fell under the sway, or yoke, of communism and are now rekindling the fires of liberty.

Still, I find it hard to ignore another factor. My mother and father came from Poland. They never thought of themselves as Poles. The Poles wouldn't let them. If you were not Christian, you were not Polish. Thus if you were Jewish and born in Poland, you were a Jew. My parents, once here, never thought of Poland except as a place from which they had escaped.

During the last seventy-two years, the Soviet Union continued to oppress the Jews, though not to the same extent—or in the same way—as had the czars, when pogroms and Cossacks were synonymous. Stalin, of course, killed his share of Jews, concentrating on leaders (Jewish communists, actually) and culminating in the so-called "doctors' plot."

When Hitler created his concentration camps, many of the worst guards were Latvian and Ukrainian SS volunteers. Vicious anti-Semitism is a part of the history of most of the countries we are now celebrating. And while we should salute their courage in breaking away from communism and toppling Moscow's quislings, we must bear in mind that anti-Semitism never died in these countries, even if under communism it was somewhat muted.

Now, with the throwing off of the communist yoke and the release of democratic forces, we also see the resurgence of popular anti-Semitism. The Jewish refugees leaving for Israel, thanks to Gorbachev's policy of unrestricted emigration, say they're not simply leaving, but fleeing, afraid for their futures, even their lives.

They describe posters on walls in Kiev, Riga, Leningrad and other cities warning Jews to "Get out," telling them to "Go to Israel," according to a recent *New York Times* story. Other recent emigrants tell of physical attacks on them or on their relatives; they even report cases of murder—all as a consequence of anti-Semitism.

Still others describe a January 18 disruption of a Moscow meeting of the Writers Union. The gang of intruders yelled, "Yids, get out to your Israel."

A Russian nationalist group called Pamyat, which openly espouses anti-Semitism, holds rallies in Moscow's Red Square. Meanwhile, Jews from various Soviet provinces report a rumor that there will be a major anti-Semitic pogrom in the Soviet Union this spring.

I recall my parents having said on many occasions how much they appreciated "the good Kaiser Franz Joseph," who, as the Austro-Hungarian emperor, ruled the part of Poland where they had lived.

I once asked, "Mama, why was he called the good Kaiser Franz Joseph?" She said to me, "Sonny, because he didn't kill the Jews." The full meaning of this response became clear to me recently, when I read a review of a new book by the historian Robert Wistrich, *The Jews of Vienna in the Age of Franz Joseph,* which affirmed that the emperor refused to tolerate Jew-baiting in his empire.

Jews who remain in the Soviet Union—sad to say—cannot count on such enlightened leadership.

This is why Diaspora Jews, particularly those of us who are first-class citizens—as we are here in the United States—have an obligation to increase vastly our financial and political support for the effort to resettle new immigrants in Israel. As so often in the past, our brothers and sisters are in great danger.

The paradox is that nations themselves freed from oppression are free once again to oppress their Jewish citizens. Fortunately for those Jews, there is now a resurrected state of Israel willing to accept them with open arms.

Over the course of more than thirty years in politics and government service, James A. Baker III has wielded significant influence on a wide range of issues and today remains a force to be reckoned with. He managed presidential election campaigns for Gerald Ford, Ronald Reagan, and George H. W. Bush, and served as White House chief of staff (for Reagan, and later for Bush), secretary of the treasury (Reagan's second term), and secretary of state under Bush. Since leaving office, Baker repeatedly has been called back for various missions, including UN envoy for the Western Sahara dispute, legal adviser to the Bush 2000 campaign, in which he led the battle over the Florida recount, and Republican presidential envoy for issues pertaining to the Iraq war. In 2006, he was named co-chair of the Iraq Study Group, which authored widely publicized recommendations to the president on U.S. policy in Iraq.

During his term as secretary of state (1989–1992), Baker adopted an unfriendly attitude toward Israel. His policies led to repeated clashes between the Bush administration and the American Jewish community.

BAKER AND THE JEWS

In early 1992, I was informed by the secretary of housing, Jack Kemp, that during a recent White House meeting, Secretary of State James Baker had made an extraordinarily harsh statement, including an obscenity, in reference to American Jews. I considered Mr. Kemp's account reliable for several reasons. First, from my own contacts with him and from the experiences of others, I knew him to be a decent, honest, and principled man. Second, the leaking of this information was a difficult and courageous thing for him to do, since it conflicted with his own personal political interests—he was risking his relationship with President Bush, potentially embarrassing his own party, and perhaps endangering his ties with Republican donors, whom he would need if he chose to seek the Republican presidential nomination (as he would indeed do, in 1996). Third, the statement he said Baker had made was consistent with the secretary of state's own record of unfriendliness toward Israel.[1]

My revelation of Baker's statement quickly became the subject of international controversy, media attention, and public debate. While it is hard to measure the long-term impact of this episode, and there had already been a number of clashes between the Bush administration and American Jewry regarding Israel, I believe that the Baker controversy contributed to the further erosion of American Jewish support for the administration. It was undoubtedly one of the factors that resulted in the extremely low level of Jewish support for President Bush in the 1992 election—the lowest for a presidential candidate since Barry Goldwater.

Here is the column that started it all.

Column originally published in the *New York Post*, March 6, 1992.

––––––

I am angry with President Bush, Secretary of State James Baker, the *New York Times,* the *Washington Post, Times* columnist Anthony Lewis and former Ambassador Rita Hauser.

They all have contributed to the current divisive rhetoric about Israel, and its loan-guarantee request, funds which are needed to assist in relocating the Soviet and Ethiopian Jews. Unless Israel defaults on the loan—and it has never defaulted in the past—it won't cost taxpayers a nickel.

U.S. support of Israel has changed dramatically under Bush and Baker. The latter showed his hostility toward Israel often when he was chief of staff under President Reagan, a friend of Israel—but Reagan always overrode him. Now that Baker has the dominant position in U.S. foreign policy, he is able to act on his hostilities.

In fact, when Baker was criticized recently at a meeting of high-level White House advisers for his belligerent attitude toward Israel, he responded, "F— 'em. They [the Jews] didn't vote for us." Baker uses every opportunity to denounce Israel's right to allow Jews to live on the West Bank. According to Sen. Patrick Leahy, in addition to blocking the loan guarantees, Baker wants to cut Israel's existing foreign aid as a penalty for constructing settlements on the West Bank.

Bush succeeded in intimidating many American Jewish leaders by implying that their opposition to his policy on Israel was a demonstration of dual loyalty. What an outrage! His later apology did not undo the harm.

While Bush and Baker should be condemned, Israeli Prime Minister Yitzhak Shamir is not without fault. Shamir has failed to adequately present Israel's case because he is so convinced of the rightness of his cause. It's understandable because he is responsible for protecting the lives of four million Israelis, and security has to be uppermost in his mind. He believes—as I do—that Jews have the right to live on the West Bank, and that Israel needs the depth of the West Bank in order to have time to mobilize its army.

Anthony Lewis and Rita Hauser take every opportunity to attack Israel and extol the Palestinian cause. In Hauser's case, she embraces PLO leader Yasser Arafat and praises him for his moderation. Was she at all moved by Arafat's latest comments when he characterized the Jews as "Dogs! Filthy! Dirt! . . . Trash is always trash . . . the rotten Jews with whom we will settle accounts in the future"?

If there ever is—and I believe there will be—a Palestinian state, separate or aligned with Jordan, its first governmental act should be to honor Lewis and Hauser with the "Sheik of the Week" award.

Is it wrong for American Jews to be critical of Israel? Of course not. Criticism is warranted, and I have criticized Israel. But there are Jews who carry the guilt of the world on their shoulders, which requires them to regularly excoriate Israel and blame themselves and Israel for the ills of the world.

Bush, Baker and the others mentioned have let loose a whirlwind. Their continuing assaults on Israel and their constant demands for concessions from Israel without counter concessions from the Arab states fan the flames of blatant anti-Semitism.

Bush has the right to urge that conditions be placed on the loan guarantees. But supporters of Israel have the right to disagree while still maintaining their total loyalty to the United States. Congress also has the right to oppose the president and support Israel's request. It is unconscionable for the president to demand that Israel accept the premise that any part of the world should be "Judenrein." If that is the price for the guarantees, then Israel must decline and pursue another route.

Jews and supporters of Israel should not hesitate during the current political debate and election to let the candidates know that the security of Israel is a top priority for them. Other groups advance their priorities without fear of intimidation. Why not supporters of Israel?

BAKER AND THE JEWS: AFTERMATH

The following excerpt was originally published in the *New York Post*, March 13, 1992:

> In the aftermath of my column reporting what Secretary of State James Baker said concerning Jewish voters, I have been criticized by some leaders in the Jewish community—publicly, privately, directly, indirectly—for having revealed what most of them agree is undoubtedly true. But they ask: "Why say it?"
>
> My response: Would they be asking that if Baker's remarks had been about another ethnic group? I have seen a resurgence of fear of the czar, fear of the Gentile world, fear of calling attention to ourselves. They're wrong. In the words of a Catholic hymn sung at funerals I attended for police officers: "Be not afraid."

MY EXCHANGE WITH PRESIDENT BUSH

Letters from the private files of Edward I. Koch.

THE WHITE HOUSE
WASHINGTON

March 6, 1992
(En route Baton Rouge, Louisiana)

Dear Ed,

Someone called to my attention that ugly story about Jim Baker in today's *New York Post*, by Broderick, Burke, and Goldstein. I don't accept that Jim would say such a thing. He is working relentlessly to find a solution to a difficult problem—one that will benefit Israel and the cause of peace in the Middle East. He would not have had any White House meeting on the subject of loan guarantees except in my presence; and, Ed, I never ever heard such ugliness out of Jim Baker.

As a matter of principle, I don't think it is fair to have a guy attacked like this by some nameless source. I don't know who allegedly would report to have heard such a statement, but I simply do not believe the allegation.

In your column, you also suggest that I "intimidate many American Jewish leaders by implying that their opposition to my policy on Israel was a demonstration of dual loyalty." There was a flap, and many Jewish leaders were upset with me, but it was not about dual loyalty. It was about the "lobbying" effort. Some were disturbed with my statement that led them to believe I thought lobbying was pejorative. I tried to make clear, in the attached letter, for example, that I did not have that in mind.

But, again, the charge of "dual loyalty" was never made, and I have been very careful about mentioning faith. People might disagree with me on issues, but that is far different.

Ed, you know I respect you, and I hope you will accept the truth of these statements that come from the heart.

Warm Regards,
George Bush

(P.S. In spite of this "flap" your #1 fan remains BPB—she sends her best)

March 13, 1992

The Honorable George Bush
President of the United States
The White House
1600 Pennsylvania Avenue, N.W.
Washington, DC 20500

Dear Mr. President:
I want to thank you for taking the time to send me your extraordinarily gracious note. I think you know that I have great affection for both you and Barbara, and I have on many occasions praised your leadership. What you did in marshaling the forces of the free world against Saddam Hussein—against all the odds— was remarkable. Most of the members of my party opposed you, but I condemned them and supported you.

You say that your comment concerning the lobbying of supporters of Israel was not intended to convey a charge of dual loyalty. I accept your statement while recognizing that it was subject to such a pejorative interpretation. That matter is now behind us.

Regarding Secretary of State Jim Baker and his alleged remarks, which I reported in my column, you must know that if I did not have total confidence in my source, who was present when the remarks were made, I would not have reported it as such. Believe me, the source is impeccable and is one that even you would find totally credible.

I have gone out of my way to say I do not perceive Secretary Baker's remarks as anti-Semitic, but rather as crude, political comments, writing off Jewish voters, which I am sure is not what you would want. Two newspapers corroborated my references that Jim Baker made such statements. The *New York Post,* a conservative, overwhelmingly Republican-directed paper which supports your candidacy, ran an editorial showing that they were independently aware of Secretary Baker's comments. In *The Forward,* a moderate Jewish-oriented paper, probably supportive of your election, there is further confirmation of Secretary Baker's views, similarly expressed on another occasion. Those articles are enclosed.

Now that I am no longer a party official but rather, in addition to other things, a journalist, I do not perceive my party affiliation to be my primary political loyalty. It is hard for Democratic officials to understand that I might very well vote for you in November, but despite my Democratic inclination, my mind is open. However, I'm sure you understand that every ethnic and religious community has its priorities. One of my priorities is the security of the State of Israel. I believe the special relationship between the United States and Israel, which began with Harry Truman and continued through Ronald Reagan, has been considerably weakened. I hope I'm wrong.

Please do give my very best to Barbara. I hope that you and she are in the best of health and that our friendship endures.

All the best.
Sincerely,
Edward I. Koch

———

THE WHITE HOUSE
WASHINGTON

March 23, 1992

Dear Ed:
I read with interest your latest letter. You know that I respect your views, but this is one area where I strongly

disagree because I also know the heart of Jim Baker. No one has worked harder for peace between Israel and its neighbors—a peace that holds so much promise for Israel—than Jim Baker.

I assure you that the security of Israel is a priority of the United States today, just as it has always been; and it will remain a priority as long as I am President. One can disagree with a particular policy of Israel's without casting doubt upon one's basic commitment to its welfare. Moreover, and as you know, it is long-standing U.S. policy—under Democratic and Republican administrations alike—that settlements in the occupied territories are counterproductive to peace. We are not following a new policy, nor will we. I want to find a way to help Israel with its humanitarian needs, but peace, too, is a humanitarian objective. I am hopeful this can be worked out, but even if not, I am confident that once we get past all the rhetoric, you will see that the bonds of friendship between Israel and the United States remain constant and strong.

Best wishes, in which Barbara joins.
George Bush

P.S. I really appreciated the "spirit" of your first letter.
P.S.S. Don't think I'm trying to become a penpal. GB

What can be done to combat anti-Semitism? In the essays that follow, Koch proposes a number of steps, including pressing for the adoption of resolutions against anti-Semitism by bodies such as the United Nations Human Rights Commission; urging the international community to recognize that anti-Semitism is not just a Jewish problem but a worldwide problem; and boycotting France to bring about the dismissal of a French diplomat who made an obscene remark about Israel.

GERALDINE FERRARO AND THE U.N. VOTE
ON ANTI-SEMITISM

Originally published in the *New York Post*, March 25, 1994.

This is the untold story behind the recent resolution by the United Nations Human Rights Commission condemning anti-Semitism. The vote was unanimous, with the exception of Japan and Malaysia, which abstained.

In January, following Geraldine Ferraro's appointment as head of the U.S. delegation to the commission, Edgar Bronfman of the World Jewish Congress, and later Morris Abram of United Nations Watch, asked her to press the commission to include anti-Semitism in its expected resolution condemning racism, apartheid and other forms of discrimination.

Ferraro declined, indicating that she was more concerned with women's issues and supporting a positive message on the Israel/PLO peace process—even though such a resolution had already been passed by the U.N. General Assembly.

It was just short of a miracle that Turkey, which was in charge of writing the resolution, moved to save the situation by proposing the anti-Semitism condemnation. However, without U.S. support, it was going nowhere. Ferraro was instructed by the State Department—which had been deluged with complaints about her inaction—to work on getting the resolution passed. Ferraro did so, but she was outraged that the Jewish community had brought her inaction to the State Department's attention.

Of course, now she will claim it as her victory, when it really belongs to Turkey and the other prime sponsors, Romania and Finland, and, of course, to Bronfman and Abram, who never gave up.

ANTI-SEMITISM REQUIRES A WORLDWIDE RESPONSE
Originally published in *Newsday*, November 24, 2000.

On September 5, 1972, eleven Israeli athletes were taken hostage in the Olympic Village at Munich, Germany, by eight members of the Palestine Liberation Organization. Two Israelis were murdered immediately and nine held prisoner.

The German authorities, unprepared to deal with this crisis, botched the rescue attempt, and the terrorists murdered the Israeli athletes. Five terrorists were killed by the Germans and three were captured.

Willy Brandt, the German chancellor at that time, colluded with the PLO. Brandt purportedly agreed to fake the subsequent taking of twelve German hostages by the PLO. The German "hostages" were then exchanged for the three Palestinians awaiting trial.

This disgraceful series of events is the subject of a first-rate documentary, *One Day in September,* now playing at the Film Forum in Manhattan. In this film, we also learn that the Israelis hunted down and killed two of these terrorists. The third, interviewed for the film, is in hiding.

Seeing the film account of the murders of these innocent Israeli athletes made me think about the current state of anti-Semitism in Germany and elsewhere in the world. A few months ago, the *New York Times* reported that one of Germany's most prestigious literary prizes was awarded to "a historian who has sought to justify the Holocaust." The article reported that: "[t]he historian Ernst Nolte received the Konrad Adenauer Prize for literature, given 'for works that contribute to a better future.'" A Harvard historian, Charles Maier, commented, "The award of the prize to Nolte was a clear political statement intended to promote the view that there is no particular stigma to Nazism. . . . It's also really scandalous."

At the end of World War II, it was thought that anti-Semitism would never again play a role on the world stage. We were wrong. Many of the Allied nations that defeated Hitler are themselves now experiencing a virulent revival of anti-Semitism.

In a recent article in the *Weekly Standard,* Michael Gurfinkiel described the current rise of Jew-hating in France this way: "On the Richter Scale of anti-Semitism, France has just registered a major quake. From October 1 to October 18, in the space of just two and a half weeks, six synagogues were burned down and another twenty-four synagogues and Jewish schools were targets of attempted arson. Stones were thrown at people outside synagogues, and Jewish kids were hounded or molested on their way to school."

French President Jacques Chirac and Prime Minister Lionel Jospin took twelve days to issue denunciatory statements about these anti-Semitic actions and, as Gurfinkiel noted, "even then, they refrained from the customary symbolic gestures, such as a visit to a burned synagogue or an address to the nation."

This is the same French government that has joined Britain and other members of the United Nations Security Council in denouncing the Israelis for using "excessive force" against the Palestinians, who are waging a Jihad (holy war) against Israel. Neither France nor Britain has noted, however, that: thirty Israelis have been killed; 308 Israelis have been injured; and the tomb of Joseph, which is holy to Jews, was deliberately destroyed by Palestinians since the current Jihad began in late September. Was the failure of France and Britain to condemn the Palestinians for their use of force and terror partly responsible for the amputations suffered by several innocent Israeli children riding on a school bus and the deaths of two Israeli adults Monday?

In Canada, according to an article published last Wednesday in the *New York Times*: "During the last six weeks, about 45 anti-Jewish incidents—arson, assaults, verbal abuse and death threats—have been recorded." The article also reports that "many Canadian Jews are livid over what they describe as a tepid response by politicians."

There are a few rays of light. The Anti-Defamation League recently reported that "the number of Americans who hold strongly anti-Semitic views has dropped from twenty percent to twelve percent since 1992," and that in 1999 there was a "downward trend that has resulted in a two percent drop in anti-Semitic incidents nationwide over the last five years."

Anti-Semitism is not simply a Jewish burden. As a worldwide phenomenon, it requires a worldwide response. In the 1930s, the western European countries concluded Jew-bashing was unimportant. Their inaction ultimately resulted in not only the rise of Nazism in Germany, but willing collaborators in their own backyards.

CAUSE FOR BOYCOTT: FRANCE'S ANTI-SEMITISM
Written December 2001, from the private files of Edward I. Koch.

All supporters of Israel should boycott French wine, cheese, perfume, and clothing, as well as refuse to visit France as tourists, until the French government recalls its ambassador to Britain, and either cashiers or demotes him.

Last week, the recently appointed French ambassador to Britain, Daniel Bernard, attended a reception at the home of Conrad Black and his wife, Barbara Amiel. Black is the publisher of newspapers in Canada, the United States, Britain, and Israel. Amiel, a reporter in her own right, said that at the party Bernard called Israel a "shitty little country," adding, "Why should the world be in danger of World War III because of those people?"

Bernard does not deny he made the statements, and his spokesman stated that Bernard was "absolutely shocked" by suggestions he was anti-Semitic. Really? He must be thin-skinned indeed to be so easily shocked. That little country and the Jewish nation, which he described in such vulgar language, never more than one-third of 1 percent of the world's population, gave birth to Moses, King David, King Solomon, Jesus, Freud, and Einstein, as well as approximately 20 percent of the world's Nobel Prize winners.

The response by Benjamin Disraeli, prime minister of Britain during the reign of Queen Victoria, to an anti-Semite seems particularly appropriate, "Yes, I am a Jew, and when the ancestors of the right honorable gentleman were brutal savages in an unknown island, mine were priests in the temple of Solomon."

Bernard used to serve as France's delegate to the United Nations. One can safely assume he supported with pleasure the prejudiced resolutions against Israel offered time after time by the Arab countries, effectively supporting Palestinian terrorism against the civilian population of Israel, while denouncing Israel because it exercised its right of self-defense.

That support shouldn't shock us. After all, wasn't it in Vichy France during World War II that French cops rounded up and delivered 61,000 Jews at Drancy to the Nazis without a request by the Nazis that they do so? Those Jews were then shipped to Nazi death camps where they were gassed.

We now know, notwithstanding herculean efforts to cover up the history of the Nazi occupation, that large numbers of French collaborated with the Nazis, and only a small number—many of them Communists responding to the orders of Stalin—continued to fight underground.

It was the French government of twenty years ago that financed and built the Iraqi nuclear bomb plant that—fortunately for the allies in the Gulf War of 1991—no longer existed because Israel bombed and destroyed it in 1981.

It was France that made a bargain with the PLO in the 1970s that it would not arrest Arab terrorists using France as their base planning attacks on Israel and Jews so long as they did not engage in terrorism on French soil. And it is France at the United Nations that now opposes requests by the United States and Britain for additional sanctions against Iraq for its refusal to admit U.N. inspectors required by U.N. resolutions.

French anti-Semitism is well known. I have no doubt that had Bernard been alive during the infamous Dreyfus Trials, he might well have defended the French government with something like, "Why is that shitty little Jew protesting his innocence when the French government and the French army says he is guilty of treason?"—as did so many others.

If a French ambassador had assailed Saudi Arabia—a country that exports not only oil, but terrorists—in the same way the French government would have fired him on the spot. Incidentally, fifteen of the nineteen who blew up the World Trade Center and hit the Pentagon were Saudis.

Where are the supporters of Israel willing to stand up and actively lead boycotts and picket lines against France until it fires Bernard?

Boycott, boycott, boycott France.

BOYCOTTING FRANCE: MY EXCHANGE WITH WOODY ALLEN

From the private files of Edward I. Koch.

A wave of anti-Semitic incidents erupted in France in the spring of 2002, coincidentally around the time of the Cannes Film Festival, which the actor and film director Woody Allen attended.

Mr. Allen was quoted in the *New York Times* (May 16, 2002) as saying, "I never felt that the French people in any way were anti-Semitic. . . . I think one can be very proud of France for the way they've acquitted themselves in the last election and I don't think a boycott is in order. I just don't feel that it's right. . . . I think any boycott is wrong. Boycotts were exactly what the Germans were doing against the Jews."

I happen to be one of Mr. Allen's fans, and I had the honor and pleasure of making a cameo appearance in his film *Manhattan Stories* when I was mayor. I also run into him on occasion because our taste in restaurants is apparently rather similar.

So, in the spirit of admiration for Mr. Allen as an entertainer but profound disagreement on this particular issue, I wrote him a letter that read, in part, as follows.

Some who disagree with you, not only now, but in the past as well, have referred to you as a "self-hating Jew." I think that is unfair. Your humor, movies and scripts all convey in an intelligent and humorous manner your positive Jewish identity. I also believe you are wrong in your comments about the French.

While you defended the outcome of the last election and Le Pen's defeat as a "clear-cut response to the extreme right," Le Pen received 18 percent of the total vote. If a party whose leader is widely recognized even in France as a defender of the Nazi regime were to receive 18 percent of the vote for president here in the United States, would you feel proud of America or would you sit up and take notice?

Were you not offended when the French ambassador to Great Britain, Daniel Bernard, recently attending a dinner party, called Israel "a shitty little country," adding, "Why should the world be in danger of World War III because of those people?" The implication to many was that Ambassador Bernard thinks Jewish lives lost in terrorist suicide bombings are not as precious as others requiring our concern. It is a fact that during World War II, French cops in unoccupied Vichy France rounded up and delivered 61,000 Jews to the Nazis at Drancy without a request by the Nazis that they do so. Those Jews ended up in Nazi death camps where they were gassed. It is generally accepted that the French in large numbers were collaborators with the Nazis. And a relatively small number continued to fight underground before France was liberated as a result of the D-Day invasion. In January of this year, Israel's Deputy Foreign Minister, Michael Melchior, singled out France as the European country where the greatest number of anti-Semitic attacks have occurred.

Historically, one of the most outrageous acts of French anti-Semitism is the infamous Dreyfus Trial followed by [Dreyfus's] imprisonment on Devil's Island before his exoneration. Dreyfus was lucky that Emil Zola was on the scene and not intimidated or infatuated with the French government of his time.

Many knowledgeable observers believe anti-Semitism in France and elsewhere in Europe is equal to what it was in 1939. I do too.

Abraham Foxman, national director of the Anti-Defamation League, has denounced French anti-Semitism and the lack of governmental response, saying, "Time and again, we have called on President Chirac to come forward with strong denunciations of the violence and incendiary anti-Semitic and anti-Israel rhetoric, and take responsibility for Jewish citizens by better protecting them."

Apparently, the French government (Chirac having been re-elected after Jospin, the socialist prime minister was defeated in the first election by LePen) is now acknowledging and taking appropriate, albeit belated action to protect its Jewish citizens and their synagogues from assault and arson. Apparently, most of the incidents are perpetrated by the French Muslim population.

Last year, Roger Cukierman, president of CRIF, the Representative Council of the Jewish Organizations of France, asked his French countrymen and the French government to recognize the seriousness of the anti-Semitic acts targeting Jews in France. He wrote in Le Monde in February 2001, "The leaders of the country like to play down anti-Jewish acts. They prefer to see these as ordinary violence. We are deluged with statistics designed to show that an attack against a synagogue is an act of violence and not anti-Semitism. Some Jews who have lost touch with reality like to buttress their personal status by turning a deaf ear and a blind eye to danger, in order to curry favor with the public consensus. The media like to give the widest exposure to voices critical of Israel and Jews, all the more so when these voices are Jewish. This way, media can't be charged with anti-Semitism or anti-Zionism. Judicial authorities don't like to mete out strong punishment for acts of anti-Jewish violence, even when the perpetrators are caught redhanded: a three-month suspended sentence or nothing for an attack on a Jewish place of worship, compared to a year in jail for burning a straw cottage in Corsica."

It is true that Mr. Cukierman, with whom I have had correspondence, is currently opposed to a boycott, writing to me on

April 8, 2002, "Things have changed in two ways. First, we have more and more anti-Semitic acts, clearly connected with the Middle East situation. We are fortunate that we have no death casualty. Secondly, the Prime Minister and the President have changed, at last, their attitude. They stopped minimizing and are now taking the situation seriously." I responded on April 15th, "Silence never works. I understand your needs living in France, and I can appreciate your frustration and inability to respond the way people like me, living in a free, democratic country where anti-Semitism is at an all-time low, will respond."

There are those equally concerned with the protection of French Jews who join Mr. Cukierman in opposing a boycott at this time, e.g., the national director of the ADL, Abraham Foxman. So, in opposing a boycott, you are not alone. But your explanation and reasoning are badly flawed. What do you mean when you compare a call by Jews for a boycott against the French with the Nazi boycott against the Jews? Do you really believe that all boycotts are the same? Did you oppose the boycott of South Africa in order to end apartheid? Did you oppose Martin Luther King's support of a boycott of segregated buses in Birmingham, Alabama, as well as a boycott of the white commercial establishments in that city?

I believe a boycott directed at the French government, until it apologizes for its ambassador's scurrilous comments, is in order. Those comments, still not repudiated by the government, when viewed in the context of the physical assaults on French Jews, convey gross hostility and indifference on the part of the French toward Jews in general.

I am convinced that your comments have given the French people and their government undeserved cover for their tolerance of anti-Semitic behavior and shamefully inadequate response to it.

———

I concluded my letter by asking Mr. Allen to reconsider his defense of France.

A short time later, he wrote back.

He made four interesting points.

The first was that when he spoke to the *New York Times,* his main purpose was to publicize his movies and provide what he called impromptu replies to complex questions about various subjects In other words, the nature and setting of the interview did not really give him enough time to fully explain his view. Fair enough. I've had my share of similar experiences, where a reporter looking for a sound byte, rather than an in-depth discussion, uses a quote that doesn't really do justice to the person's position.

That said, Mr. Allen still stood by his main point: "I do not believe the French are anti-Semitic because I know a number of French Jews who strongly believe they are not anti-Semitic." Anti-Semitic utterances by a few prominent people should not be considered reflective of widespread sentiment, he argued.

His third point was particularly interesting: "The truth is much of the world is anti-Semitic and to single France out with a boycott seems wrong to me." I did not realize he felt that strongly about the general international climate toward Jews, so it turned out we had more in common than I thought, despite our disagreement on the specific question of boycotting.

But on that point, Mr. Allen proved more flexible than I expected. He conceded that my point regarding boycotts was "a good one." He said that although, in general, he disapproved of boycotting one's political opponents, he did agree with me that, at least "in certain extreme cases," boycotting is a legitimate means of protest.

To which I replied: "Even if we are not in agreement on whether or not the French are anti-Semitic, your letter states your position in a very rational and responsible manner. I do hope that we will have an opportunity to pursue the matter, perhaps one night over dinner."

To my regret, we never did have that dinner. I hope one day we will.

*The ever-changing face of anti-Semitism assumed a new visage in the months pre-
ceding the U.S. war against Saddam Hussein in 2003. Some antiwar activists alleged that Jewish advisers to President Bush, together with some American Jewish
groups, were trying to drag America into the war because it would benefit Israel.
The accusation was reminiscent of charges made by isolationists who claimed, on
the eve of World War II, that American Jews were dragging America into a war
that would benefit Jewry by defeating Hitler. In the letters to follow, Koch challenged one of the accusers, U.S. Congressman Jim Moran, and urged his political
allies to speak out against him. Moran did not reply to Koch, although he publicly
denied that his letter was anti-Semitic. Moran's constituents evidently did not regard the matter as decisive; they subsequently reelected him.*

THE IRAQ WAR AND THE "DUAL LOYALTY" CHARGE:
THREE UNANSWERED LETTERS

From the private files of Edward I. Koch.

March 11, 2003

*The Honorable James P. Moran
U.S. House of Representatives
2239 Rayburn House Office Building
Washington, D.C. 20215*

Dear Congressman Moran:
I read with great interest your comments, reported in
the *Washington Post,* holding "the Jewish community" responsible for "this war with Iraq." You admit telling a
forum on March 3rd, "The leaders of the Jewish community are influential enough that they could change the
direction of where this is going, and I think they
should."

You believe that your comments, while insensitive, were not anti-Semitic.

I served in the Congress for nine years. I am very proud of that service. I also served as Mayor of New York City for twelve years and am very proud of that service. I am Jewish and proud of my religious and eth- nic traditions. In neither of my elections was I elected or opposed because of my religion and in neither did Jews comprise a majority of the voters. Further, all of the polls in my reelection campaigns for mayor showed that I did better among Italian and Irish Catholics than among Jewish voters. Among the former, I received 81 percent of their vote; among the latter, 73 percent. I mention these facts because I want to convey that, while of course there is some anti-Semitism in this country, it is very limited, and people of good will take great pride in our having trounced the devils of anti-Semitism and racism. So, for you to reintroduce, particularly as a member of Congress, anti-Semitism in your appeals to your con- stituency is extremely troubling and appalling.

How can you say that your comments were simply insensitive, but not anti-Semitic? Your language is really another version of the blood libel. After World War I, the Germans, pre- and post-Nazism, blamed the Jews for their defeat. There was no basis for that allegation, but the German public was receptive.

You seek to blame the Jews for the oncoming war that President Bush has said must be waged against Iraq if it does not fulfill the obligations of the ceasefire it en- tered into in 1991 requiring it to destroy its weapons of mass destruction. Iraq's failure to carry out these obliga- tions were cited in Resolution 1441, which was unani- mously adopted by the fifteen members of the Security Council. As you also know, a huge majority of both Houses of Congress authorized the President to deter- mine when military force should be used against Iraq to compel its destruction of weapons of mass destruction. Yet, you blame the Jews for the impending war.

In today's *New York Times,* a poll shows that "55 percent of respondents . . . would support an American invasion of Iraq, even if it was in defiance of a vote of the Security Council." The *Washington Post* reports: "A January poll commissioned by the American Jewish Committee found that 59 percent of American Jews supported war against Iraq, a percentage not appreciably different from that of Americans generally."

As you undoubtedly know, there are many Jews who have participated in antiwar demonstrations around the country for which they are libeled by some as unpatriotic. Jews, like everyone else, have a right to their opinions, individually and collectively. What your comments, and I suspect your intent, convey is that if there are casualties, as there surely will be in any war, "blame the Jews."

I support the war, if the President believes that is the only way left to best protect America and disarm Iraq. I do not think it is unpatriotic to be on the other side of the issue. This is a judgment call. However, for you to say, in effect, that the actions of President Bush and his Cabinet, including Vice President Dick Cheney, Secretary of State Colin Powell, Defense Secretary Donald Rumsfeld and National Security Advisor Condoleezza Rice, are controlled by the Jewish community is an outrage. Not one of those individuals is Jewish; nor is British Prime Minister Tony Blair; nor is Prime Minister Aznar of Spain. To accuse these leaders of taking orders from a segment of their communities—Jews—who are divided on the issue like all Americans, is simply seeking to employ an ancient anti-Semitic technique. In earlier times, it was the forged *Protocols of the Elders of Zion.*

The *Washington Post* article indicates that you have had personal financial problems and been the subject of ethics complaints, suggesting that may be in part responsible for your outburst. We know that when an equally vile racial statement was made by Senator Trent Lott, he was compelled to resign as Majority Leader. You hold no such position of leadership, so perhaps you should resign from the Congress itself.

All the best.
Edward I. Koch

———

March 11, 2003

The Honorable Nancy Pelosi
U.S. House of Representatives
2457 Rayburn House Office Building
Washington, D.C. 20215

Dear Nancy:
The statements of Representative James P. Moran, as reported in the *Washington Post,* are a disgrace. I have sent a letter to him, a copy of which is enclosed, urging that he resign. I hope that you, as the Minority Leader and head of the Democratic Party in the House, will rise in appropriate wrath and demand he do so. I believe you demanded that Trent Lott resign as Majority Leader for his racial slurs. I did.

All the best.

Sincerely,
Edward I. Koch

———

March 12, 2003

Lawrence Framme
Virginia Democratic Party Chairman
1108 East Main Street, 2nd Floor
Richmond, VA 23219

Dear Mr. Framme:

I read your comments on the statements made by Congressman James P. Moran in the *Washington Post.*

Do you believe that an apology, no matter how profuse, is adequate? Didn't Trent Lott apologize five times and profusely? Didn't you agree that, nevertheless, he should resign?

I thought that you would be interested in two letters I have written: one to the Congressman and the other to Nancy Pelosi, leader of the Democrats in the House of Representatives. I am interested in your further insights now that the matter is being discussed nationally.

All the best.

Sincerely,
Edward I. Koch

REFLECTIONS ON THE JEWS AND THEIR ENEMIES
Essay written October 2003, from the private files of Edward I. Koch.

Each year on Rosh Hashanah, I am asked by Rabbi Arthur Schneier to deliver a short statement to the congregation of the Park East Synagogue. I have done that for nearly twenty years and did so again this year.

My remarks are always extemporaneous and no notes are used, nor is my speech recorded. When I finished, Rabbi Schneier said, and I believe he meant it, "This is your best one yet, particularly because of the intensity of the delivery." A friend of mine, the former parks commissioner Henry Stem, was in the congregation and later offered this comment, "It was a heartfelt and well-reasoned statement delivered extremely well." I thought I should try to recall the speech, write it down and use it as my commentary this week. The following is what I recall saying:

———

Several weeks ago, Mayor Michael Bloomberg called and asked if I would like to join him on his scheduled trip to Israel. He was using his private plane and intended to visit some of the survivors of the recent Jerusalem bus bombing who were receiving treatment at Hadassah Hospital. Twenty-one people had been killed and one hundred injured, many of them children. I was delighted to accept his invitation.

At the hospital, we talked with recovering victims who exhibited great bravery and clearly intended to resume their normal lives, voicing the feelings that by going on, they were not yielding to the terrorists, and that the government would do everything possible to protect them and others from future incidents. Later in the evening, we spent an hour on Ben Yehuda street, a pedestrian mall where thousands of Israelis were attending a handicraft exhibit, again showing they would not be cowed by the bombers.

In the course of the service each year, we ask God to bless our leaders, the president, vice president, and the Cabinet. I read the prayer and added my amen to the blessing. I want to thank our government for standing up in support of Israel, using its veto at the U.N. Security Council, even when we had to stand alone, because the rest of the world is in such fear of the Arab countries and their oil resources, and are worried they could be deprived of oil for their economies if they didn't go along.

The latest U.N. resolution offered was deemed by the United States as grossly unfair in that it did not denounce terrorism or the Palestinian terrorist organizations on the West Bank and in Gaza—Hamas, Islamic Jihad and al-Aqsa Martyrs Brigade—which engage in the deliberate killing of innocent Israeli civilians. As usual, the U.N. condemned Israel alone. The United States also cast a "no" vote on a similar one-sided resolution adopted by the U.N. General Assembly, stating it was unfair.

I particularly condemn those Jews who align themselves with Israel's enemies, but I recognize that every group has its own self-haters and betrayers. The *New York Times* reports that the State Department is interviewing Muslims all over the world to ascertain why they hate us. A Muslim panelist who criticized the United States as being too preoccupied with Islamic fundamentalists said that "Every country has fundamentalists. I think Billy Graham Jr. is a fundamentalist." She was referring to Franklin Graham. His father, Billy Graham, is a fundamentalist and even more famous. Billy Graham may not like Jews, but he doesn't want to kill us, and the Islamic fundamentalists do. And that is a big difference.

You don't have to be a genius to know why the Arabs hate us. They envy our standard of living; they resent our democracy and all it means for the liberation of women and minorities; they are angry that the Islamic world, once an intellectual center, stopped being so and drifted into third-world status when they lost the great battle of civilizations in 1683 at the gates of Vienna.

There have been people in the State Department forever who have sought to placate the Arabs. Indeed while I will always revere President Franklin Roosevelt for saving the United States and the world from fascism, I will never forget and will always condemn the fact that he, along with the State Department, refused available visas to Jews who could have left Germany and been saved. Instead, they were left there to be killed. I appreciated the Polish government's decision to allow two Israeli planes to fly over Auschwitz-Birkenau during recent memorial services held for more than a million Jews gassed and cremated there by the Nazis. The head of the Israeli Air Force recently told me that the fly-over was symbolic, showing what would have occurred if Israel had been in existence then, at a time when the United States and England refused to bomb the railways to Auschwitz or the camp itself to help the Jews escape.

Wahhabism, the national religion of Saudi Arabia, is spreading like wildfire. Wahhabists believe they have a right to kill Hindus, who are polytheists, because they don't believe in one god. Wahhabists accept the monotheistic religions of Christianity and Judaism, but believe they have the right to kill us unless Christians and Jews also, according to Dr. Bernard Lewis, one of the foremost authorities on Islam, "accept the supremacy of Islam and the rule of the Muslim state."

So again I think of the prayer we recite today invoking God's blessing on our president, our vice president and the Cabinet, and I say, amen, amen.

IT'S TIME TO SOUND THE ALARM

Essay written in October 2003, from the private files of Edward I. Koch.

An editorial in the October 18 *New York Times,* captioned "Islamic Anti-Semitism," got it right. The *Times* said, "It is hard to know what is more alarming—a toxic statement of hatred of Jews by the Malaysian prime minister at an Islamic summit meeting this week or the unanimous applause it engendered from the kings, presidents and emirs in the audience. The words uttered by the prime minister, Mahathir Mohamad, in a speech to the fifty-seven member Organization of the Islamic Conference on Thursday were sadly familiar: Jews, he asserted, may be few in number but they control the world.

"The Europeans killed six million Jews out of 12 million, but today the Jews rule the world by proxy," the prime minister said. "They get others to fight and die for them." Muslims are "up against a people who think," he said, adding that the Jews "invented socialism, communism, human rights and democracy so that persecuting them would appear to be wrong, so that they can enjoy equal rights with others."

The false and evil words of Mahathir Mohamad and their enthusiastic acceptance by Muslim leaders the world over will, without doubt, be responsible for the persecution if not the deaths of innocent Jews living in Muslim nations and elsewhere. Just as troubling is the muted response from Europe and the United States. According to the *Times* editorial, "The European Union was asked to include a condemnation of Mr. Mahathir's speech in its statement yesterday ending its own summit. It chose not to, adding a worry that displays of anti-Semitism are being met with inexcusable nonchalance."

At the European Union, the Italian foreign minister, Franco Frattini, sought to have the E.U. deplore the Malaysian prime minister's call to arms against Jews everywhere. Frattini's effort was rejected by French president Jacques Chirac. According to the *New York Post,* Chirac "convinced members [of the E.U.] to leave any criticizing of Mahathir to Italy." Why? "It would not have been appropriate for the European Union, a French official said." Subsequently, Chirac issued his own letter, which is worthless, given that he conveyed his true feelings with his earlier action.

President Bush rebuked Prime Minister Mahathir Mohamad directly, stating that his comments were "wrong and divisive," and that they stand "squarely against what I believe in." Our president's response, while appreciated, is not what is required. A clarion call, equivalent to Emile Zola's *J'Accuse,* directed to the world community is what is needed.

Where are other respected leaders of the world who surely would be speaking out if Mahathir Mohamad had denounced Christians or blacks or other minorities? Where are the voices of Pope John Paul II, Nelson Mandela, Tony Blair? Where are the leaders of the Eastern Orthodox churches? Where is Rev. Billy Graham?

Is it any wonder that sixty years after World War II, Jews and righteous gentiles are thinking "here we go again." Most occupied

European nations collaborated with Nazi Germany during World War II, delivering their own Jewish citizens to the Nazis for transport to the death camps. This was especially true of France, which offered up its Jews even before being asked to do so.

I will not forget that Franklin D. Roosevelt, who was one of our greatest presidents and who saved the world from being conquered by the Nazis, nevertheless failed to grant U.S. visas to European Jews before World War II began, a humanitarian act that could have saved many Jews who were later murdered in Nazi extermination camps.

Besides focusing on "Islamic Anti-Semitism" in its editorial, the *Times* should have included a ringing denunciation of the virulent anti-Semitism that can now be found in nearly every country at levels not reached since shortly before the outbreak of World War II. So-called "Islamic anti-Semitism" is no different than the Jew-hatred that now pervades Britain and France, much of it disguised as "anti-Israeli" or "anti-Zionist" statements. Even France's ambassador to Great Britain, Daniel Bernard, referred to Israel as "that shitty little country."

We Jews are no better than any other people, but we are as good as any, and we deserve dignity, security, and respect as individuals and for the Jewish State of Israel. We can match our accomplishments with any other group. From our loins came Moses, who gave the world the Ten Commandments; Jesus, who gave the world Christianity; Freud, who gave the world psychotherapy; and Einstein, who gave the world unmatched insights into mathematics, science, and physics; and so many other intellectual giants. From our people came more than 16 percent of the Nobel Prize winners, even though we have never been more than one-third of 1 percent of the world's population. We are, as Pope John Paul II described us, Christianity's "elder brother."

Today, that brother needs support and embrace. The world should remember at its peril the lament of the German pastor Martin Niemoller after World War II: "When the Nazis came for the communists, I remained silent; I was not a communist.

When they locked up the social democrats, I remained silent; I was not a social democrat. When they came for the trade union- ists, I did not speak out; I was not a trade unionist. When they came for the Jews, I remained silent; I wasn't a Jew. When they came for me, there was no one left to speak out."

Recently, a friend sent me the remarks of former CIA direc- tor James Woolsey, who said, "I sometimes get asked these days if I'm Jewish. It's my neoconish views on defense and foreign af- fairs, I suppose. For a while I would just say, 'No, Presbyterian,' but I've started saying instead, 'Well, I anchor the Presbyterian wing of the Jewish Institute for National Security Affairs.' What with anti-Semitism growing in Europe and a hideous variety thereof metastasizing in the Middle East, not to speak of the American Left's (and a small part of the Right's) hostility to Is- rael, which sometimes veers off into anti-Semitism, it seems to me our Jewish friends could use a bit of solidarity these days. Today, the first day of Rosh Hashanah, celebration of the Jewish New Year, is as good a time as any to explain why." My heartfelt thanks, Mr. Woolsey.

"Never Again" is the lesson of the Holocaust. Today, those words ring hollow. Once again they're getting ready to come for the Jews. It's time to sound the alarm.

New manifestations of anti-Semitism require new strategies of defense. In the spring of 2004, a Rutgers University student newspaper published a grotesque cartoon ridiculing the Holocaust. In a country where the Constitution protects virtually every expression of opinion, no matter how insulting or vile, can anything be done about something such as the Rutgers outrage? Seeking counsel from some of the nation's brightest minds, Koch wrote to a number of scholars and university presidents, inviting their comments on how to respond to the cartoon. His original letter, and a selection of the responses Koch received, follow.

DESECRATING THE MEMORY OF THE HOLOCAUST: SHOULD THERE BE LEGAL LIMITS?

An Exchange with Noted Scholars and University Presidents

From the private files of Edward I. Koch.

April 23, 2004

Richard McCormick
President
Rutgers, The State University of New Jersey

Dear Mr. McCormick:

I read an article in today's *New York Sun* entitled "Astonishment, Fury as Anti-Semitism Rakes Rutgers. Knock a Jew in the Oven!" I am enclosing a copy for your ready reference.

It reported that "The illustration featured on the cover of a Rutgers University student newspaper shows a frightened Jewish man suspended on a carnival-style contraption. Below him is a burning oven. 'Knock a Jew in the oven!' reads the caption underneath the cartoon. 'Three throws for one dollar!' A contestant is throwing a ball at a target. The headline reads: 'Holocaust Remembrance Week: Springfest 2004.'"

In response, you are reported as saying that "though the cartoon desecrates the memory of six million innocent Jewish people, the newspaper is protected by the First Amendment."

The article reports that the university would not consider cutting the funding the paper receives from student activity fees. I assume that those fees include payments by Jewish and non-Jewish students who are offended by the cartoon simply because they do not support bigotry directed towards Jews or any other ethnic or racial group. If you believe the student newspaper is not subject to penalty because of this article and the First Amendment, tell me please, is there any situation that would cause you to take punitive action? If the article showed a black man hanging from a tree and an exhortation to lynch more blacks, would it warrant the imposition of a penalty by you? You have embarrassed by your inaction both the university and the State of New Jersey.

Editors of the school paper defend themselves by saying that the paper is "the entertainment weekly of giving birth to a retarded child." That same paper apparently printed in the past an anonymous personal ad that read: "This personal is dedicated to all the darkies and sons of slaves out there on Livingston campus. . . . Don't you have women to rape, or presidents to mug." Can you tell me what your response was to that anti–African American ad? If you published a response, may I have the actual text? Frankly, I don't understand your point of view that student fees must be paid under these circumstances to finance bigotry.

May I also remind you that free speech does not include the right to cry "Fire!" in a crowded theater. It was less than sixty years ago that millions of Jews were being "knocked" into real ovens. The cartoon and the attitude that led to its creation do not simply dishonor the memories of those who were murdered. By trivializing genocide, at a time when governments and private backers are reviving "The Protocols of the Elders of Zion" and other hate propaganda that made the Holocaust possible, the cartoon threatens Jews who are alive today.

I am writing to Governor McGreevey to ask if this situation isn't comparable to that involving Amiri Baraka, poet laureate of New Jersey, who used his position to publish an anti-Semitic poem. The New Jersey State Legislature took action against him at the Governor's request, ending the position. Perhaps it will take appropriate action regarding the state's ties with the university.

For a university to support with funding bigotry directed at blacks, women, gays, Jews and other traditionally victimized groups is unacceptable in my book.

Serendipitously, it happens that this weekend I will be leaving for a conference in Berlin sponsored by the Organization for Security and Cooperation in Europe (OSCE). The organization, made up of fifty-five nations, will be addressing the issue of rising anti-Semitism in Europe which is reaching heights not seen since the thirties. Apparently it is also rising at Rutgers University as well.

All the best.

Sincerely,
Edward I. Koch

———

April 29, 2004

Dear Mayor Koch:

Thank you for writing to me about the student publication that ran a deplorable cartoon making light of the Holocaust and about my administration's reaction to the incident.

How I wish I could do more. My initial reaction was that we have to shut down this loathsome publication, which has repeatedly published material that is racist, anti-Semitic, homophobic, and otherwise offensive to large groups of people. My legal staff advised me, however, that such action would be struck down in court based on their interpretation of the First Amendment and ample case law. As a public institution, Rutgers is subject to protections of the First Amendment; some private educational institutions are not subject to the First Amendment and can, therefore, restrict student speech in ways that Rutgers cannot.

Because this student-run publication is funded by student fees, I also asked whether student governing associations, which administer these funds, could deny funding to the publication. Again, the law forbids denying funding of a student organization based on its viewpoints.

As you will see from the enclosed copy of my earlier reaction to offensive material published in *The Medium,* the publication was brought under campuswide scrutiny just a few months ago, and it is deeply disappointing that the students have learned nothing from that controversy.

The editors of the publication have issued an apology for their decision to run the cartoon. An apology is not enough, but it is a start. At least in the case of this attack on human decency, the perpetrators recognized that they had erred badly and are sorry for their actions. Whether this contrition translates into greater sensitivity in their editorial choices remains to be seen.

I agree with you that student fees should not be paid to finance bigotry, but until we can find legal grounds on which to deny funding to student organizations for this reason, we cannot pursue the avenues that you suggest. We can and will, in the meantime, continue to denounce, as strongly as we can, such hurtful and offensive material. In addition, we will encourage students of good will to become involved in changing the culture of this publication, which by regulation must be open to every student at Rutgers.

We will also continue to develop programs that promote understanding and tolerance of people of different races, religions, backgrounds, colors, and sexual orientations.

Just a few days before the cartoon was published, I spoke at a Yom HaShoah commemoration event on our campus and stated that we at Rutgers "recognize our obligation to remember always the consequences of allowing hatred and intolerance to go unchallenged." I am determined to take every action we can—within the confines of the law—to speak out against acts of bigotry and to work toward greater editorial responsibility on our student publications.

I have the greatest respect for your insights and your experience in dealing with these issues. I would like to discuss the matter further with you at your convenience. If you are agreeable, please have your office call my assistant, Carol Koncsol.

Again, thank you for writing.

Sincerely yours,
Richard L. McCormick, President
Rutgers, The State University of New Jersey

———

May 3, 2004

Richard L. McCormick
President
Rutgers, The State University of New Jersey

Dear Mr. McCormick:
Your letter makes your case. If the law bars you from taking rational action to deal with the despicable act of students in putting out a university-subsidized student newspaper with a cartoon that can only be described as degrading to the memory of the six million Jews murdered in the Holocaust, then you are off the hook.

I will now have to find out if Charles Dickens' Mr. Bumble's statement, "the law is an ass," was accurate or our interpretation of the law flawed.

All the best.
Edward I. Koch

———

May 14, 2004

Dear Mayor Koch:
Thank you for sharing your correspondence with President Richard McCormick of Rutgers University. Your question is an important one, and I fear there are no simple answers to the dilemmas posed by the bigotry of certain members of our society.

I am dismayed that a cartoon of this nature was published at all, let alone in a student publication. I like to think that the maturity and decency of our students will prevent a similar occurrence here, but one can never be certain.

President McCormick is correct in asserting that private institutions such as Princeton University are not bound by the terms of the First Amendment, so we could, in theory, close a publication that conducted itself in the manner of *The Medium*. However, I must also say that as an academic community predicated on unfettered communication, we aspire to conduct ourselves in a manner consistent with the First Amendment. So, in some respects, the challenge we would face in such a situation is greater than the one that Rutgers is confronting. We have the power to close a student publication, but to use this power to censor the printed or spoken word raises a host of ethical, if not legal, issues.

What then, if any, are the remedies? I believe, in answer to your question, that as educational institutions and as a society, we can and must address affronts to the dignity of our fellow citizens whenever they occur. We must employ the very freedom of speech that shields the offender to uphold the interests of the offended. We must use such incidents, repellant though they are, to educate and galvanize the apathetic and indifferent. Censorship is punitive and may well occasion satisfaction in some quarters, but it does little to expose and combat the underlying causes of bigotry, and it often gives birth to martyrs who scarcely deserve this status. Perhaps the strongest guarantee that free speech will survive in this country is that people will from time to time abuse it. Only then, it seems, do many people exercise their right to speak and denounce the act of defamation that has taken place.

It is relatively easy to mobilize opinion in the face of egregious manifestations of hatred, but this is only a short-term remedy. It is no less important, though much more difficult, to create a climate on our campuses and in our society that is respectful of human differences, sensitivities, and historical wounds. This is where universities must take the lead in combating hatred—in purging prejudices that students bring to campus and giving them the intellectual and moral strength to combat these prejudices when they encounter them in later life.

One of the most moving annual events at Princeton is a solemn reading of the names of Holocaust victims—a twenty-four-hour litany that takes place in a central courtyard through which hundreds of students pass each day. Flags, representing the numbers and categories of Hitler's victims, are also erected near our campus center, which means that very few students can be oblivious to the terrible legacy of Nazi Germany. This public recognition of and solidarity with the Jewish experience is one of the ways in which we can combat the equally public venom of newspapers such as *The Medium,* not only in the wake of a specific outrage but also from day to day and from year to year.

I realize that these remedies are far from foolproof, but they are far, far better than passivity and, in the long term, may well prove more effective than curbing the scope of the First Amendment. I appreciate this opportunity to reflect on something that is close to your heart and should be close to everyone's.

With every good wish,

Sincerely,
Shirley M. Tilghman
President
Princeton University

———

May 17, 2004

Dear Mr. Mayor:
Thank you for your letter and for sending me the materials regarding the anti-Semitic cartoon published in the student-run publication at Rutgers University.

While the First Amendment protects the rights of the paper to publish a cartoon such as the one published in *The Medium,* it does not preclude the community from taking action. The Rutgers community has sent a clear message that it will not tolerate hate speech. You are clearly doing the same. I applaud your efforts.

Best wishes,
Lawrence H. Summers
President
Harvard University

———

May 24, 2004

Dear Ed:
This is in response to your letter of May 4 about the Rutgers student newspaper.

Without *reaching* President McCormick's lawyers' view that Rutgers could not shut down the paper, or prevent student funds from supporting the paper—which appears to be a recidivist on despicable speech—I thought the President failed adequately to do what the First Amendment clearly permits, and—as Holmes/Brandeis taught us in dissent long ago—encourages: fight bad ideas with better ideas. (See *Abrams v. U.S.,* 250 U.S. 616, 630 (1919).)

As expressed in your letter of April 23, all he said was "though the cartoon desecrates the memory of six million innocent Jewish people, the newspaper is protected by the First Amendment." If that is all he said, it is, to say the least, pretty pale tea. Moreover, it is less vehement than his November 24, 2003, paper ("Addressing Concerns about *The Medium*") that he attached to his letter to you of April 29.

Finally, just focusing on his pale-tea words, is he saying "Knock a Jew in the Oven" would be ok if there had not been a holocaust?

Clearly, the President could and should have been more critical. Moreover, even assuming (as I guess I do) that under the First Amendment, a state university cannot shut a publication or *prevent* students from funding it, the First Amendment surely does not stop the university president from urging students not to use their money this way. How best to say that might take some care, so as not to have an opposite reaction. But, particularly when the paper (under, I assume, the same editors) has been grossly offensive before, he could have started a useful and educational student dialogue with some sharper words and suggestions of his own.

We can recognize someone's *right* to speak; but we do not have to spend our money buying offensive garbage.

On another note, when Jack Rosenthal introduced me as one of the *American Lawyer*'s first twelve "Lifetime Achievers," he included a quote from you, which I much appreciated. I enclose a copy of Jack's remarks.

Best wishes.
Sincerely,
Frederick A. O. Schwarz, Jr.
Brennan Center for Justice
at NYU School of Law

———

June 23, 2004

Dear Ed,
You have written me twice asking for my views of the violently anti-Semitic cartoon that appeared in *The Medium,* the student newspaper at Rutgers. I am sorry I am late responding and even sorrier I didn't pay attention to this as the story was breaking. An apology is not enough. The paper should be closed and no university funding ever provided to the students who were responsible. This would be my minimum response.

I hope you are well. . . . I do love hearing your voice.

J. Robert Kerrey
President
New School University

———

May 11, 2004

Honorable Edward I. Koch
1290 Avenue of the Americas—30th Floor
New York, NY 10104

Dear Ed:
You ask me whether consistent with the First Amendment there is anything Rutgers can do to limit the use of University funds to school publications that are offensive to religious or ethnic groups.

The Supreme Court's unanimous decision in *Board of Regents of the University of Wisconsin System v. Southworth,* 529 U.S. 217 (2000), does indeed protect the First Amendment rights of the student newspaper. I am enclosing a copy of the opinion. First Amendment interests are protected by the requirement of "viewpoint neutrality," which means that the school must disburse funds for student activities without regard to the viewpoint expressed in those activities.

You might note, however, that a university could, but need not, opt to protect the First Amendment interests of dissenting students in another way as well. At page nine of the opinion (headnote [4]), the Court writes that if "a university decided that its students' First Amendment interests were better protected by some type of optional or refund system, it would be free to do so." But the Court refused to mandate such a system because of the likelihood of disruption and expense. Under such a system, students who objected to the viewpoint of a particular student activity, including a publication, would be able to request that none of their mandatory fees be used to support the particular activity.

I hope this helps. Best wishes.

Stephen Gillers
Vice Dean and Professor of Law
School of Law
New York University

Two years later, the Rutgers cartoon affair took on new significance in the wake
of the controversy over a Danish newspaper's publication of cartoons about
Muhammad. In an essay published in The Forward *on August 4, 2006, Ed*
Koch and Rafael Medoff wrote, in part:

As mobs throughout the Muslim world assault European targets
in response to the publication of caricatures of Muhammad, an
Iranian government newspaper has offered its own bizarre response to the controversy: It has announced a contest for cartoons mocking the Holocaust.

In their fevered imagination, the Iranians believe they will
expose a double standard, according to which—they claim—the
West tolerates cartoons offensive to Muslims but will not tolerate cartoons deriding the Holocaust.

What Teheran apparently does not realize is that Americans
already grappled with this issue two years ago—and responded
very differently.

On April 21, 2004, *The Medium,* a student newspaper at Rutgers University, published a cartoon under the headline "Holocaust Remembrance Week: Springfest 2004." It portrayed a
carnival-style scene of a bearded Jewish man sitting above an
oven, with a person throwing a ball at him. The caption read:
"Knock a Jew in the oven! Three throws for one dollar! Really!"

Rutgers president Richard McCormick criticized the cartoon as "outrageous in its cruelty" and asked the editors to apologize, but concluded there was nothing he could do to punish
the newspaper. The First Amendment's guarantee of free speech
would prevent a state university such as Rutgers from shutting
down *The Medium* or even cutting off its funding "based on its
viewpoint," McCormick said, citing a memorandum by his legal
staff.

Instead of circling the wagons, the university's lawyers
should have engaged in a little creative thinking. There was, in
fact, a variety of ways that Rutgers could have responded to the

cartoon [such as withdrawing university funding from the newspaper or permitting students to request that their student fees
not go to the newspaper]. . . .

Neither the public nor a university are required to quietly
accept any outrageous action in the name of free speech. There
are appropriate, peaceful, legal ways to register one's displeasure
over a grievous insult.

Nobody responded to the Rutgers cartoon with arson attacks or stonings or violence of any kind. The editor of *The
Medium* was not jailed. No legal restrictions were imposed upon
the newspaper or the university. Instead, reasonable people engaged in a thoughtful discussion within the context of complete
respect for freedom and the law.

That is the standard according to which a civilized society
should conduct itself. And it is a standard to which everyone
should be held, regardless of the depth of their religious sentiments or the extent to which their feelings have been injured.

The administration of George W. Bush demonstrated the seriousness it ascribes to the issue of anti-Semitism by sending Secretary of State Colin Powell to address an international conference in Berlin on anti-Semitism in 2004, and appointing a high-level delegation, headed by Ed Koch, to accompany him. Koch's description of the background and purpose of the conference is followed by the text of his address to the event, and then his post-conference reflections.

A NEW CHAPTER IN THE FIGHT AGAINST ANTI-SEMITISM

Written in April 2004, from the private files of Edward I. Koch.

The Organization for Security and Cooperation in Europe (OSCE), little known by the U.S. public, is preparing to confront anti-Semitism in the region encompassing the organization's fifty-five member states. Those states extend from Vancouver through Europe and Eurasia to Vladivostok.

The OSCE was created in 1994 but has its origins in a historic agreement signed in 1975 by the leaders of thirty-five states—including the then two superpowers—the United States and the Soviet Union—the members of NATO and the Warsaw Pact, and the neutral and nonaligned countries. It became the OSCE at the Budapest Summit in December 1994.

Quietly working to resolve old conflicts and prevent new ones, the OSCE has an agenda that encompasses three major aspects of European security: political/security issues, including the struggle against crime and terrorism; the promotion of economic development and environmental protection, and the promotion of human rights and democracy.

Last year in Vienna, for the first time ever, the OSCE held a conference specifically devoted to the issue of anti-Semitism. Coined in 1879 by Jew-haters, the term was intended to describe the anti-Jew fever then sweeping the European countries as race-directed and not religion-directed. It never included

Arabs, only Jews. It was really a way to disguise the hostility directed at Jews and their religion. Jews, who trace their history back to the patriarch Abraham and his wife Sarah, are Jews by virtue of one or two aspects of their life: they are born of a Jewish mother, or they accept as their religious persuasion the Jewish religion.

Many Jews fall into both categories. There is the famous case of the Archbishop of Paris, Jean-Marie Cardinal Lustiger, born a Jew, converted to Catholicism during the Holocaust who describes himself as both a Jew and Catholic, and the two words are not inconsistent with one another.

Hating Jews and persecuting them has a history of at least 2,000 years. The longest-lived false charge against the Jews is the cry of the mob, and often the priest, "They killed God": deicide. The second myth is they kill Christian children to use their blood to make matzos for Passover. More recently, Muslims have incited hate against Jews by making the same false charge, alleging the killing of Muslim children for that same purpose—the blood libel. The third charge is that Jews secretly control the world and meet every year to decide its fate. This fabrication was included in the *Protocols of the Elders of Zion,* a hoax created and published by the Russian Czarist police in 1911 to encourage pogroms. The Russian word "pogrom" denotes physical attacks upon Jews often, but not exclusively, inspired by government action and direction.

In the 1930s, the Nazis began their assault upon the Jews, intending to murder every one of them, and before killing them, to dehumanize them. The Nazis required by regulation on August 17, 1938, that every German Jew take an additional name effective June 1, 1939. The regulation provided "males will take the given name Israel, females the given name Sara."

The world has seen over these last sixty years a rebirth of anti-Semitism in the very countries that defeated the Nazis. The new anti-Semitism is to be found not only in so-called skinhead groups, but is now most acceptable in intellectual leftist circles. In addition to the crescendo of physical assaults directed at Jews in Europe, the Middle and the Far East, there has been a rising Muslim intolerance and fury inflicted on Jews because of the existence since 1948 of the reborn State of Israel. That small country has survived for the last fifty-six years because of the courage of its sons and daughters and some—the religious—would say because of the protection of God who had promised Abraham and his descendants, "To your progeny I will give this land."

Building upon the Vienna conference last year, the German government offered to host a second conference on anti-Semitism in 2004 to give a further boost to the OSCE's important work in this area. At their annual meeting, which took place in December 2003 in the Dutch city of Maastricht, the ministers of all fifty-five OSCE countries welcomed the German invitation to host the Berlin conference of 2004. Under the leadership of Secretary of State Colin Powell, the U.S. delegation argued persuasively that there was much unfinished business and a need to further discuss and adopt measures to track and combat the growth of anti-Semitism in the OSCE region.

During the week of April 25, OSCE states will meet in Berlin to consider what measures, including the collection of statistics about hate crimes and the education of young people about the horrors of the Holocaust, to take to address both historic and new forms of anti-Semitism. I am particularly concerned that the newest form of anti-Semitism is to use attacks upon the State of Israel to disguise attacks on Jews simply because they are Jews.

Today, the anti-Semite will attack "Zionism." What is the meaning of Zionism? For me and many others it means support for the Jewish nation. At one time, it described a person whose intent was to leave his or her country and move to Israel, the historic Aliyah that still motivates some. Jews, in fear and subject to anti-Semitism, as they have been in Russia in previous years, do engage in Aliyah by the thousands, exercising their right of return. Others, like myself, full citizens of their country, have no desire to leave and never will, loving our country that has given us equal opportunity with our fellow citizens. Nevertheless, we also, like our fellow citizens, support the country from whose people and loins we have sprung.

I have been honored by Secretary of State Colin Powell, who has designated me as the chairman of the U.S. delegation that will attend the Berlin conference. I thank the German government for hosting the conference. While in Berlin, I will visit the Wannsee Villa where Reinhard Heydrich, Adolf Eichmann, and their Nazi colleagues planned the destruction and death of all Jews throughout the world. In order to disguise their unspeakable plan, they referred to it as the Final Solution.

The Berlin conference will, hopefully, find ways to track anti-Semitism in all of its forms in every one of the OSCE's fifty-five countries. Most important, the conference will hopefully—and here I speak personally and not as chairman—encourage member states to educate youth on the nature of anti-Semitism and where anti-Semitism can lead.

Those who lived through the transient triumph of the Nazis and saw what their *Juden hasse* caused assumed that when Hitler and his cohorts were defeated, the cry of "never again" truly reflected the agony and contrition of the individuals and nations who had contributed to the persecution of the Jews. Regrettably, Santayana's admonition, "Those who cannot remember the past are condemned to repeat it," is closer to the current state of affairs.

————

REMARKS MADE TO INTRODUCE A SESSION ON THE ROLE OF THE MEDIA IN COMBATING ANTI-SEMITISM, AT THE BERLIN OSCE CONFERENCE ON ANTI-SEMITISM, APRIL 29, 2004
From the private files of Edward I. Koch.

In the interest of expediting the debate and allowing as many interventions as possible from the floor, I will limit myself to laying out a general framework for the issues that relate to anti-Semitism and posing a number of basic questions about the role of the media in conveying and in countering prejudice.

The media can play either a positive or a negative role in the fight against anti-Semitism and other forms of intolerance.

On the positive side, there are many ways in which the media can counter prejudice and promote tolerance. They all have in common that the relevant media figures take their professional duties seriously, that they recognize their responsibility for shaping public views, and that they encourage the voices of reason and humanity.

On the negative side of the equation, we can all cite many examples of articles, broadcasts, and websites that stir up hatred and appeal to the most primitive prejudices.

So I'm going to turn over the floor to you, my dear colleagues, with the hope that together we can begin today to find constructive answers to the following questions:

> How can the media report on the activities of minority populations, and specifically of the Jewish communities in our countries, to promote better understanding among the general population?
>
> Are there ways that governments can encourage the media to report more objectively on domestic developments affecting the Jewish community, or on international developments, while fully respecting freedom of the media? What are the special responsibilities of state-owned media in this regard?
>
> How can we isolate those extremist publicists who convey anti-Semitic or other hateful messages from the mainstream of respectable, responsible media professionals?
>
> How should media respond to anti-Semitic statements and images, quickly and firmly, to make sure our populations get an objective view?

My own style is to be blunt, to confront the adversary, to "tell it like it is." If you're in the media business, I think you need to report on hate crimes in all their ugliness. But you also need to report on the joys of Jewish life, and the benefits for everyone of living in a tolerant, multicultural society.

If you're in the education business, you need to make sure that citizens know all about the horrors of the Holocaust. But you also need to teach about the positive experiences of the ensuing decades in overcoming the Nazi legacy in Germany and beyond.

If you are the public consumer of media messages, you need to reject bias and demand fairness. You need to view the media with a critical eye, and to distinguish between responsible and irresponsible journalism. Finally, when you encounter examples of intolerance in the media, even subtle ones, you need to speak out, whether through letters to the editor or e-mails to the producer, or simply by spreading the word in your community. I hope that these broad principles will help to stimulate a fruitful debate this morning.

POST-BERLIN REFLECTIONS

Written in May 2004, from the private files of Edward I. Koch.

I've just returned from Berlin, where I served at the designation of Secretary of State Colin Powell, as chairman of the U.S. delegation to the Organization for Security and Cooperation in Europe (OSCE) conference on April 28 and 29.

The regular U.S. ambassador to OSCE is Steven Minikes, to whom I first spoke about seven weeks ago in a telephone conference call among the five members of the delegation and members of Congress. He was the architect of the final language adopted at OSCE condemning anti-Semitism and imposing obligations on every one of the nations comprising the OSCE.

Frankly, I wondered how much the conference could achieve. The fifty-five nations making up the OSCE do everything by unanimous agreement and any one nation can veto proposed actions. Last year in Vienna, the conference discussed anti-Semitism but adopted no binding resolutions or measures to condemn it. There are Muslim nations, such as Turkey and the now-independent republics, formerly part of the Soviet Union, such as Tajikistan and Kazakhstan, that are part of OSCE.

However, as a result of the joint action by the United States, led by Secretary of State Powell, and the German Republic, led by its foreign minister, Joseph Fischer, a miracle was accomplished in Berlin. The OSCE, after extended discussion, unanimously adopted a decision binding on every member nation that requires that every country collect annual statistics on anti-Semitic acts, including violence against persons and the desecration of Jewish cemeteries and destruction of property motivated by anti-Semitism, and publicly report those incidents annually. Under the OSCE decision, those same nations are mandated to adopt hate crime legislation, as well as implement a number of other measures, including educational programs teaching the dangers of anti-Semitism. Difficult to achieve but achieved nonetheless was a reference to anti-Semitism resulting from the ongoing conflict in the Middle East between Israel and the Palestinians. The decision adopted on Israel is worth quoting: "OSCE participating States declare unambiguously that international developments or political issues, including those in Israel or elsewhere in the Middle East, never justify anti-Semitism."

There were many who did not believe it was possible to reach this outcome, especially with regard to the reference to Israel. The point reiterated by the U.S. delegation and others, both in floor discussions with the delegates and in meetings with delegations off the floor, was that Israel should be judged by the same standards applied to all nations, instead of the double standard currently used. What other nations do with impunity and without criticism, Israel is condemned and demonized for. This is, in effect, anti-Semitism disguised as opposition to Israel's policies. There is no doubt this provision will require daily monitoring by advocate organizations to report on breaches of the provision.

We won the battle and achieved an enormous success. It would not have happened had not President Bush and Secretary Powell lobbied successfully to hold a second conference on anti-Semitism this year in Berlin. The conference was agreed to, notwithstanding some objections, because of their leadership and the offer by German foreign minister Joseph Fischer, known affectionately as Joschka, to host the conference in Berlin. Indeed, one of the often-stated comments by delegates was how appropriate it was, because of Germany's historic role in causing the Shoah, to hold the conference in Berlin. The conference was held in a building, under the jurisdiction of the foreign ministry, that was used by the Nazis during World War II. There is no doubt that many delegates, including me, at moments during the conference imagined Nazis walking through those halls. I speculated about their conversations concerning Jews in the very hall in which I was sitting, and in which the world was now considering how to end anti-Semitism, forty miles away from the Wannsee Villa where Heydrich and Eichmann planned the Final Solution: the mass murder of all Jews worldwide.

My week in Berlin will always remain indelibly fixed in my mind. The single most poignant moment for me occurred not at the conference but at an event honoring Foreign Minister Fischer. In his remarks, he talked of how important it was to hold the conference and adopt the decisions here in Berlin because of all that occurred there before and during World War II. He acknowledged, as he has on so many other occasions, the debt Germany owes the Jews of the world for the horrors inflicted upon them. He said he was dedicated to doing whatever he could to make amends. I was called upon to respond for the assembly.

I said that I believed the Jews were saved from total destruction primarily because of God's intervention and the victory of the Allies, primarily the United States, Great Britain, and the U.S.S.R. But there were also the actions of righteous Gentiles who saved individual Jews and to whom all Jews will be eternally grateful. I went on to say Joschka Fischer is such a righteous Gentile who, even now, is saving Jews. It was hard not for me to cry.

Adding to the excitement at the Berlin conference was an evacuation of our hotel because of a bomb threat. We were not able to return for five hours, while each room was inspected by the German police and a bomb-sniffing dog. No bomb was found.

In recent years, anti-Semitic violence, often but not exclusively perpetrated by local Muslim youths, has reached near-epidemic proportions in some West European countries. France has been the subject of much international attention in this regard, both because of the frequency of anti-Semitic incidents there as well as the severity of episodes, such as the torture-murder of a young French Jew, Ilan Halimi, by anti-Semitic Muslims in 2005. Our exchange of correspondence with the French ambassador to the United States, concerning the level of anti-Semitism in his country, raised more questions than it answered.

ANTI-SEMITISM IN FRANCE: RISING OR FALLING?

From the private files of Edward I. Koch.

October 25, 2006

His Excellency Jean-David Levitte
Embassy of France
4101 Reservoir Road, NW
Washington, DC 20007

Your Excellency:
We are writing with regard to your recent statements concerning anti-Semitism in France. According to the *New York Sun* (Oct. 23), you said in remarks at the Young Israel of Pelham Parkway on October 22 that there has been a "48% decrease in reported anti-Semitic incidents over the past year." You acknowledged that there had been a wave of anti-Semitism in France back in 2001–2002, but you emphasized: "Yes, we had a problem, but it has abated. It's not over, but the trend is encouraging."

A recent report by another observer, however, presents evidence that is anything but encouraging. Arnaud de Borchgrave, editor at large of United Press International and the *Washington Times*, reported just last week that "Anti-Semitic incidents have proliferated in France in recent times, but the news seldom makes it across the Atlantic. . . . A Jewish sports club in Toulouse attacked with molotov cocktails; in Bondy, 15 men beat up members of a Jewish soccer team with metal bars and sticks; a bus that takes Jewish children to school in Aubervilliers attacked three times in the last 14 months; synagogues in Strausbourg and Marseilles and a Jewish school in Creteil firebombed in recent weeks; in Toulouse, a gunman opened fire—all ignored in mainstream U.S. media. The metropolitan Paris police tabulated 10 to 12 anti-Jewish incidents per day in the last 30 days throughout the country." (*Washington Times*, Oct. 16, 2006)

While every decrease in anti-Semitic attacks is of course welcome news, a rate of ten to twelve anti-Jewish attacks daily—even if that does represent the 48% decrease to which you reportedly referred—is still intolerable and deserves the immediate and unrelenting attention of the French authorities.

We would be grateful if you would please let us know if you were quoted accurately in the *Sun* article; if you would please clarify the apparent discrepancy between your statements and those of Mr. de Borchgrave; and if you are able to ascertain and tell us if recent anti-Semitism has had any effect upon the exodus of French Jews to other countries.

Cordially,
Edward I. Koch
Mayor of New York, City, 1978–1989
Member, United States Holocaust Memorial Council

Rafael Medoff, Ph.D.
Director, The David S. Wyman Institute for Holocaust Studies

———

After a month passed with no reply, we wrote to the ambassador a second time, reiterating our original points and adding:

———

In the four weeks since our first letter to you, the following incidents have been reported by the Jewish Telegraphic Agency and other media:

- On November 8, 2006, arsonists attacked and damaged Merkaz HaTorah, a Jewish school in the Paris suburb of Gagny.
- On November 12, 2006, the European Jewish Congress released a report which found that between April and August of this year, there were sixty-one anti-Semitic incidents, "an increase of 79 percent over the same period last year."
- On November 23, 2006, a mob of French soccer fans shouting "Filthy Jew!" assaulted an Israeli man in a Paris restaurant, compelling the police to use lethal force to stop the attack.
- Speakers at a conference held in November by the umbrella group of French Jewish organizations, CRIF, reported "that in many suburbs of Paris, few Jewish young people still attend public school because of violence or threats of violence, mainly from African and North African Arab students. Jewish parents have placed their children in private Jewish schools, many of which were established in the past few years."

Mr. Ambassador, we again respectfully ask you to let us know if you were quoted accurately in the *Sun* article; if you would please clarify the apparent discrepancy between your statements and those of Mr. de Borchgrave; and if you are able to ascertain and tell us if recent anti-Semitism has had any effect upon the exodus of French Jews to other countries. In addition, would you please let us know if the aforementioned report by the European Jewish Congress about a 79% increase in anti-Semitic incidents from April to August 2006 is, to the best of your knowledge, correct; and if so, how does this square with your own reported statement of a recent decrease in anti-Semitic incidents.

———

Finally, on December 5, 2006, the ambassador replied. In his letter, he quoted a statement by French president Jacques Chirac condemning anti-Semitism and a statement by Israeli prime minister Ehud Olmert praising Chirac's stance. And he quoted a poll showing most Frenchmen think favorably of Jews. As for the substantive issues, the ambassador quoted statistics on anti-Semitism that indeed show a 47 percent decrease, as he had claimed—but for an earlier time period than the one about which we inquired. When he quoted the figures for the time period that we were asking about, the numbers were drastically different from the ones that he had been quoted (by the *New York Sun*) as citing.

So we wrote again:

———

December 13, 2006

His Excellency Jean-David Levitte
Embassy of France
4101 Reservoir Road, NW
Washington, DC 20007 / Fax (202) 944–6166

Your Excellency:
Thank you for your letter of December 5, 2006, in response to our letters of October 25 and November 27

regarding the problem of recent anti-Semitism in France.

Pardon us for seeking further clarification, but it seems to us that the information contained in your letter did not entirely address our questions.

You were quoted in the *New York Sun* on October 23, 2006, as saying (at the Young Israel of Pelham Parkway on Oct. 22) that there has been a "48% decrease in reported anti-Semitic incidents over the past year." In your letter of Nov. 27, you write: "I confirm what I said in my remarks at Young Israel of Pelham Parkway on October 22."

Yet the information you cite in your letter does not seem to support the statement you made at Young Israel. You write in your letter, "anti-Semitic acts in France declined 47 percent in 2005 compared to 2004." So 47 percent is the figure for 2005. But at Young Israel, you said you were referring to anti-Semitism "in the past year," meaning between October 2005 and October 2006. Concerning that period, you write in your letter, "By the end of October 2006, 436 anti-Semitic incidents had been reported (compared with 450 for the same period in 2005)." That figure of 436 represents a decrease of only 3 percent. While of course any decrease is welcome, a 3 percent decrease is a far cry from a 48 percent decrease.

There are two additional points in our earlier letters that we still hope you will address:

1. In our letter of October 25, we asked if recent anti-Semitism has had any effect upon the exodus of French Jews to other countries. We would still very much like to know your answer to that question.
2. In our letter of November 27, we noted that speakers at a conference held in November by the umbrella group of French Jewish organizations, CRIF, re-

ported "that in many suburbs of Paris, few Jewish young people still attend public school because of violence or threats of violence, mainly from African and North African Arab students. Jewish parents have placed their children in private Jewish schools, many of which were established in the past few years." According to your information, is this description accurate?

Cordially,
Edward I. Koch
Mayor of New York, City, 1978–1989
Member, United States Holocaust Memorial Council

Rafael Medoff, Ph.D.
Director, The David S. Wyman Institute for Holocaust Studies

———

On December 28, Ambassador Levitte replied. To our disappointment, he wrote that he did "not wish to go into a point-by-point discussion" of the issues at stake. Instead, he chose to briefly reiterate that "substantial progress" has been made in France in the fight against anti-Semitism "over the last few years." He said that these gains, "which were spectacular in 2005, look like being [*sic*] confirmed in 2006." He concluded: "Even so, the French government is not satisfied with the present situation and remains fully determined to keep up a tireless fight against anti-Semitism."

While we appreciate that pledge, we are concerned that the government's efforts may be undermined by statistics such as those that appeared in the ambassador's letters to us. In the very same letter, he wrote that he stands by his claim of a 48 percent decrease in anti-Semitism over the past year, and then he wrote that there has been a 3 percent decrease in anti-Semitism over the past year. Will the French government really commit substantial resources to fighting anti-Semitism if it believes that it has already dropped by 48 percent?

We are likewise troubled by the ambassador's decision not to address our questions about the rate of French Jewish emigration and the reports of many French Jewish parents withdrawing their children from public schools because of anti-Semitism. These are important questions that deserve answers.

In late 2006, one of Koch's fellow members of the U.S. Holocaust Memorial Council, Los Angeles radio talk show host Dennis Prager, ignited a controversy by asserting that Congressman-elect Keith Ellison, a Muslim, should not be permitted to use a Koran in his swearing-in ceremony, on the grounds that it conflicts with America's Judeo-Christian values. Koch condemned Prager's statement as bigotry and urged that he be removed from the council. It was not within the council's power to do that, since it is a presidential appointment and only the president can remove a member. But the council, at Koch's urging, did publicly criticize Prager, which was a highly unusual step.

DENNIS PRAGER AND THE KORAN

Written in December 2006, from the private files of Edward I. Koch.

A number of Americans of different faiths are demanding that syndicated columnist Dennis Prager step down or be removed from the board of the U.S. Holocaust Memorial Council, the governing body of the U.S. Holocaust Memorial Museum.

The reason for the demand is that a newly elected congressman from Minnesota, Keith Ellison, who is Muslim, has stated he wants to use the Koran to take his oath of office on January 4 and Prager has written in his column, "He should not be allowed to do so—not because of any American hostility to the Koran, but because the act undermines American civilization."

Prager's statement is both foolish and erroneous. Having been sworn in five times as a member of Congress, I am familiar with the protocol. The entire House of Representatives is sworn in at the same time, and members are not asked to place their hands on either Bible—the Old or New Testament—as Prager noted in a subsequent column. The members are called to order by the Speaker of the House, who administers the oath to members who swear or affirm to uphold the U.S. Constitution. Following that, the House adjourns and the members who choose to do so then meet with the Speaker for a private swearing-in at which pictures are taken. This will all be done on January 4, 2007.

I was first elected to Congress in November 1968. Remember that year? The Democratic candidates—Hubert Humphrey and Edmund Muskie—lost, and the Republican candidates—Richard Nixon and Spiro Agnew—won.

At the private ceremony, the member is again sworn in, in the presence of his or her family, with a family member generally holding a Bible, sometimes a family Bible brought by the newly elected member. But members are not required to use a Bible. It is a matter of choice. Prager, I believe, is simply distressed that a member of the Muslim faith won the congressional election in Minnesota.

Had I lived in that district, based on what I've read about Keith Ellison, I probably would not have voted for him. So what? The people who live there did vote for him, and he is entitled to place his hand on the Bible—Old or New Testament—or any other holy document, including the Koran, at an official or private ceremony when reciting his oath of office. If holy books were used at the official ceremony, he would and should have the right to swear or affirm on a document of his choice, recognized by the world as a document of faith, but, as Prager pointed out in his subsequent column, the documents are in fact used at private ceremonies.

Dennis Prager's columns on this issue convey bias and bigotry directed at Mr. Ellison, his faith, and at all Muslims who revere the Koran and demand using it at their being sworn, as Christians revere the Old and New Testaments and Jews revere the Old Testament and demand those holy books be used when they are sworn.

Prager is not qualified to serve on the board of the Holocaust Council. The purpose of the Holocaust Museum is to teach the world's adults and children how wrong it was for the Nazis to wage a war of extermination against Jews, gypsies, homosexuals, political opponents, and dissenters. Members of the commission, of which I am one, have, I believe, the obligation to extend this message of tolerance to the farthest reaches of the world. Prager has not done that when tested in this matter.

A voice from history, that of the first Jew in England to be elected to Parliament in 1847, is relevant. I recalled when commencing the writing of this commentary that there had been an incident concerning the oath taken by him which prevented his being sworn in—the Internet provided the information in an article that appeared in the European Jewish Press discussing Lionel Nathan De Rothschild (1808–1879). The article stated, "In 1847, Rothschild was first elected to sit in the British Parliament but could not do so as he refused to take the oath that spoke of Christianity as 'the true faith.' After many attempts to change the law in 1858, Rothschild with a covered head and using the Hebrew term for God was able to claim his seat and became the first openly Jewish parliamentarian."

The same European Jewish Press referred to another Jew who served as one of England's great prime ministers. The reference is a delight. "Although he was Jewish by birth and circumcised, former British prime minister [Benjamin] Disraeli was baptized by his father at the age of thirteen. To be allowed to sit in the British Parliament, Disraeli had to belong to the Church of England, but his allegiance to his ancestors was an open secret. When responding to an attack on his Jewishness, Disraeli replied: 'Yes, I am a Jew and when the ancestors of the right honourable gentleman were brutal savages in an unknown island, mine were priests in the temple of Solomon.' Disraeli first became Prime Minister in 1868 and served again from 1874–1880."

My advice to Dennis Prager is, reconsider your position. Prager should recognize that bigotry is wrong when directed at anyone because of their religion and that, notwithstanding the current battle of civilizations occurring across the world with radical Islam and its use of terrorism, Islam and its largest grouping of Muslim adherents are part of the world's great monotheistic religions. Interestingly, Isaac, whose descendants became the Jews, and Ishmael, whose descendants became the Arabs, both sons of Abraham, are brothers.

ARE JEWS SUPPRESSING FREE SPEECH?

By Edward I. Koch and Rafael Medoff

Written in December 2006, from the private files of Edward I. Koch.

From Tehran to Plains, Georgia to the hallowed halls of Harvard, a new cry is heard in the land: The Jews are suppressing free speech!

In recent weeks, Iranian president Mahmoud Ahmadinejad, former U.S. president Jimmy Carter, and academics John Mearsheimer and Stephen Walt have all claimed to be victims of a conspiracy by Jews to keep them from speaking out.

According to Ahmadinejad, the Tehran conference of Holocaust deniers that he organized was necessary because the Jewish-influenced governments of other countries prevent public discussion about the Holocaust.

The Iranian president apparently hasn't done the math. Only twelve countries have laws that in some way restrict public denial of the Holocaust or other genocides. That's less than 7 percent of the 192 member-countries of the United Nations, leaving more than 90 percent of the globe free for Ahmadinejad and his acolytes to spread their hatred without legal encumbrance.

The United States has no laws prohibiting Holocaust denial, although if Tehran conference speaker David Duke decided to return to his old Ku Klux Klan ways, he would run into problems in some parts of the country: Twenty states have legal restrictions on burning crosses or wearing Ku Klux Klan–style hoods, regarding those activities as terroristic intimidation. But thirty states do not, meaning that Duke and company can still operate with complete freedom in 60 percent of the country (with, of course, freedom of speech and assembly everywhere else).

Former President Carter, for his part, has authored a provocative book, *Palestine: Peace Not Apartheid,* which is, to put it mildly, harshly critical of Israel. That, of course, is his right. But Mr. Carter crossed a line when he charged recently that universities "with high Jewish enrollment" had refused to let him speak on their campuses. The implication is that the Jews are trying to silence him. Expanding on this allegation in an interview in the latest issue of *Tikkun,* Carter added this howler: "One of the things that's missing is any voice in the Jewish community who dares to be at all critical of anything that the right wing in Israel does."

Apparently Carter forgot to whom he was speaking. *Tikkun* is one of the leading voices in the Jewish community critical of "the right wing in Israel." In fact, it has also been critical of the Israeli center, and sometimes even the Israeli left. Not only is *Tikkun* critical in its articles; it organizes meetings and rallies on the same themes, and has even lobbied Congress. And, of course, anyone even remotely familiar with the American Jewish community knows of the numerous organizations, leaders, writers, and other voices critical of the Israeli right. The notion that American Jewry, like Carter himself, has been cowed into silent acquiescence to "the right wing in Israel" would be laughable were it not so pernicious.

Mearsheimer and Walt are, respectively, professor at the University of Chicago and professor and former academic dean at Harvard University's Kennedy School of Government. The Kennedy School's website recently published their controversial eighty-two-page paper, "The Israel Lobby." They contend that American Jews, some American Christians, and pro-Israel elements of the media have colluded to bring about a pro-Israel U.S. foreign policy that was detrimental to America's own interests. Moreover, they allege, "the Lobby" works assiduously to "prevent critical comments [about Israel] from getting a fair hearing" in the media and other public forums.

"The Lobby" also tries "to blacklist and intimidate scholars" who are critical of Israel, they report; although, in contrast to

Jimmy Carter, Mearsheimer and Walt claim the pro-Israel forces have "had difficulty . . . in stifling debate on university campuses."

The irony is that Mearsheimer and Walt's allegations have received extraordinarily wide attention in the supposedly Zionist-dominated media. Their paper appeared in full not only on Harvard's website but in the *London Review of Books* as well. It was reported extensively in the world's press and discussed just as extensively on the op-ed pages of numerous prominent daily newspapers. And they have landed a book deal with a major publisher, Farrar, Straus and Giroux. But facts do not seem to get in the way of Mearsheimer and Walt, or Carter or Ahmadinejad, for that matter.

It is, of course, important to be cautious about drawing comparisons between public figures. Overwrought analogies have soiled public discourse on more than one occasion in recent memory. Ahmadinejad is a genocidal maniac, and obviously Carter, Mearsheimer, and Walt are not. But that is what makes their allegations all the more disturbing: Their irresponsible utterances are dragging the good name of the office of the presidency and Harvard University through the mud of Tehran.

CHAPTER THREE

CONFRONTING THE HOLOCAUST

During the years Ed Koch served as mayor of New York City, 1978 to 1989, Holocaust-related issues repeatedly attracted public attention. Just as he spoke his mind frankly on other issues, Koch soon became known as a leading voice on issues concerning the Holocaust. These included the controversy over President Reagan's visit to the cemetery in Bitburg, Germany, where SS men are buried; U.S. efforts to capture Nazi war criminals; and the emergence of a new form of anti-Semitism—Holocaust denial. At the same time, it was a period of increased awareness of the courageous few who risked their careers, and sometimes even their lives, to rescue Jews from the Nazis.

In the writings and speeches included in this chapter, Koch discusses the Latin American diplomat George Mantello, who surreptitiously provided documents that saved thousands of Jews, and Raoul Wallenberg, the Swedish diplomat who rescued thousands of Jews in German-occupied Budapest in 1944–1945 before being taken prisoner by the Soviets. This chapter also sheds light on Koch's role in the Brooklyn Holocaust Memorial Park, the first permanent commemoration in New York City of the Shoah. The chapter concludes with writings on more recent matters of public interest, including the controversy over Holocaust-era assets in Swiss banks; the failure of the Allies to bomb the Auschwitz death camp; the involvement of Koch's predecessor, Fiorello La Guardia, in promoting rescue of refugees from the Holocaust; and new research revealing that the Allies had early, and detailed, knowledge of the mass murder of the Jews.

AN OBLIGATION TO REMEMBER

Remarks at the annual assembly of the American Gathering of Jewish Holocaust Survivors, April 13, 1983, from Box 080065, Folder 4, EIK.

Z'chor!

Gedenk!

Remember!

That is why we have gathered here: to remember. To remember the Holocaust, a horror and death that took the lives of six million European Jews, that destroyed their religious and cultural institutions and—this is often forgotten—came close to destroying the Yiddish language itself.

A Holocaust doesn't just happen. It is a deliberate, calculated act of mass murder, in which the murderers are not only those who do the killing, but those who stand by and do nothing to stop it.

Throughout the ages, there have been acts of savagery and barbarism taken against individuals and groups, but never in recorded history has one nation sought to totally exterminate another people based solely on their religion.

Yes, it is true that early followers of Muhammad put people to the sword unless they would convert. But the option of conversion was available.

Yes, it is true that Spain in 1492 sought to expel the Jews unless they converted. But the option of conversion was available.

Other persecuted groups can point in their history to attempts of an enemy to subjugate them. However, there never was a plan, that I am aware of, to totally exterminate a nation simply because of their religion.

And that is why the word "Holocaust" is unique to the Jewish experience in Nazi Germany. Indeed, at Yad Vashem, in Israel, is the actual plan from the German archives giving their strategies and dates for the extermination of the Jews in every nation of the world. I was horrified when Gideon Hausner, the prosecutor of Eichmann, pointed to a document listing the United States and American Jews—all of us—already marked down in the Nazi extermination books.

When I walk through Yad Vashem, as I have on several occasions, each time I stand transfixed at the picture of a young Jewish boy of perhaps ten years of age with his hands raised as the Nazi soldiers herded him and his family and other Jews into the boxcars for extermination. Imagine that ten-year-old Jewish boy was the enemy for those Nazi beasts.

That picture has now been seen around the world and it will never leave the mind of anyone who has ever seen it. It will certainly never leave my mind. That picture is even more apt to bring tears to my eyes than pictures of bodies in concentration camps because seeing all those bodies is an unbelievable sight. One simply cannot comprehend it. But seeing that boy with his hands raised, and his eyes filled with fear, is overwhelming because it is so human—so real.

So horrible, so monstrous were those years of the Holocaust that we sometimes think of Germany and Eastern Europe as one enormous death camp. It wasn't so. Much of the time, ordinary people were going about the ordinary business of everyday life.

The railroad lines that carried Jews to the death camps also carried German civilians in comfortable passenger trains. There were people traveling on business, tourists on vacation, children visiting grandparents, grandparents visiting children. Some of them may well have passed through the town of Auschwitz. The Auschwitz railroad station was one mile from the death camp. The stench of burning bodies spread throughout the area. Local citizens complained—about the stench, not about the slaughter of Jews. And when it was over, they said they didn't know. They didn't remember anything about it.

But we know. We remember.

And what we remember, the world will remember, whether it wants to or not.

Because remembering is a personal obligation. A moral obligation. A national and international obligation. And we must not only remember how it ended but also how it began. We must remember how to recognize the early symptoms of this hideous disease.

The early symptoms of Nazi evil were always there to see. Long before he came to power in Germany, Hitler made it clear what he intended to do. In his book, *Mein Kampf*, published in 1925, Hitler was already talking about the idea of killing Jews with poison gas.[1]

From the day he was elected chancellor of Germany in 1933, Hitler began his campaign to terrorize the Jews. The Nuremberg Laws of 1935 turned Jews into non-people. This was all part of the plan to make the murder of Jews acceptable to German citizens.

On the infamous Kristallnacht, 191 synagogues throughout Germany were burned to the ground. Thousands of Jews already in concentration camps were murdered, and thousands more were sent to the camps to be killed. In Austria, Nazis burned synagogues and, in some communities, every male Jew was sent to a concentration camp.

There was nothing secret about these atrocities. American diplomats in major German cities sent detailed reports to the State Department of what they and their staffs had seen. Every American consulate was jammed with Jews seeking visas to emigrate to the United States. Jews waiting in the streets to be admitted to the consulates were beaten by Nazi mobs.

The Germans themselves knew very well what was taking place. As Jews were driven from their homes to be transported in what the Nazis called "resettlement," German citizens formed their own lines—to apply for permits to move into Jewish homes, knowing the previous occupants would not be returning.

The world knew. The world knew, and the world did nothing. There were some halfhearted attempts to deal with the Nazi menace. President Roosevelt organized an international committee to handle refugee problems.[2] But he refused to formally recall the American ambassador to Germany, a move that would have signaled strong American disapproval of Nazi savagery and that might have slowed it down. Instead, President Roosevelt simply asked the ambassador to come to Washington to give a "firsthand report."

The president did criticize the German government, but, when asked if America would take special measures to help Jewish refugees, the answer was negative. No modification of American policy was contemplated. Refugees could have been saved. In May 1939, a luxury liner called the *St. Louis* sailed from Germany with 930 Jews on board. They were heading for safety in Cuba, but the Cuban government would not allow them to land. And neither would the American government.

Still thinking there might be a change of heart in Washington, the captain of the *St. Louis* drifted off the coast of Florida, close enough for the passengers to see the lights of Miami. But America's only response to this crisis was to dispatch a coast guard cutter to shadow the *St. Louis* to make certain that none of the passengers tried to enter the country by swimming. The ship returned to Germany.

The world knew, and the world did nothing.

And Canada, which until recently prided itself on being a haven for all refugees, has now been shown to have excluded Jews attempting to flee the Nazis.[3] Two top Canadian leaders, Mackenzie King and Lester Pearson, held out hope to Jewish groups while silently working behind the scenes to appease anti-Semites and severely limit Jewish immigration to Canada. In December of 1939, the *Times of London* published an article detailing the early operation of Nazi death camps. Pinpointing one area in which they were located, the *Times* specifically refuted German propaganda that these were "resettlement" camps and identified them as "places for gradual extermination" and "mass massacre" of the prisoners. But the world did nothing to stop it.

We know. We remember. Some of us learned of these horrors from family and friends, some from books. But some were actually there, and saw with their own eyes the death machine at work—that's one reason why this gathering is so important. People may wonder about stories they hear from family and friends. They may wonder if the books are accurate. But the direct testimony of those who were there leaves no room at all for doubt.

It is difficult to conceive of a fate worse than being sent to a concentration camp, but perhaps there is one thing worse. And that is to survive the camps and live to see a day in which some people claim that the Holocaust never happened.

And yet today there are people—dangerous people—who make that very claim. They want to persuade us that the Nazi death camps are a myth. They want to erase the bloodstains from the pages of history.

Today, survivors of Auschwitz and Buchenwald see the sickening spectacle of American citizens parading the streets in Nazi uniforms. "They are crackpots, a lunatic fringe," we are told. But Hitler was called a crackpot, too, and by the time people realized that insanity can be an infectious disease, it was too late. Today, for you and me, and for all of us, it is not too late.

We will remain vigilant, ever alert, to the threat of those who skillfully stoke the fires of anti-Semitism. In some cases, their tactics have changed. Sometimes they use new code words to convey their message. In the United Nations, they pass anti-Semitic resolutions and call them "anti-Zionist." They seek to isolate Israel in the world community, to turn Israel into a "non-nation" just as the Nuremberg laws turned Jews into "non-people."

They don't want peace in the Middle East. They want Israel destroyed. They may talk peace, just as Hitler talked peace at Munich. But their real objective is the destruction of Israel. There are those who—intentionally or perhaps unknowingly— give acceptability to the enemies of Israel. Unfortunately, President Reagan stated that PLO radicals were refusing to join with King Hussein at the peace table, thereby implying that the majority of the PLO is non-radical.

The fact of the matter is that the PLO are terrorists who murder and maim women and children, and whose greatest dream is to finish what Hitler started. America must never give acceptability to those who want to destroy Israel, the Jewish people, and our very memory.

But Israel lives and Israel with Jerusalem as its undivided capital will continue to live. Your presence here this evening confirms that fact. Those who love freedom, those who battle against oppression and bigotry, draw strength from your victory. You walked through the fire and survived. Your survival is our survival. We thank you. We salute you. Am Yisroel chai! Gedenk! Remember! God bless you.

While Holocaust education has traditionally focused on the German perpetrators and their Jewish victims, new research during the 1970s and 1980s shed light on the activities of a third group: those who tried to rescue Jews. One of the best known of these rescuers is Raoul Wallenberg, a Swedish businessman who was sent to Nazi-occupied Budapest in the spring of 1944 by the U.S. government's War Refugee Board (which itself was created as a result of a struggle between Treasury Department officials seeking to promote rescue and State Department officials trying to obstruct it). With American funds and Swedish diplomatic protection, Wallenberg saved many thousands of Jews by sheltering them in safe houses, and in some cases literally pulling Jews off trains bound for Auschwitz. When the Soviets liberated Budapest in early 1945, they arrested Wallenberg. He was never heard from again, and the Kremlin never provided a satisfactory explanation as to what happened or why.

Among those Wallenberg rescued were future U.S. Congressman Tom Lantos, then sixteen, and Lantos's future wife, Annette. Four decades later, at Lantos's initiative, Wallenberg became only the second person to be made an honorary U.S. citizen. He was also named one of the "Righteous Among the Nations" by Israel's Holocaust center, Yad Vashem, and was the subject of numerous books as well as a television miniseries. But the question of Wallenberg's fate remains one of the great unresolved mysteries of World War II.

WHERE IS RAOUL WALLENBERG?

Remarks at a press conference marking the fortieth anniversary of the disappearance of Raoul Wallenberg, City Hall, New York City, January 17, 1985, from Box 080078, Folder 5, EIK.

It was forty years ago today, while on one last mission to save the Jews of Budapest from Nazi gas chambers, that Raoul Wallenberg vanished into the so-called protective custody of Soviet authorities. But he did not vanish without a trace.

For one thing, he has left us the legacy of his accomplishments, the shining example of a humanitarian who would not stand idly by while the Jews of Europe were being slaughtered. Raoul Wallenberg was as courageous as the bravest soldier in the fiercest battle of that war. His memory will endure long after military campaigns have been forgotten.

Raoul Wallenberg left us with something else, too. The nature of his disappearance makes him a personal metaphor for a bitter truth about World War II. For millions of people, victory over Nazi tyranny was followed by tyranny of another kind. One vicious totalitarian system was overthrown. Another rose to take its place. Raoul Wallenberg became a victim of this new tyranny. He was detained without cause and imprisoned without explanation. He was never charged with any crime. His Soviet captors later claimed he died as their prisoner, and have never offered so much as a word of apology or remorse for what they did. It is a cruel irony that Raoul Wallenberg risked his life to save thousands of strangers from the death camps, only to be lost himself in the camps of the Gulag Archipelago. Those who tried to silence Raoul Wallenberg have failed. Forty years after his disappearance, his memory and the meaning of his life live on. Through each and every one of us, his voice grows stronger with each passing year.

Free people throughout the world will never yield in the effort to find him, know his fate, and force his captors to admit the full extent of their shame. In closing, I have a specific suggestion as to just how I think that can be accomplished. The Russians despise public opinion, because they despise personal freedom. No matter what the Russians claim, however, they listen to what the world is saying, especially when attention is focused on something that embarrasses then. Well, I propose that we embarrass them. I propose that all of us here today begin a very simple campaign in which our weapon will be postcards—sending one ourselves, and asking others to do the same. These postcards should be sent to the Soviet Union's Mission to the United Nations, located at 136 East 67th street, New York, New York 10021. And on those postcards should be written these four words: "Where is Raoul Wallenberg?"

Probably no single controversy during the Reagan years upset American Jews as much as Bitburg. The little-known German cemetery where forty-nine SS members are buried was included on the itinerary of President Reagan for his 1985 trip to West Germany. His hosts thought it an appropriate site to visit on the fortieth anniversary of VE Day. When the nature of the cemetery became known, the lines of angry debate were drawn. The American Jewish community, large majorities in both houses of Congress, and many others regarded the bestowing of honor on SS men as an insult not only to the victims of the Holocaust but also to the American GIs who fought against the SS. On the other side stood Reagan's advisers, Pat Buchanan prominent among them, who contended that canceling Bitburg would insult the Germans and undermine American-German relations. It was at the peak of this dispute that Elie Wiesel, standing alongside President Reagan at a previously scheduled White House ceremony, boldly declared, "That place, Mr. President, is not your place. Your place is with the victims of the SS." Reagan did not appease many critics by agreeing to visit the site of the Bergen-Belsen concentration camp in addition to Bitburg, and in fact compounded matters by remarking that the SS men buried in the cemetery were "victims of Nazism just as surely as the victims in the concentration camps."

REAGAN AT BITBURG

Remarks at the Briarwood Jewish Center, Queens, NY, April 14, 1985, from Box 080078, Folder 5, EIK.

In the last few days, we've heard a lot of criticism about President Reagan's plans for the fortieth anniversary observance of the end of World War II. It was announced that the president will visit the graves of soldiers who fought for Nazi Germany, but will not visit a concentration camp. Some of the president's advisers seemed genuinely puzzled by the uproar that followed this announcement. It is disturbing that some people still don't understand—even at this late date—the significance of the Holocaust. They don't understand the full horror of what happened, or just how helpless were the Jews who found themselves caught up in the undertow of Nazi terror.

In the May issue of *Harper's* is an excerpt of a Holocaust memoir by an Israeli author named Roman Frister. At age sixteen, he was imprisoned in a Nazi work camp in Poland. As the Russian army approached, rumors spread that the prisoners would be sent to Auschwitz. Escape into the nearby forest, where Polish partisans were active, seemed to be the only hope. One night, the young man joined an escape party and was shot in the leg. But he and others made it to the forest. They found the Polish partisans and were given food and coffee.

The boy went to a nearby stream to wash his wound. While he was gone, he heard gunfire. From the bushes, he saw that the camp prisoners had all been shot by the partisans and were being buried in a mass grave. The partisans hated the Germans, but they hated Jews just as much. The boy didn't know what to do. There was no place to turn for help. That night he did something that reveals just how vulnerable and trapped the Jews of Europe were. He snuck back into the concentration camp. He had no other place to go. As it turned out, he was indeed sent to Auschwitz.

But he survived. He survived. And today he is an Israeli. Today, he and millions of others who remember the Holocaust wonder why President Reagan can't find it in his heart to visit a concentration camp. I think that the president is a decent man. I hope he will change his mind. Some of his advisers may wish to forget the Holocaust, but we will never forget. Never.

DITA'S MOTHER DIDN'T COME HOME

Remarks at Warsaw Ghetto Commemoration Day, Madison Square Garden, New York City, April 17, 1985, from Box 080078, Folder 5, EIK.

Fellow Jews, fellow mourners: Being mayor of New York City is like being a Jew. It brings with it many happy times, it brings with it very sad times. One of my saddest duties of late has been dealing with the scourge of child abuse. The entire nation is now struggling with the problem. Social workers and psychologists are wondering—as I wonder—what kind of parents neglect, abuse, even murder their own children? What kind of people abuse other people's children?

On this anniversary of the Warsaw Ghetto uprising and commemoration of the Holocaust, we must ask ourselves an even more horrible question: What kind of people tortured, used as guinea pigs, shot, gassed, burned, and slaughtered one million Jewish children? Yet as each year goes by, Jews and non-Jews ask: "How long must we go on remembering? Isn't it time to forgive and forget?" Our answer is this: We will remember forever. We will remember as long as we live and as long as civilization survives.

Our civilization can survive only if we don't forget. If we forget, we become like the murderers, because we make it possible for it to happen again, we remember today with deep sadness in our hearts and tears in our eyes—and yet with a sense of triumph, for "am Yisrael chai," "the Jewish people live." And there is a muted feeling of joy, for what is it that makes the Jew mourn if not the realization of the joy of life, of the richness that life offers each of us, of the blessings that God bestows on us. Else why do we feel sad when life comes to an end? So the Jew laughs through his tears and cries through his laughter. As each additional year goes by, we understand better what it is we are remembering. We understand better what really happened in the past. That's the basic law of history: We don't see too well from close up. Only the passing of time helps us to see better—to understand better. And, often, new events, new developments make us see the horror of what we were too numb to understand and to feel forty years ago.

Some three years ago, I created the New York City Holocaust Memorial Commission, which is composed of members of the Jewish community and charged them with the mission of establishing in the city of New York a living memorial to the martyrs of Hitler's genocide. That commission, under the able leadership of George Klein and Robert Morgenthau, has taken a major step forward in the realization of this effort.

After collective discussions involving the city, the state, and the Battery Park City Authority, Governor Cuomo has authorized the Authority to begin negotiations immediately with the commission for construction of the memorial in Battery Park. It is our feeling that this option will provide a quicker and more expeditious method for completing the Holocaust memorial. It is my prayer that all of us will stand together next year at the very site of the future memorial to commemorate Yom Hashoah. We need this memorial, because, to some, the vision of the past becomes blurred. I am thinking now of the people who advised President Reagan to visit a German military cemetery on his forthcoming trip to Europe, but who also advised him not to visit a concentration camp or other memorials to the victims of the Holocaust.

The president is a decent man. He has reconsidered the advice he received. He will visit a Holocaust memorial. I hope he will also make it clear that he has no intention of honoring German soldiers who belonged to the SS. The SS were murderers in uniform. Never, never should their memory be honored, and especially not by an American president. Recently, something occurred that gives us yet another insight into what happened forty years ago and how the world responded to bringing the German murderers to justice. Remember—there's that word again—remember 1960? Israeli agents captured that arch murderer Adolf Eichmann.

Arch murderer? There is no adjective strong enough to place before his name. When Israel announced that Eichmann would be tried for his crimes, the lawyers began to fuss. They talked about "jurisdiction," about "crimes against humanity." The lawyers in 1960 said: How dare Israel try Eichmann for crimes committed when Israel did not yet exist? And how dare Israel try Eichmann when his crimes were committed not against Jews alone, but "against humanity"? And there were people who took the lawyers seriously.

Yet today, as we look back, we see more clearly that those acts were not only committed against humanity but by humanity! Now I am not a prophet, but when you get to be sixty years old, you just get to be able to understand how people's minds work, and how the world works, and how "humanity" works. And I think I can tell you what might have happened if Israel had weakened and turned Adolf Eichmann over to "humanity" for trial. The lawyers would have raised more questions, and for several decades Eichmann would have been in a prison eating three meals a day, with a private exercise yard for his daily walks. He might have written his memoirs, and the memoirs might have been turned into a miniseries for television.

And, as he grew feeble, he might have been released on "humanitarian" grounds. And a protocol officer would have met him at the airport to welcome him back to the fatherland—just like the Nazi war criminals who were released back to Austria from an Italian prison. But we didn't forget what Eichmann did. Eichmann—and all that he represented—stood trial. And justice was done.

In the city of Prague, there is a synagogue with a clock on its tower. The Hebrew letters that represent the numbers from one to twelve read from the left around to the right. Near the synagogue is the old Jewish cemetery of Prague, where lies buried the great sixteenth-century rabbi Yehuda Loew, so great a defender of his people that he came to be known as a "wonder-rabbi." After the war, someone found a sliver of paper jammed between the stones of the statue of Rabbi Loew. Written in a childish scrawl was this message, which I would like to read to you: "Dear, kind, wonder-rabbi: please, I beg you, help me. Let mother come home this week. Don't let them take her in the transport. Yours, Dita." Dita's mother didn't come home. A million Jewish children's mothers and fathers didn't come home.

As long as life has meaning for us, as long as we treasure life, we will mourn our murdered children and their mothers and fathers. We don't want to forget. We cannot forget. We dare not forget. We never will forget.

THE TEMPTATION TO FORGET

Remarks at the East 55th Street Conservative Synagogue, April 21, 1985, from Box 080078, Folder 5, EIK.

I would like to say a few words about something that I know concerns us all. President Reagan dug himself into a deep hole last week by announcing that he would visit a German cemetery where SS troops are buried, but would not visit a concentration camp or other memorial to the victims of the Holocaust. He tried to get out of the hole by changing his plans and announcing that he would indeed pay tribute to the victims of the Holocaust. But he fell right back in the hole again when he stated that dead German soldiers were just as much victims of Nazism as the millions who died in concentration camps. The question is obvious: How could he possibly say such a thing?

I think the president is a decent man. I don't think he intended an offense. Nevertheless, what he said was offensive in the extreme. What could have been going through the president's mind to allow him to say such a thing? I'm not a psychoanalyst, but let me offer an opinion on a possible motivation for the president's outrageous remark.

The Holocaust is unlike any other event in history. The nation of Germany declared war against people of Jewish religion, culture, or descent.

It didn't matter what nationality they were. It didn't matter if they were rich or poor. It didn't matter if they were loyal to Germany. If they were Jewish, they were dead. Some historians believe that the real reason Hitler attacked other nations was not to conquer territory, but to get his hands on more Jews. It was a time of horror, a time when modern technology was combined with a pagan mentality to produce a massacre of unprecedented dimension.

It was so horrible that even today, forty years later, the human mind instinctively tries to block out the terrible suffering—the millions of tragic and cruel deaths. Like many others—some of them Jews—President Reagan would probably like to forget the horror of the Holocaust. Not because he is a bad man, but because he finds it painful and upsetting to stare into the face of evil—even at this distance in time, he would like to forget. I think he knows now, however, that we are not going to let him forget. The Holocaust happened because the world looked the other way.

We are not going to look the other way now. We are not going to forget. There are people today who actually publish books which state that the Holocaust never happened. Their motive is all too clear. They want us to believe that the Holocaust never happened because they want it to happen again. They will never succeed. We will never forget.

And, if the president of the United States succumbs to the temptation to forget, we will remind him. We will make our voices heard.

ISRAEL'S SECRET

Remarks at Yad Vashem, Jerusalem, Israel, May 10, 1985, from Box 080078, Folder 6, EIK.

It is an honor to be here today.

The millions who died during the Holocaust perished under conditions of unsurpassed horror. The horror went beyond their physical torment. Their days on earth came to an end in the midst of an immense pogrom that was intended to engulf the entire world. Some historians believe that the Nazis' main motive in attacking other countries was not to conquer more land, but to get their murderous hands on more Jews. To concentration camp victims, cut off from any contact with civilization, it must have seemed as if the insanity of the Nazi onslaught was a contagious disease destined to infect every corner of the globe. With few exceptions, the last words and thoughts of the murdered Jews of Europe will never be known. They died at the hands of barbarians who were intent upon erasing every trace of them, even their thoughts and prayers.

Strengthened by their faith, the martyrs of the Holocaust must have faced death with all the courage they could summon. But many may have been overwhelmed by despair. All around them were signs of Nazi triumph. They had nothing left at all but hope. Not hope for themselves, but hope that somehow, somewhere, the light of Jewish religion and culture would continue to glow against the night. At the height of the Nazi madness, SS troops rounded up the Jews of a small town in Poland and ordered them to be shot. As a small girl was dragged away by the killers, she looked back at her mother and asked in a terrified voice, "What shall I do?" Her mother replied, "Before you die, say Shema Yisrael."

That girl's entire family fell before the Nazi guns, but, as fate would have it, the girl herself survived. So, in this case, we know her last words, and therefore we know the last words of her mother, her father, her sisters and brothers, and perhaps of her entire village. And the words were "Shema Yisrael." Those words of prayer did not go unheard. Amplified by a thousand, by a hundred thousand, by six million, they echoed to the heavens and they echo still in our hearts. They echo here in Yad Vashem.

Yad Vashem is our way of showing that we hear the cries of the martyred. The existence of Israel is how we know that those cries were not in vain, for out of the fire of murder and genocide came a nation devoted to peace. A nation dedicated to preserving the light that the Nazis tried to extinguish, a nation with the courage to be strong. Since 1948, Israel has successfully defended herself against all enemies, often when the odds were heavily against her. Some people wonder, "What is Israel's secret?" I've thought about that question, and I think I know the answer. You can see it here at Yad Vashem. The Israeli army is much larger than most people realize, because no matter how many soldiers you see in Israeli uniforms, the true strength of the army is always six million more.

FORGETTING IS THE FIRST STEP TOWARD REPEATING

Remarks at the Holocaust Memorial Park, Brooklyn, NY, June 9, 1985, from Box 080078, Folder 6, EIK.

Last March, when I signed the Holocaust Memorial Mall bill into law, it was a moment of great satisfaction for me. First, I was very proud of Ira Bilus and the Holocaust Memorial Committee for doing such an excellent job in the planning, organizing, and establishing of this memorial mall. I was very appreciative of the outstanding support provided to this effort by Senator Donald Halperin, Councilman Sam Horwitz, and so many others, most of whom are with us today.

But I was especially pleased at this additional proof that, even though the generation that experienced the Holocaust is getting older, the memory of the Holocaust will never fade. Some people in Washington were surprised by the intensity of the public outcry against President Reagan's visit to a cemetery containing graves of SS troopers in Bitburg. Were we overreacting when we urged the president to reconsider his ill-advised trip to Bitburg? No, we weren't.

We understand the necessity of making peace with the past, but we also understand that we can never—never!—make peace with the Nazi monsters who murdered the Six Million. Therefore, as one generation grows older, it is our moral responsibility, our solemn duty, to keep alive the memory of the Holocaust for the generations that will follow. Why? Because we know that forgetting is the first step toward repeating. And as much as we might wish it weren't true, we must be aware that there are those who want the world to forget the Holocaust. There are those who would like to see the Holocaust repeated.

Books have been published in Canada, Sweden, France, and right here in America that claim that the Holocaust is a myth—that it never happened. We are also seeing the rise of neo-Nazi and ultra rightwing groups that not only imitate and mimic the uniforms and ideology of Hitler, but also support the same kind of anti-Semitism. They spew forth hatred of the Jews with the venom and barbarity of the Nazis. All they are waiting for is a sign of weakness, a sign of tolerance, and a sign of forgetfulness so that they can advance their evil plans.

They will find no weakness here. They will find no tolerance here. They will find no forgetfulness here. We will always remember. The Holocaust will never happen again. In closing, I want to take this opportunity to say that plans for the Holocaust Living Memorial in Manhattan are moving forward. We expect to sign a lease for the site at the Battery before the holy days this year. Next year, we want the Warsaw Ghetto commemoration to take place on this site and have asked the survivors' organizations to act on this request. Again, my thanks and congratulations to everyone who helped to make this memorial mall a reality.

JEWS WHO FOUGHT BACK

Remarks on the anniversary of the Warsaw Ghetto Uprising, Metropolitan Synagogue, New York City, April 19, 1987, from Box 080078, Folder 8, EIK.

I am pleased to join with you today in marking the forty-fourth anniversary of the uprising in the Warsaw Ghetto. The heroic struggle in Warsaw was more than an uprising. It was a battle. It wasn't the first time that Jews struck back against the Nazi murder machine. It wasn't the last time, either. But it was a shining moment that clearly signaled to the rest of the world that Jews were taking charge of their destiny. It was a message of hope not only to other Jews, but also to oppressed people of all nations and religions that a new day was coming. If a mere handful of Polish Jews could not only survive in the very jaws of death itself, but fight back as well, then others could follow their example.

The road to freedom begins when we no longer accept oppression. The road to freedom begins when we fight back. I doubt the Nazis ever recovered from the shock of Warsaw. They were accustomed to murdering defenseless people in secret.

They were stunned that it took the full might of their military strength to conquer a small number of Jews. And when the fighting was over, they leveled the ghetto. Some say they did it as an act of contempt, an act of revenge. I don't agree. I think they did it in an effort to cover up a stinging defeat. Because for the Jews of the world, and for the cause of freedom and justice, the battle of the Warsaw Ghetto was not a defeat. It was a ringing victory!

We celebrate that victory today. We celebrate the courage and heroism of those who fought and died. And we honor the partisans who took up arms, we honor those who fought the battle of the concentration camps. I call it a battle because you did more than simply survive. You fought for life. You fought to deny the Nazis the one thing they wanted most: to eliminate all Jews from the face of the earth.

And because you won that battle, you were able to bear witness to what had happened. What you saw, and what you experienced, helped to reshape the conscience of the world. During my recent trip to Poland, I was honored to meet Dr. Marek Edelman, one of the leaders of the battle of the Warsaw Ghetto. You all know what Marek Edelman did. You know because many of you helped him do it, with your support and encouragement, and for that I thank you. Marek Edelman fought the battle of the Warsaw Ghetto, but there are many, many others who fought at his side. Were you at the battle of the Warsaw Ghetto? Was I at the battle of the Warsaw Ghetto? Were our friends and neighbors at the battle of the Warsaw Ghetto? My answer is this: Every Jew was at the battle of the Warsaw Ghetto. The victory that was won there was a victory for all of us.

Z'chor!

Gedenk!

Remember!

Remember and be proud.

WHAT THE FLAMES COULD NOT CONSUME

Remarks on the forty-fourth anniversary of the Warsaw Ghetto Uprising, Madison
Square Garden, New York City, April 26, 1987, from Box 080078, Folder 8, EIK.

Distinguished guests, members, and friends of the Warsaw
Ghetto resistance organization, fellow New Yorkers: On the eve
of Passover, 1943, the surviving Jews of the Warsaw Ghetto
struck back at the Nazi murder machine. They faced the savage
and heavily armed forces of Hitler's Germany.

Even the most optimistic of the Jewish heroes could hardly
have hoped for more than a brief display of defiance, but the
hours stretched into days, and the days into weeks. The light of
Israel refused to die. The Nazi troops were astonished by the
courage and tenacity they encountered in the ghetto. By the time
the last shot was fired, the entire world was beginning to understand that something momentous had taken place in the ghetto.
The Jews of Warsaw, inspired and strengthened by their faith,
showed the world that a new determination and spirit had been
born in the very midst of the Holocaust.

The *Book of Daniel* tells us that three sons of Israel survived the
flames of Nebuchadnezzar's furnace. Hitler's Holocaust con-
sumed millions, but the flames of the concentration camps and
the fire of countless guns did not consume the faith of Israel.
And they will never consume the faith of Israel. They will never
consume the State of Israel. We suffered terrible losses in the
Holocaust, but those losses were not in vain. Hitler's war against
the Jews was intended to destroy us all. Instead, we emerged
from the flames with a new strength that inspired us to complete
the job of building the State of Israel; we came out of the fire
with fire in our eyes. Never again will the forces of hatred and
bigotry take us by surprise, never again.

Those who attack us do so at their own peril. Karl Linnas
found that out a few days ago. The long arm of moral justice
reached out and seized this mass murderer by the throat.[1] There
can be no safety for people who have evil in their hearts. Today
we remember those who fought, and those who died, in the

struggle that led to victory. We will never forget them. We will honor them always.

A VISIT TO HELL

Remarks at Holocaust Memorial Day, Garden Jewish Center, Queens, NY, April 26, 1987, from Box 080078, Folder 8, EIK.

I am honored to be here with you this evening to share in re-membering the victims of the Holocaust. As many of you know, I journeyed to Poland this past winter, where I visited Auschwitz-Birkenau. . . . It will remain a vivid memory for the rest of my life. As we entered, there was a great deal of snow on the ground, and the snow continued to fall. The barracks, little more than shells, were totally unheated and, even though I was wearing a heavy coat, I was still very cold. Prisoners were counted in the early morning every day, where they stood out-side in the worst of weather, with many dying as they stood in place.

When you enter, you are shown a forty-year-old film made by the Soviets. The film is narrated in different languages and shows the liberation of the camp. What it does not do, however, is indicate that most of the people in the camp were Jews. Every life is precious, and all those who lost their lives at these death camps must be remembered and mourned. But the sheer horror of the genocide committed at Auschwitz-Birkenau is lost when the overwhelming number of victims are not identified as Jews—since it was their very Jewishness, which they could not shed if they wanted to, which caused their terrible deaths.

Several years ago, the Polish government created exhibitions in various barracks, and one of them memorialized the killing of Jews. In that barracks there were areas displaying hundreds of suitcases with the names of those who were brought to the camps, thinking the Nazis were only going to resettle them. An-other exhibit contained the hair of women who had been shorn; the hair had turned gray with time. The most piteous exhibit contained thousands of little shoes, belonging to the children killed there.

At one point they took us to the wall of death, where prisoners were brought for execution after some infraction of the rules. I felt a compulsion to touch the wall with my hand, as though with a kiss after touching my lips. When I was asked later why I did that, I said it was to establish contact with all those who had been put to death at that site. I thought of what we do when we go to touch the Western Wall in Jerusalem, or when the Torah is carried through the synagogue.

Throughout history, there have been acts of savagery, but never had one nation sought to literally exterminate another people based solely on their religion. Not until Nazi Germany. Not until Auschwitz-Birkenau. So we must have more remembrances like this one, while the generation of survivors still lives to tell what happened. We must build our living memorial to the Holocaust, and to the vanished life of Eastern European Jewry, that will preserve the story of what happened. And we must always keep in mind that forgetting is the first step to repeating.

Z'chor!

Gedenk!

Remember!

The primary Nazi death camps were set up in Poland, and a significant number of Poles collaborated with the Germans in persecuting the Jews. The prevalence of anti-Semitism in prewar Polish culture undoubtedly affected the level of collaboration. At the same time, there were a number of individual Poles who risked their lives to save Jews. After the war, Polish government officials and Polish groups abroad sought to emphasize the notion that the Poles were victims of Nazism, not its facilitators. The Polish public was infuriated by the award-winning 1985 Claude Lanzmann documentary, Shoah, because they felt it put too much emphasis on anti-Semitism among ordinary Poles as a factor in the Holocaust. Polish anger was stirred anew by a 2001 book revealing that the 1941 massacre of Jews in the Polish town of Jedwabne was perpetrated by Poles, not Germans, as Polish institutions had always claimed.

More recently, the Polish authorities went so far as to ask UNESCO, in early 2006, to change the name of the Auschwitz death camp site on the U.N.'s world heritage registry to "Former Nazi German Concentration Camp Auschwitz-Birkenau," to emphasize that it was a German, not Polish, institution.

In the letter that follows, Polish American activist John Gmerek presented his perspective on Poland and the Holocaust to the Catholic Church's senior representative in the United States, Cardinal John O'Connor. Cardinal O'Connor shared Gmerek's letter with Koch, whose comments follow below Gmerek's.

POLAND AND THE HOLOCAUST: TWO LETTERS

From the private files of Edward I. Koch.

September 17, 1987
His Eminence John Cardinal O' Connor
Catholic Center
1011 1st Ave.
New York, NY 10025

Your Eminence,
We are very grateful of having been invited to appear before your office to present our feelings and concerns

over the manner in which Polish Christians, the Church and the Vatican have been described in the media, press, films, documentaries, novels, plays and educational materials relative to the Holocaust. There is cause for alarm.

Poles have often been described as collaborators, not victims; death camps have often been described as "Polish camps" not Nazi camps in occupied Poland; Poles have often been described as insensitive to Jewish suffering, yet Poles had the largest organized underground system in occupied Europe to render aid to the Jews; the suffering and genocide of the Jews has often been described as unique, yet approximately half of the six million Polish citizens, murdered victims in Nazi death and concentration camps in occupied Poland were Christian, mostly Catholic. In addition, the entire Polish nation was terrorized during the war, and ultimate Nazi plans were to annihilate Polish culture and its people. Seldom are such facts readily available to the American public.

Our committee has also served approximately five years as an advisory group to the New York State Department of Education in helping prepare teaching guidelines on "Teaching About the Holocaust and Genocide." As advisors, we managed to correct many initial misconceptions about the Polish role in the Holocaust, and introduced into the final version many vital facts which had been originally missing from the earlier drafts. On Catholic and Vatican issues in the Holocaust, we closely cooperated with the Catholic League for Religious and Civil Rights.

We are aware that preparations are currently underway to develop a Holocaust curriculum for all levels of the Catholic educational system. We have included a detailed news item about it in the given folder.

We respectfully request assurance that appropriate Polish Christian review committees are included in preparing and evaluating the contents dealing with Polish experiences in the Holocaust. Pope John Paul II recently urged in Miami that leaders of both faiths, Catholic and Jewish, teach future generations about the Holocaust so that never again will such horror be possible. We agree, and thus an accurate presentation of both sides must be made and be reflected in any responsible development of a curriculum on the Holocaust. In this regard, our committee could be of service.

We are hopeful that a wider knowledge of Polish-Christian suffering, and aid provided to the Jews, as reflected by the high number of Poles honored as "Righteous Gentiles" at Yad Vashem, the Jewish Holocaust memorial in Israel, will be further advanced through diocesan programs, forums, television presentations, special or annual masses, homilies and school events.

We too trust that material in the folder which includes numerous letters to the editor dealing with both the Holocaust and the Polish image; comments about the film *Shoah*; supportive letter to Right Reverend Pete Finn; testimony of Mr. Michael Preisler and Mr. Aloysius Mazewski before the U.S. Holocaust Commission in Washington, D.C. in February 1987; contents of a lecture series on Polish-Jewish-Holocaust topics at the Kosciuszko Foundation in 1985, and letter nominating Mr. Walter Kuskowski, a member of our committee, for the Louis E. Yavner award for distinguished teaching about the Holocaust in New York state, will help promote a deeper and fuller understanding of our concerns. Two books are also offered: (1) *The Forgotten Holocaust* by Richard C. Lukas and (2) *Poland's Way of the Cross,* by Franciszek Proch, to further augment understanding of the "other" Holocaust.

Although Your Eminence's busy schedule during the Papal visit removed the opportunity for joint discussions, we nonetheless declare our deep appreciation for the sympathetic attention given to us by your executive secretary, Brother William J. Martyn, S.A., who will carry our message to you for your consideration and whatever action deemed advisable.

With deepest gratitude and respect,

Sincerely,
John J. Gmerek
Chairman
Holocaust Committee

Committee members participating in discussions:
Mr. Walter Kuskowski, Holocaust teacher (Ret.)
Mr. Michael Preisler, survivor of Auschwitz

THE CITY OF NEW YORK
OFFICE OF THE MAYOR
New York, N.Y. 10007

November 9, 1987

His Eminence
John Cardinal O'Connor
Archbishop of New York
1011 First Avenue
New York, N.Y. 10022

Your Eminence:
Thank you for sharing with me the letter you received from John Gmerek, Chairman of the Holocaust Committee of the Kosciuszko Foundation. I read his letter with great interest and concern. I would like to offer my reactions.

Mr. Gmerek is concerned that "Poles have often been described as collaborators, not victims." Of course, the picture of Poland during World War II is complex, as Mr. Gmerek suggests. But it is certainly more complex than Mr. Gmerek states here.

His implication that Poles were victims is only part of the story. By all accounts, Polish anti-Semitism was intense. Though more traditional and less systematic than Nazi anti-Semitism, hostility in Poland toward Jews was widespread. It is a question not of Poles for or against the Nazis, but rather the degree of collaboration with Nazism.

Likewise the case of rescuing Jews. Mr. Gmerek's observation that Poles "were the largest organized underground system in occupied Europe to render aid to the Jews," if true, should not blur the fact that those who rescued Jews were the exceptions.

No one wants to diminish the suffering that Poles experienced during the war, nor deny that there were those among them who saved Jews. But those observations are neither definitive nor conclusive.

The complexity of the situation in Poland demands a deeper assessment. I feel confident you will help.

Sincerely,
Edward I. Koch
Mayor

cc: John Gmerek

KRISTALLNACHT: THE BEGINNING OF THE END

Remarks at a preview screening of the film *More than Broken Glass: Memories of Kristallnacht*, Temple Emanu-El, New York City, October 25, 1988, from Box 080078, Folder 9, EIK.

Fifty years ago, synagogues all over Germany and Austria—temples of the Lord, just like the one we sit in here tonight—fell victim to Nazi goon squads rampaging through the Jewish quarters of every major city in the Third Reich. The homes and shops, the very lives of millions of Jews were wrecked, never to recover. A beautiful way of life was ending. The Final Solution was coming.

Kristallnacht was not something that happened because of the assassination of one Nazi official in Paris,[1] or because of the Treaty of Versailles,[2] or any other specific cause. It occurred because justice, and freedom, and mutual respect had become dead values in Nazi Germany.

It occurred because decency had retreated in the face of force. It occurred because the German people no longer thought of themselves as "one out of many," as we aspire to in America. Instead, they became convinced it was "us" and "them," that there were "true Germans" and "others" living in Germany. They began to listen to demagogues who convinced them to shun, to turn against, and eventually to kill their equally German neighbors.

We must always remember that it happened not so long ago. We must make all the historical records we can while the generation of survivors can still bear witness. And we must never let it happen here.

THE LESSON OF KRISTALLNACHT

Remarks to the Council of Jewish Organizations in Civil Service, New York City, October 30, 1988, from Box 080078, Folder 9, EIK.

Ten days from now we will be marking the fiftieth anniversary of Kristallnacht. The observances have already begun, of course, and in a very real sense they will never end. But we will gather in solemn remembrance of this anniversary as a way of paying special tribute to the victims of Kristallnacht, and to renew our vow that never again will we allow such an atrocity to take place.

The Nazis took control of Germany in 1933; from the very beginning it was clear that they meant to persecute the Jews. But people argued about just how far the Nazis intended to go. Hitler and his henchmen were careful to gloss things over as much as they could.

The 1936 Olympics were a showcase for the Nazi regime. Efforts were made to keep the world from knowing the truth. But if any doubts still remained, they were swept away by the horror and savagery of Kristallnacht. At last it was obvious what the Nazis had in mind. They not only meant to persecute the Jews, they meant to kill them. And what was the reaction of other nations to Kristallnacht? Shock and outrage in some quarters, to be sure. But was there a sudden and dramatic shift in world opinion? Were there changes in foreign policy? Did the world mobilize to save the Jews?

The answer is no. In fact, six months after Kristallnacht, the ocean liner *St. Louis* set sail from Germany carrying 930 Jews who had visas for Cuba. The Cuban government, citing a technicality, would not allow them to land in Havana. The ship was turned away. While the *St. Louis* drifted off the coast of Florida, pleas were made to let the passengers land in America. But Washington refused.

In fact, America sent a coast guard cutter to make sure that none of the refugees tried to enter the United States by swimming. If anyone had tried to swim ashore, they would have been swimming for their lives, because the *St. Louis* returned to Nazi Germany, where most of the Jews on board were swept away by the Holocaust.[1] Kristallnacht was an early warning sign that mass murder was on the way, and the world did nothing. America wouldn't even let 930 refugees come ashore.

I point this out because we must never forget the lesson we learned fifty years ago. If we wait until the executioner is at the door, we have waited too long. The time to fight is when we still have a chance to win. Today, we hear loud and shrill criticism of Israel for resolutely defending itself against terrorism. The recent killing of Israeli soldiers shows that the terror gangs are still at work; the organized riots and demonstrations in the streets are another form of war against Israel. And Israel is reacting strongly to these assaults.

Israel has learned the lesson of Kristallnacht: Do not wait until the executioner is at the door, because then it's too late.

A MAN WHO ACCOMPLISHED MIRACLES

Remarks at a ceremony honoring George Mantello, New York City Board of Estimate chamber, March 13, 1989, from Box 080078, Folder 10, EIK.

Distinguished guests, members of the diplomatic corps, fellow New Yorkers. Good afternoon. I am very pleased to welcome you to City Hall for what can only be described as a truly extraordinary occasion. We are here today to honor and salute Mr. George Mantello, one of the great heroes of our time. During the Second World War, Mr. Mantello saved tens of thousands of Jews and non-Jews from the Nazi death camps. Greatness does not always bring fame. Many of us are not familiar with Mr. Mantello's story. So let me begin today's ceremony by briefly describing what he did. From 1942 to 1945, Mr. Mantello served as the first secretary of the consulate of El Salvador in Switzerland. Neutral Switzerland was, at that time, entirely surrounded by Nazi forces. The Holocaust was claiming thousands of victims a day in Germany and Nazi-occupied Europe. In Hungary alone, up to 10,000 Jews a day were being deported to Auschwitz.

It wasn't until two prisoners escaped from Auschwitz and revealed the story of what was happening there that the full truth about the death camps was known. The atrocities were described in detail in a thirty-page document called "the Auschwitz protocol,"[1] but the report did not receive sufficient notice until George Mantello brought it to the attention of

Swiss theologians and the press. As a result of Mr. Mantello's campaign, there was an international outcry against the death camps. In July 1944, the Hungarian regime responded to the growing diplomatic pressure by halting the deportations. Some 150,000 Jews still remaining in Budapest were saved from the gas chambers. It is George Mantello whom they—and we—have to thank for their lives.

Mr. Mantello saved thousands more by producing and distributing El Salvadoran citizenship papers to both Jews and non-Jews who were in danger. Consular officials from some neutral countries made fortunes selling passports and other documents to refugees. But George Mantello provided El Salvadoran papers without charge. Thanks to George Mantello, about 15,000 people were provided with El Salvadoran documents, and almost all of them survived the Holocaust. Mr. Mantello also helped the Allied war effort by smuggling chronographs from Switzerland, in diplomatic pouches, to the United States and British authorities.

Mr. Mantello is now eighty-seven and lives in Rome. I am honored to welcome him, and the Mantello family, to City Hall. His inspiring story is virtually unknown. Today, we will help to correct that oversight in the history books, as we honor and pay tribute to a truly remarkable man.

Sometimes we all feel overwhelmed by the pressure of daily events. The world is filled with struggle and conflict. Can one person make a difference? The answer to that question is with us today. George Mantello has shown that one person can accomplish miracles in the face of overwhelming odds. It takes courage. It takes a commitment to justice. Mr. Mantello had both.

That's why today I am very honored to present Mr. Mantello with the Eleanor Roosevelt Human Rights Award, and to read the following inscription: "To George Mantello, courageous humanitarian, who awakened the world to the atrocities of the Holocaust, saving the lives of countless people throughout Nazi-occupied Eastern Europe. Edward I. Koch, Mayor, March 13, 1989."

HEROES WHO UNDERSTAND HISTORY

Remarks at Holocaust Memorial Program, Hebrew Institute of Riverdale, Bronx, NY, May 3, 1989, from Box 080080, Folder 6, EIK.

It is an honor to be here in the company of Beate Klarsfeld, who, along with her husband Serge, bravely tracked down the infamous Klaus Barbie, and had the Butcher of Lyon brought to justice at last. If that had been the only Nazi war criminal Beate had hunted down, her life's work would have been worth it. But, as we know, other criminals of the Holocaust have met their match in this passionate, superb, incorruptible woman. And, as ever, of course, it is a pleasure to be back here once again with my friend, Rabbi Avraham Weiss. Rabbi Weiss, too, can claim credit for the exposure of a major Nazi—Valerian Trifa, the Iron Guard commander who lied his way into a life of postwar comfort right here in America.[1]

The rest of the world turned its back, not wanting to deal with the fact of the Nazi horrors until it was too late, until those horrors had spread beyond Germany's borders. Can we ever forget the fate of the doomed Jews on board the S.S. *St. Louis*, denied entry even by our own country? Today, a half-century later, the world again prefers to forget. It prefers to focus its anger on Israel—on Israel's efforts to defend herself, to stave off those who would use rocks and propaganda to undermine her very existence.

The countries that spread this propaganda have some of the worst human rights records, not just in the Middle East, but in the entire world. And the countries that buy this propaganda are the ones that thought it best to avoid getting involved with what was happening to Germany's Jews in the 1930s and 1940s.

If history has told us one thing, it is that we Jews must depend on ourselves for our survival—today, tomorrow, and forever. And if the lives of Beate Klarsfeld and Avraham Weiss tell us one thing, it is that we Jews have heroes who understand our history.

Z'chor!

Gedenk!
Remember!

HAUNTING REMINDER OF THE HOLOCAUST

Originally published in the *New York Post*, September 5, 1995.

There should be a fifth question asked at the Passover Seder:
Why is the Holocaust visited on the Jews more appalling than
other acts of genocide the world has witnessed?

I believe the difference lies in the magnitude of Hitler's
plan. In the case of the Jews, the Nazis were embarked on what
they called "The Final Solution" of the Jewish "problem." No
Jew was to live, not even to be used for labor. No Jew was to be
allowed to convert to Christianity and live or, if a child, be
adopted and thus saved.

In short, every Jew—man, woman and child—under Nazi
control was under a death sentence.

The victims of other historical genocidal acts were targeted
for a variety of purposes: land, monetary, political or to be sold
into slavery. But with the Jews, it was killing for killing's sake—
an effort to totally annihilate a particular people.

I recently saw a film on the Holocaust that for me more than
rivals *Schindler's List*. Not that the film, *Chronicle of the Uprising in the
Warsaw Ghetto,* is a better film. From a technical point of view, in
fact, it isn't even close—but it brings you nearer to the reality of
the Holocaust because it portrays real people, not actors playing
roles.

Schindler's List is a docudrama with all that implies: a script
that builds with dramatic Hollywood crescendos. *Chronicle* is
an actual documentary: far more muted, presenting what happened on a random basis, leaving so much more to your imagination.

It relies on inadequate and amateur film footage taken by
Nazi soldiers who, in all probability, were either on duty in the

ghetto or visiting as tourists to see the "subhuman" Jews in their enclosure.

The film begins in 1940 and takes us to that extraordinary day when the Nazis sought to liquidate the entire ghetto and ship the remaining 60,000 Jews off to the Treblinka concentration camp to be gassed in pursuit of The Final Solution. Every Jew should know that he or she was on the Nazi death list, no matter what country any one of them called home.

None of the meager footage depicts the actual battle between the German SS and the few hundred Jews who desperately fought, equipped with a few dozen guns and a meager number of Molotov cocktails, to defend the thousands of men, women and children—if only to keep them alive for a few more days.

They vainly hoped they would be rescued, either by Polish Christians living on what the Germans and their captive Jews referred to as the Aryan side of the wall, or by the Soviet Army.

But it was not to be: The Polish Christian partisans provided little assistance, leaving the Jewish defenders to make to do with the few guns they had. The Soviets were of no help, nor did they aid the Polish partisans when they subsequently rose up in a later Warsaw revolt and were destroyed by the Nazis.

The film's narrator, Marek Edelman—one of the leaders of the Warsaw Ghetto uprising—describes the final battle, which took place at the resistance headquarters bunker at 18 Mila Street. He speaks of how he and forty survivors escaped the Nazis—who were burning the ghetto to the ground—by entering the sewers, which took them outside the ghetto walls.

Edelman sardonically describes the physical condition of he and the other survivors, who literally emerged from the muck of the sewers, as "filthy, dirty Jews." Anonymous rescuers picked up the escapees in broad daylight and drove them across half of Warsaw to safety.

Viewing the footage, I saw faces resembling the faces of my two young grandnieces, whose pictures sit on my desk; also youngsters and adults who could be my relatives or children of friends.

An elderly Jewish woman is stopped by a Nazi soldier, who maliciously brandishes his riding crop in her face, then disarranges her coat with it. She looks at him without fear, in total submission and resignation, knowing he could kill her then and there—and if he didn't, someone else would later, after she endured even more suffering.

Edelman recounts how the fighters, so few in number and so young, died while the vast majority of the Jews who had looked to those precious few "Maccabean" resisters for protection were shot in the streets or marched off to the Umschlagplatz for shipment to Treblinka.

We see them being marched to the boxcars, guarded by Nazi soldiers, Polish police officers, Lithuanians and Estonian guards. There is a little girl holding her mother's hand. She can't keep up, so another woman takes her other hand and both pull her along. A man, clean shirt and tie neatly in place, walks along as though alone—thinking perhaps that he is being sent to a work camp, as the Nazis had told him, not realizing that his true destination was the gas chamber.

This story is stark and totally true—there is no conjectured dialogue. Sitting there in the dark, before the house lights came up, I was for a moment filled with anxiety, anger and fear. I thought how sad it was that, while the Jews were dying in the ghetto, the Poles on the other side of the wall were bringing their children to a carousel that was so close, Marek Edelman could hear its music.

What continues to haunt the Jewish consciousness is that the world stood by, averting its eyes—its leaders lying about efforts to save the Jewish community—while millions of Jews who could have been rescued instead died.

I'm now reading *The Secret War Against the Jews* by John Loftus and Mark Aarons. What is remarkable is that, after all this, the Jews have survived and are still making positive contributions to the world's civilization of a magnitude that far exceeds our numbers.

Fifty years later, the Jewish nation—resurrected in Zion—kicked off a year of celebrating the 3,000th anniversary of the establishment by King David of Jerusalem as the capital of the Jewish nation.

But Martin Indyk, the U.S. ambassador to Israel, failed to attend the opening ceremonies. He claimed it was a cultural event more appropriate for the embassy's cultural attaché. Shameful.

There will be some who perceive this column as a Jewish lament, filled with self-pity. I don't believe it is. Even if it were, however, is it so wrong on occasion to remember and recall to a new generation what took place?

JEWS, BUSH, AND ISRAEL

Originally published in *Jewish World Review*, August 27, 2003.

I think it is critical that Israel be supported during these trying times. In the aftermath of the recent bus bombing in Jerusalem which killed twenty-one people—including seven children, and injured one hundred others, including about forty children—the Israeli government demanded that the Palestinian Prime Minister Mahmoud Abbas take immediate action against Hamas and Islamic Jihad, both of which took responsibility for that heinous terrorist act.

Prime Minister Abbas requested twenty-four hours to take police action against the terrorists. The Israelis took no military action during that period. When the Palestinian Authority failed to act, the Israelis exercised their right of self-defense and eliminated a top Hamas leader, Ismail Abu Shanab.

The terrorist organizations and the people of Gaza poured into the streets during Shanab's funeral, threatening revenge. That should not give the Israeli army pause. If they hadn't killed Shanab, would Hamas and Islamic Jihad suicide bombers have refrained from engaging in any more such attacks? Of course not. And Shanab would be planning them.

The goal of all Palestinian terrorist organizations is the destruction of the State of Israel.

Under the road map, the government of Prime Minister Abbas was required to begin to dismantle the terrorist infrastructure. It has not done so. The Israelis have no choice but to pursue the terrorists directly.

In President George W. Bush, Israel has a friend and supporter who has exhibited more concern for the Jewish state than any other president, Republican or Democrat. President Reagan was a firm supporter of Israel. But George W. Bush is far and away more willing to stand up for the Jewish state and support its right to a secure existence.

Israel's security should be a very high priority for American Jews. When Jews were persecuted and murdered in Nazi-occupied Europe, almost no one was willing to help them or give them refuge. During the Holocaust, from 1941 to 1945, six million Jews were murdered. The citizens of almost every country occupied by the Nazis, particularly France, collaborated with Hitler and turned their Jewish fellow citizens over to the Germans for extermination in the gas chambers.

Had the State of Israel existed in 1939, when Hitler offered to allow Jews to leave Germany if any country would accept them, ultimately six million Jewish lives would have been spared. Today, Europe again abounds with anti-Semitism not seen since the 1930s.

The American Jewish community adored President Franklin D. Roosevelt. He was one of our greatest presidents, ranking with Washington, Jefferson and Lincoln. Our vote for him was monolithic. Yet, it was not until mid-1944, two years after he knew that Hitler was intent on killing off every Jew on the planet, that he spoke out decisively against the Nazi campaign to exterminate the Jews.

And yet—except for 1,000 Jewish refugees admitted in 1944—FDR kept America's doors overwhelmingly closed to most of Europe's Jews, who could have escaped death had he allowed them to enter the United States.

President Harry S. Truman, for American Jews an icon in the pantheon of presidents and, for me personally, a hero, was recently revealed in a newly-discovered diary written in his own hand to have held Jews in great contempt. Will we learn as a community to never again walk in lockstep with a single party, undeviating in our support, and instead, hold those at the top of our government accountable for how they feel about our community's worldwide security and concerns? How public officials feel about abortion and taxes is important, but not as vital as how they feel about our living and dying.

The American Jewish community appreciated the support President Reagan gave to the Jewish state and it responded with 39 percent voting to reelect Reagan in 1984, whereas normally Democrats receive up to 90 percent of the Jewish vote. I believe that next time around, the American Jewish community will express its appreciation to President Bush by voting for him in even greater numbers than was the case with President Reagan.

Before *Wall Street Journal* reporter Daniel Pearl was decapitated by his Muslim abductors, who videotaped the atrocity, he was compelled to say with his last breath, "My mother is a Jew. My father is a Jew. I am a Jew." Every Jew should embrace his or her identity with pride and vote their conscience. I remain a Democrat, but have supported candidates from other parties when my conscience so dictated. So let me now proclaim, "My mother of revered memory was a Jew. My father of revered memory was a Jew. I am a Jew."

AMERICA AND THE HOLOCAUST: REFLECTIONS ON THE SIXTIETH
ANNIVERSARY OF THE LIBERATION OF AUSCHWITZ

Excerpts from interviews with Ed Koch conducted by Israel Television and Italian

National Television, January 2005, prepared by The David S. Wyman Institute for

Holocaust Studies.

Q: International leaders will be gathering at Auschwitz
at the end of January, to mark the sixtieth anniversary of its liberation by the Allies. What would you
say to those leaders?

A: The deaths of millions of Jews has to weigh on the
consciences of the many nations that could have
made a difference by giving refuge to the Jews. It
would be a small atonement, but the world leaders
who attend the Auschwitz ceremony should get
down on their knees and ask God to forgive them
for how their countries acted during the Holocaust.

Q: What was it like for you, the first time that you visited the former death camps?

A: I went to Auschwitz, to Poland, to see the camp—
this was when I was mayor. And I went during the
winter and that is when I think the experience has
its greatest impact. Because the inmates, the prisoners, were not given winter clothing. They walked
around in pajama-type clothing. And when you go
there in the winter—they have harsh winters in
Poland, and there's snow on the ground. You go into
the barracks and in the barracks there's no heat, you
know what they suffered.

What was interesting when I went—it's changed
since then—you wouldn't have known that
Auschwitz was created primarily to kill Jews, because
the word "Jew" wasn't there. They had barracks in
which the Jews were kept, but instead of designating
the barracks as Jewish-occupied, they said "French,"
"Belgian," and other countries from which the Jews

had been taken by the Nazis. But all of these people were Jews.

In one barracks, they had the hair that was shorn from the heads of, I guess, primarily women but maybe men as well. And then they had a collection of suitcases taken from those newly arrived at the camp. And then they had shoes, and for whatever reason, in that particular group of shoes that I saw, they were primarily children's shoes.

While it's now more than fifteen years ago that I went to that camp, I remember that I wept as I saw these things. I saw the ovens where Jews were murdered and incinerated. It was an experience I will not forget.

Q: Should the Allies have bombed Auschwitz?

A: There is no question that many lives would have been saved if the Allies had bombed the railways leading to Auschwitz, or the gas chambers.

[The Roosevelt administration] said that the planes could not be used for that purpose, since they had to be used exclusively for destroying German projects and supporting attacks on the German-Nazi army. Most people today would say that was a false excuse. And that it would not have adversely affected our attacks on the German army or Germany if planes specially had been sent to bomb the rail lines and the death camps or to combine an action where the planes were flying nearby and to have them to do the same—destroy the railroad lines and the barracks.[1]

Q: You have said that Roosevelt must be in Purgatory, for his sin of abandoning the Jews. What did you mean?

A: I think it's a Catholic expression. I'm not Catholic, I'm Jewish. I don't think Jews have purgatory. I'm not really sure, I'm not religious myself, although I

believe in God. But "Purgatory" is a well-known expression, meaning that you have an opportunity to
deal with your sinful life and ultimately get to
Heaven. You're not excluded, but you have to spend
a time in Purgatory, winning the right to enter
heaven.

Franklin Roosevelt did many, many good things.
He saved the world from fascism, certainly the
United States. It was as a result of his leadership that
the United States participated in the ultimate destruction of the Nazis. And we owe him a great debt,
all Americans do. He saved the United States from
the Depression.

He had an opportunity to save Jews before
World War II, and in particular the best illustration
of his refusal to do that—which any decent human
being would have done at the time—was when the
ship the *St. Louis* had gone to Cuba, thinking that
Cuba would take in the refugees. There were a little
over 900 of them, Jewish, and the Cubans for whatever reason wouldn't do it, and the ship was compelled to go back. As the ship was going back, they
could see the lights of Miami, Florida—Cuba is not
very far from Florida—and great efforts were made
by the Jewish leadership to ask the president to allow
these Jews to land and to be given sanctuary. He declined. The State Department was anti-Semitic at
the time, and they didn't do anything to assist the
refugees. Also, the president failed to insist that the
State Department provide visas, even without expanding the number of visas—although that should
have been done as well—but the State Department
refused to give visas that were available.[2]

And he didn't help in the worldwide conference
that was held [at Evian]. He and the Canadian prime
minister misled the world, conveying that action had

been taken, when in fact there was an agreement that they would not provide sanctuary. Adolf Hitler had said before 1939, when World War II commenced, "I will let the Jews leave, if there is any country that will take them, come take them." And no country would. No country did. He knew that when he made the offer he was showing how hypocritical the rest of the world was. I know that had Israel existed as a country, it would have taken every single Jew offered the opportunity to leave. Six million of them. Whether they were poor, whether they were sick, whether they were old, wouldn't make any difference. That is the mission, to provide sanctuary to Jews as well as to build a Jewish state.

When Israeli planes conducted a symbolic fly-over above Auschwitz, in 2003, I read about it in the newspaper, and I applauded, even though I was alone in the room. It said to me that never again, so long as there is a State of Israel, will the Jews be abandoned as they were during the Holocaust.

Q: In the face of so much anti-Semitism in America, what could Roosevelt really have done?

A: Yes, there was a lot of anti-Semitism in America in those years, but that is no excuse for Roosevelt's inaction, which was vile. A leader has to lead. He has to try to change minds.

Apologists for FDR say that because of the anti-Semitism in the 1930s, if he were to take measures to save the Jews then under terrible attack by the Nazis, there would have been no opportunity to create a climate where the American public would want to take on Hitler because he had attacked Great Britain and France and other European countries. I don't accept that. I believe that the American public could have accepted saving Jews. Now that couldn't possibly mean the United States taking all the Jews that were offered by Hitler to leave, but it could have meant, as we have done many times since, for other groups since World War II, calling various countries together and have them all take a number of people, just the same way we took the Vietnamese that wanted to leave from South Vietnam and other countries in a similar way.

Q: Is it that FDR didn't feel the unprecedented horror of the Holocaust?

A: I can't tell you what he felt or didn't feel. Undoubtedly he shared in the social anti-Semitism of that era—yes, Jews can live, but not on his block; yes, Jews can send their kids to school, but not to his children's school. Like many non-Jews who were wealthy and "well-born," as they say, in the top layers of our society—there was a certain social anti-Semitism. Jews were not their friends. But not the kind of anti-Semitism you had in Europe, where they wanted to kill Jews.

Q: Did American Jewish leaders do everything they could to influence Roosevelt to save refugees?

A: Jewish leaders did not do enough. Did they get arrested? Maybe they would have, if some other group was being persecuted. Some of them thought, the less they said, the better—or that they shouldn't say as much as they would like because it would increase anti-Semitism. They should have stormed the gates of the White House to demand action. But they were afraid of anti-Semitism—afraid they would "make things worse." Only a few people spoke out, like Ben Hecht, and of course Henry Morgenthau, the secretary of the treasury, whom we revere for his role in convincing Roosevelt finally to create the War Refugee Board, which saved some Jews late in the war.[3]

Q: Sixty years have passed since the liberation of Auschwitz. When you look at events in Rwanda,

Sudan, and elsewhere in recent years, can you say that the international community has learned any lessons from the Holocaust?

A: They've learned some things, but Darfur, in Sudan, is an illustration of how the world will turn its back out of fear. Economic fear—the third world vis-à-vis the Arabs, the Muslim countries. They don't want to antagonize the 1.2-billion Muslims in the world. So the black African Christians and animists who are living in Darfur and are being murdered, enslaved, harassed, and assaulted are for the most part left alone and not protected, notwithstanding the fact that both the United States and France asked the U.N. to take action and were told that sanctions, let alone military action, were not acceptable, and so all that they could get passed was a resolution condemning but taking no action.

The United States' and other countries' response to natural disasters is much better. Countries send billions of dollars, and they even send in military people to help in relief efforts—the best illustration being the tsunami and our response and the response of countries all over the world. You would hope that when the catastrophe is the result of human actions, as in the case of Sudan, or China in Tibet—where they destroyed the Buddhist temples and the lamas were murdered and so forth—nobody wanted to do anything. They were afraid of alienating the enormous economic power of China.

NEW REVELATIONS ABOUT THE ALLIES' KNOWLEDGE
OF THE HOLOCAUST

Written in August 2005, from the private files of Edward I. Koch.

The Allies received detailed information about the Holocaust earlier than is generally realized, according to a new U.S. government report. And that has important implications for our understanding of how the Allies responded to the Holocaust.

Sam Roberts reported in the *New York Times* on July 31 on a Holocaust-related report written by Robert J. Hanyok, a member of the staff of the National Security Agency's Center for Cryptologic History. Hanyok's analysis shows that the Allies, including the United States and Great Britain, had information detailing the Nazi genocide against the Jews as early as January 1943.

The information was provided through an intercept. Sam Roberts writes, "For instance, one message, declassified in 2000 and barely noticed except in scholarly journals, was intercepted on Jan. 11, 1943. It specified the number of Jews killed under 'Operation Reinhard' at four death camps—Lublin, Belzec, Sobibor and Treblinka—through 1942: 1,274,166."

This is the latest smoking gun that refutes the claim of apologists for President Roosevelt, that the Allies did not know of the death camps or the systematic extermination of the Jews until the end of the war and, therefore, bombing the train tracks to the Auschwitz death camp or the camp itself was not an option. The latest revelations show the Allies did know, and they knew early on.

According to the *Times*, the very first indication that the Nazis had embarked on wholesale killing of the Jews was "July 1941: The first intercept: a report of a massacre of Jews by German police in the western Soviet Union." A later intercept in October 1942 stated: "A report is intercepted detailing the slave labor population at Auschwitz." Then came the January 11, 1943, intercept giving the horrifying number of 1,274,166 Jews killed by the Nazis, who kept meticulous statistics recording the deaths.

The Hanyok analysis states, "Both President Roosevelt and Prime Minister Churchill were often hampered in their limited efforts to alleviate some of the suffering by the general anti-Semitic sentiment in both nations." But was the fault really just with the public, and not the Allied leadership? The National Security Agency's records contained an internal British government memorandum providing an insight into the official British mind-set on the killing of the Jews: a September 11, 1941 memorandum from a British cryptologic official with this comment on German massacres of Jews in Soviet territory: "The fact that the police are killing all Jews that fall into their hands should now be sufficiently well appreciated. It is not therefore proposed to continue reporting these butcheries unless so requested." Out of sight, out of mind. And all the while, the British continued to close off Palestine to Jewish refugees.

Jan Karski, a Polish Christian affiliated with the Polish underground, was spirited into the Warsaw ghetto in 1942, where he saw Nazi atrocities firsthand. When Karski went to England, he met with Foreign Minister Anthony Eden, who said that Great Britain had already done enough for Jewish refugees. Karski traveled to the United States and met President Roosevelt at the White House on July 28, 1943. According to a later *New York Times* account, Karski "told Roosevelt about Auschwitz and said that 1.8 million Jews had already been killed in Poland. He said that commanders of the underground Home Army were estimating that if there were no Allied intervention in the next year and a half, the Jews of Poland would 'cease to exist.'" Roosevelt responded by assuring him that the Allies would win the war. The President said nothing about rescuing the Jews. Rescue was not on his agenda. After the war, Karski summed up his feelings concerning the destruction of the Jews as follows, "This sin will haunt humanity to the end of time. It does haunt me. And I want it to be so."

The Sam Roberts article includes a positive reference in the Hanyok report to Pope Pius XII's statements and actions vis-à-vis the Jews during the Nazi period. Roberts writes, "It also offers a revealing exchange involving Pope Pius XII, who some historians say did not use his influence to halt the killing of Jews." The conversation, relayed by an Ecuadorian envoy, was between the Vatican ambassador and Marshal Henri-Phillippe Petain, the French collaborationist leader. Over lunch at a Vichy hotel in July 1942, Marshal Petain said he was consoled that the pope approved his policy of deporting Jews. The ambassador corrected him, saying, "The Holy Father does not approve." If the Vatican had announced that it would excommunicate Petain or any other Catholic who took part or assisted in the slaughter of the Jews, one can only wonder what the impact would have been.

The world's political and religious leaders, in Washington, London, the Vatican, and elsewhere, could have done so much more to impede the Nazi slaughter of the Jews. The Hanyok report is a grim reminder of that painful fact.

LA GUARDIA AND THE HOLOCAUST

Remarks made at the third national conference of The David S. Wyman Institute for Holocaust Studies, held at the Fordham University School of Law, New York City, September 18, 2005, from the private files of Edward I. Koch.

I am very pleased to participate in this important conference. The David S. Wyman Institute for Holocaust Studies is doing unique and important work by teaching the lessons of America's response to the Holocaust. Professor Wyman, who will be here a little later today, has every reason to be proud of the work being carried on by the institute that bears his name and is based on his landmark book, *The Abandonment of the Jews.*

I am particularly impressed by the Wyman Institute's efforts to bring attention to those Americans who did speak out for rescue from the Holocaust. Regrettably, there were all too few, which makes it even more important that today's generation learn about the handful of courageous men and women who would not be silenced. Fiorello La Guardia was one of those few brave individuals.

As a youngster, I idolized La Guardia. Growing up in New York City in the 1930s and 1940s, it was La Guardia to whom I looked as my role model when I first began to think about a career in government. I am speaking here of his extraordinary accomplishments for the city of New York.

I did not know then, and most people still do not know today, about what La Guardia did to promote the rescue of Jews from the Holocaust. And that is what the speakers in this panel will address this morning, shedding new light and educating us about this important but little-known chapter in the life of the man we affectionately called "the Little Flower."

I don't know if what I accomplished as mayor of New York City will ever be compared to what La Guardia achieved during his terms in office. Of course every mayor dreams of being compared to La Guardia, but that is for historians to judge. But it does seem to me that in at least one area, La Guardia's inspiration was reflected in something that I did.

I am referring to the phenomenon of mayors of this city being involved in foreign affairs. This is not exclusively a New York phenomenon, but it is primarily a New York phenomenon, for several reasons.

The first is that this city is home to some of the largest and most politically influential ethnic communities in the country— Jews, Irish, Italians, Germans, and today, the largest ethnic and racial groups are African Americans and Hispanics. They naturally have a strong interest in the affairs of their ancestral homelands, and they sometimes look to the mayor of their new home city to take an interest, too. Earlier in the city's ethnic history, it was de rigueur that mayors would visit the three "I" countries—Israel, Ireland, and Italy. Today, the three countries are Israel, Puerto Rico, and the Dominican Republic. A trip to South Africa—home of Nelson Mandela—is now recommended as well.

David Dinkins, when he became mayor, decided to remove the picture of Fiorello La Guardia from the mayor's office and placed there instead the picture of Nelson Mandela. I had seen

La Guardia's picture hanging on the wall of the mayor's office during the administrations of John Lindsay and Abe Beame and it was there when I took office in 1978. I brought La Guardia's desk back into the mayor's office when I became mayor. It had been removed by Abe Beame, who gave it to a secretary in an outer office. I recognized it because it had a metal plate stating it had been La Guardia's. I had to have the desk top raised by New York City carpenters so that my knees could slip under the desk. David Dinkins removed the desk from the mayor's office when he succeeded me.

After the revolution in Tiananmen Square was bloodily put down by the government of the People's Republic of China, I proposed to the City Council that we honor the students by placing a new street name sign at the corner of 12th Avenue and 43rd Street, designating it "Tiananmen Square." The Chinese Mission to the U.N. was located at that corner. I placed the sign there myself with great pleasure. On one occasion, the sign was stolen, by whom I do not know, and I personally replaced it. Regrettably, it is no longer there.

The second reason New York City's mayors are sometimes drawn into foreign affairs is that, as the location of the United Nations, New York City is also home to a large community of foreign diplomats with whom the mayor inevitably has to interact.

A third reason is that New York is the center of the world's news media, headquarters to the *New York Times,* the major television networks, and so forth. So naturally whatever goes on here tends to attract greater public and media interest.

Most of us know, and many of us personally remember, how outspoken Mayor La Guardia was against Hitler and the Nazis. La Guardia was really the pioneer when it comes to American mayors and foreign affairs. And to me, he was an inspiration in his willingness to say and do what he did, especially when his political friends and allies, including President Roosevelt, were not willing to speak out. That took courage. To speak his mind knowing that the State Department might come down on his head—that was admirable.

I carried with me the memories of La Guardia when I found myself confronted, in 1979, by the policies of a president from my own party who was going back on his promises regarding Israel and taking action that was undermining America's traditional friendship with the Jewish state. I had more than my share of clashes with the Carter administration regarding Israel. And there were plenty of people in my own party who did not want me speaking out. But I don't regret what I said or did, and I would like to think that I was acting in the tradition of Fiorello La Guardia.

MIXING POLITICS WITH BUSINESS? LA GUARDIA, THE NAZIS, AND THE TRIBOROUGH BRIDGE

By Edward I. Koch and Rafael Medoff

Written in March 2006, from the private files of Edward I. Koch.

Controversy continues to swirl around the awarding of two huge New York City construction contracts to a British architect who is one of the leaders of an anti-Israel group. The city and state officials grappling with the issue may find some useful lessons in the experience of Fiorello La Guardia, who as mayor found himself face to face with a construction controversy of his own, one that also involved the Jews and their enemies.

The current flare-up centers around the prominent British architect Richard Rogers, who has been awarded contracts to expand the Jacob K. Javits Convention Center in Manhattan and the Silvercup Studios in Long Island City, Queens.

The problem is that Rogers has hosted at least three meetings of an anti-Israel organization called Architects and Planners for Justice in Palestine. The gatherings, which were held at Rogers's London office, included denunciations of what they called Israel's "oppression" of Arabs and its "apartheid system of control." Participants also discussed such actions as boycotting Israeli construction firms and expelling Israeli architects from the International Union of Architects.

When protests erupted in recent days, Rogers experienced a foxhole conversion, announcing that he opposes boycotts and is dissociating himself from the group. Silvercup Studios and Queens officials are considering whether Rogers's statements should suffice to drop their opposition. But the Empire State Development Corporation, which had awarded him the Javits Center contract, is reportedly satisfied that his new position is sincere and that the project should move forward with him at the helm.

Is it indeed possible, in such a situation, to separate business and politics?

La Guardia didn't think so.

In the autumn of 1935, the Bridge Authority purchased five hundred tons of sheet steel to build the Triborough Bridge. The steel came from Germany. Nazi Germany.

La Guardia was not about to let that pass.

Since Adolf Hitler's rise to power two and a half years earlier, La Guardia had been one of his most persistent and vociferous critics. Much to the consternation of the State Department, which was interested in maintaining good relations with Berlin, La Guardia denounced Hitler's persecution of German Jews as the work of "a perverted maniac," took part in a mock trial of Hitler at Madison Square Garden, and urged New Yorkers to refrain from purchasing goods from Nazi Germany.

Although bedridden at Mount Sinai Hospital after a painful attack of sciatica, the feisty mayor swung into action when he heard about the steel contract. In a telegram to Bridge Authority chairman Nathan Burkan, the mayor announced that he did not want that "damned steel" in his city. "The only commodity we can import from Hitlerland now is hatred," La Guardia declared, "and we don't want any in our country."

Earlier that year, mobs of German pogromists, led by Nazi stormtroopers, had rampaged through the Jewish community of Berlin, shouting "The best Jew is a dead Jew" as they viciously beat Jewish passersby and smashed the windows of Jewish-owned shops. Three months had passed since those events, but La Guardia had not forgotten.

Technically, the Bridge Authority was an independent agency that did not require the mayor's approval for its construction purchases, but the mayor found grounds to block the deal: he bore responsibility for New Yorkers' safety, and could not vouch for the reliability of Hitler's steel. As he wrote to Burkan: "I cannot be certain of its safety unless I first have every bit and piece of German made material tested before used. *Verstehen Sie* [Do you understand]?"

La Guardia took his share of heat for his one-man campaign against Hitler Germany. Six thousand German Americans held a rally in New York City and pledged to vote him out of office. Nazi propaganda chief Joseph Goebbels threatened to bomb New York City. Secretary of State Cordell Hull complained that La Guardia's actions were harming German-American relations. The Little Flower was not fazed. "I run the subways and he runs the State Department—except when I abrogate a treaty or something," he declared in classic La Guardia style.

Richard Rogers is not a Nazi, and the Jews of Israel are not the Jews of Hitler Germany. But the principle that Fiorello La Guardia defended in 1935 remains: New York City has no obligation to do business with those who trample on values that New Yorkers cherish.

Rogers's sudden "conversion," in response to the possibility of losing a $1.7 billion architectural contract, would not satisfy any reasonable person, nor should it satisfy the officials in charge of expanding the Javits Convention Center and Silvercup Studios. At this time of rising anti-Semitism in Great Britain and elsewhere in Europe—anti-Semitism that is often thinly disguised as opposition to Israel—Rogers should suffer appropriate economic consequences for his role in the deplorable activities of "Architects and Planners for Justice in Palestine." He should be dismissed as the proposed architect for the Javits Center and Silvercup.

IRAN'S HOLOCAUST CARTOON "TEST": WE PASSED

By Edward I. Koch and Rafael Medoff

Written in September 2006, from the private files of Edward I. Koch.

The Iranian government's exhibit of cartoons mocking the Holocaust, which opened recently in Teheran, was intended as a "test" of Western reactions, in the wake of the cartoons about Muhammad published by a Danish newspaper last year.

Well, the West has passed Iran's "test" with flying colors.

The exhibit in Teheran showcases more than two hundred of the entries submitted to the Iranian government's grotesque "Holocaust International Cartoon Contest." They invoke a wide range of both classical and modern anti-Semitic images: Jews with huge noses, Jews controlling the world, Jewish vampires drinking Arab blood, swastika-adorned Israeli soldiers slaughtering Arab children.

The Iranians expected this would be a way to expose Western hypocrisy: Westerners are willing to circulate cartoons insulting Muhammad, Teheran reasoned, but surely they will be outraged if cartoonists insult the Holocaust.

Yes, we are outraged. But we did not respond with riots, arson, and murder, as Islamic extremists responded to the Danish cartoons. Instead, we responded exactly as civilized people should respond when they don't like an article or a drawing: We turned the page.

We did so despite the fact that we have ample reason to be outraged.

First, because the cartoon exhibit in Iran is government sponsored. This is a critical difference between the Denmark controversy and the Teheran exhibit, something the Iranians never grasped because they are apparently incapable of understanding how free societies work.

That newspaper in Denmark is not controlled by the Danish government. It is a free, independent newspaper that can print whatever it chooses. And if subscribers or advertisers don't like what they print, they can cancel their subscriptions or advertise elsewhere. Muslims who were offended by the cartoons should have directed their protests at the newspaper or the cartoonists, not at all Danes, or all Europeans, or all Westerners. And it goes without saying that those protests should have taken the form of letters or phone calls, not rock-throwing or bomb-hurling.

By contrast, the cartoons mocking the Holocaust are being sponsored by the Iranian government. It can and does control whether or not they are disseminated. Similarly, anti-Jewish cartoons and articles appear often in government-sponsored publications in Egypt, Saudi Arabia, the Palestinian Authority, and elsewhere in the Middle East. They are totalitarian regimes that could stop the dissemination of such hateful images with the snap of their fingers.

The second reason we are outraged by Iran's Holocaust cartoons is their impact.

We have seen no evidence that the cartoons about Muhammad resulted in anti-Muslim feeling among Westerners. They certainly did not provoke anti-Muslim violence.

By contrast, the anti-Jewish cartoons that Arab governments publicize do play a role in encouraging hatred and violence. They appear in government-controlled media and schools, and are thereby legitimized by the regime's seal of approval and the endorsement of teachers and other authority figures. As U.S. Senator Hillary Clinton pointed out in a memorable speech last year, what these regimes are doing is nothing less than "child abuse." They "take young minds and twist and pervert them and create a new generation of terrorists . . . young minds are being infected with this anti-Semitism."

A frightening report appeared in the Israeli daily *Ha'aretz* on August 27, 2006, about a summer camp for disadvantaged children run by the terrorist group Islamic Jihad on the beaches of Gaza, under the Palestinian Authority. A camp director named Hisham explained what the campers are taught: "We teach the children the truth. How the Jews persecuted the prophets and tortured them. We stress that the Jews killed and slaughtered Arabs and Palestinians every chance they got. Most important, the children understand that the conflict with the Jews is not over land, but rather over religion. As long as Jews remain here, between the [Jordan] river and the sea, they will be our enemy and we will continue to pursue and kill them. When they leave we won't hurt them."

At a press conference in 1934, President Franklin Roosevelt pointed out that one of the most ominous signs of future German aggression against France was the message of militarism and martyrdom that the Nazis were imparting to German children. To illustrate his point, he told an anecdote about a little German boy so inculcated with Nazi propaganda that each night he prayed, "Dear God, please permit it that I shall die with a French bullet in my heart."

Not many people paid attention to those warning signs in the 1930s. Will our generation repeat that mistake?

WHAT CAN BE DONE ABOUT HOLOCAUST-DENIERS?

By Edward I. Koch and Rafael Medoff, originally published in the *Jerusalem Report*, January 8, 2007.

The recent conference of Holocaust-deniers in Teheran and the jailing earlier this year of British author David Irving in Austria for denying the Holocaust have stirred debate over what can be done to combat the deniers.

While Austria, Germany, France and some other European countries have enacted legislation outlawing Holocaust-denial, the United States has not. Countries on whose soil the Holocaust took place understandably feel a need to act against attempts to whitewash the Nazis' crimes. The United States, with its very different past and its stricter constitutional interpretation of free speech, has not taken such action, although many states ban or restrict either cross-burning or wearing Ku Klux Klan–style hoods.

But just because Holocaust-denial is legal in the United States does not mean that Americans are helpless to combat it.

There are many steps that the government, media, and general public can take to show America's contempt for deniers and reduce their influence.

- *Recognize that Holocaust-denial is bigotry.* Holocaust-denial expert Prof. Deborah Lipstadt has described deniers as "anti-Semites in three-piece suits" and the State Department's 2005 report on global anti-Semitism listed instances of Holocaust-denial as examples of anti-Semitic activity. They're right. It's old-fashioned anti-Semitism in a new guise. Holocaust-denial is not a legitimate part of public discourse. Deniers are not "revisionists," although they have tried to appropriate that term to give themselves a veneer of credibility. The *Chronicle of Higher Education,* the leading newspaper of the academic world, should be applauded for its recently-adopted policy of refraining from characterizing deniers as "revisionists."
- *Don't give deniers a platform.* No newspaper or magazine is legally required to accept every advertisement that is submitted. In 1992, the newsletter of the Organization of American Historians declared it would not accept ads from deniers. The political weekly *The Nation* adopted a similar policy in 2004. C-SPAN's plan, last year, to "balance" a speech by Prof. Lipstadt by broadcasting one by denier David Irving was wrongheaded and, fortunately, was reversed after public protests. One presumes C-SPAN would not "balance" a speech by a geologist with one by someone claiming the earth is flat.
- *Don't give celebrities a pass.* Soon after the controversy over the drunken anti-Semitic tirade by actor-director Mel Gibson last summer, there were two important but little-noticed reports (one in the *Melbourne Herald Sun,* the other in the *New York Post*) of his involvement with the Australian League of Rights (ALR), a group that denies the Holocaust. According to these accounts, Gibson backed the candidacy of the ALR's Rob Taylor when he ran for local

office in 1987, and in recent years Gibson attended an
ALR dinner, together with his father Hutton, an avowed
Holocaust-denier. The group's newsletter described the
Gibsons' attendance as the "sensation" of the event.

Yet there has been no serious investigation of this new
evidence. Already there are reports that Gibson's new
movie may win an Academy Award, and many in Hollywood seem ready to forgive and forget. Until Gibson
comes clean about his ties to the ALR, there is reason to
doubt the sincerity of his recent apologies.

• *Put pressure on regimes that sponsor denial.* Some governments
that the United States considers friendly, such as Egypt
and Saudi Arabia, include Holocaust-denial material in
government-controlled news media and other publications. These regimes are recipients of significant
amounts of U.S. military and economic assistance. U.S.
taxpayer money should not be subsidizing such hate. The
implicit threat of losing Western aid can work wonders.
International pressure forced the United Arab Emirates
in 2004 to shut down the Zayed Center, which had been
promoting Holocaust-denial. (Unfortunately, the State
Department sent mixed messages—while the U.S. ambassador in the UAE protested Zayed's activities, a State
Department report listed the closure as an example of
suppressing free speech.) That same year, U.S. pressure
brought about the first-ever public disavowal of Holocaust-denial by an Egyptian government official. Now
there must be follow-up.

Openly anti-American regimes such as Iran under Mahmoud Ahmadinejad may be less susceptible to foreign
pressure, but an end to Holocaust-denial propaganda
should be on the list of changes the West would require of
Teheran to shed its pariah status.

• *Insist that leaders behave responsibly.* Presidents and prime ministers set the tone for what is acceptable in public discourse. Leaders who dabble in Holocaust-denial should be

held accountable, not excused in the name of realpolitik. In 1994, international criticism compelled then–Croatian President Franjo Tudjman to publicly apologize for a book he wrote that called the Holocaust an exaggeration. Croatians got the message. Last month the new Croatian leadership opened a museum on the site of the Jasenovac concentration camp, where the Nazis' puppet Croatian regime murdered more than 90,000 Jews and Gypsies during the Holocaust.

Similarly, Palestinian Authority president Mahmoud Abbas should be urged to publicly disavow his 1982 book, which claimed less than one million Jews were killed by the Nazis and accused David Ben-Gurion of "provoking" Hitler. As Israeli cabinet minister Isaac Herzog has written, Abbas's book "is not a matter that can be brushed under the carpet, because at issue is a moral question whose importance cannot be overstated."

Yes, the Holocaust-denial conference in Teheran was an outrage. But it was also a test of the free world's resolve.

CONCLUSION

By Edward I. Koch and Rafael Medoff,

December 2007

Understanding the lessons of the Holocaust, and successfully confronting the anti-Semites who aspire to perpetrate another one, requires, first of all, a comprehension of the many and varied ways in which anti-Semitism manifests itself today. The picture is sometimes blurry, and the protagonists are not always easy to identify. If someone is anti-Israel, does that make him anti-Semitic? Can one be against Zionism without being against Jews? Are those who denounce Israel engaged in legitimate disagreement with Israeli policies—or are they expressing old-fashioned bigotry in a new guise?

With Israel and other Jewish issues constantly in the international spotlight in recent years, these questions have taken on particular urgency. They go straight to the heart of what is an acceptable part of public discourse and what is not.

In our society, criticism of the policies of the Israeli government or of a Jewish organization is legitimate and cannot be dismissed out of hand. It becomes part of the public conversation and may ultimately influence government policy. But attacks that are anti-Semitic are something else entirely. They should be regarded as bigotry and do not deserve serious consideration by the public or policymakers. The difference between the two is crucial, and the line that separates them should not be crossed. The problem we face is that the line is becoming increasingly blurry. That makes it harder than ever to know how to respond effectively.

VIOLENT ANTI-SEMITISM

When hostility to Jews is expressed violently, there is little problem understanding its source. A firebomb thrown at a synagogue or a swastika daubed on a Jewish tombstone carries with it, by its very nature, an unambiguous message of Jew hatred. While a few extremists may rationalize such behavior by claiming it is "provoked" by, for example, Israeli policies, reasonable people will agree that there is no justification for it whatsoever.

Violent anti-Semitism is essentially a problem of law enforcement, and most Western governments seem equipped and committed to combating it. Unfortunately, this does not mean that officials are always sufficiently sensitive or motivated to ensure that the culprits are properly punished. Too often, the perpetrators are seen as naive pranksters who can be straightened out by sending them for a lesson about the Holocaust with a local rabbi.

That kind of slap-on-the-wrist approach will not suffice. There must be meaningful consequences for instances of anti-Semitic violence. This is especially true when the perpetrators are teenagers; if they are not appropriately punished at a young age, they will go through life believing they can assault Jewish targets and get away with it.

The response of a German American high school principal in New York City in 1944 offers a powerful lesson. When five seniors at Andrew Jackson High School in Queens were caught painting anti-Semitic slogans in Queens Village, principal Ralph Haller announced that he would not permit them to graduate.

At a meeting with parents, Haller explained: "I consider such [anti-Semitic] activities totally in contradiction to everything that the America of today or the America which we hope to have tomorrow stands for." Since he, as the principal, was authorized to deny a graduation diploma to any student who gave evidence of "poor American citizenship," he vowed to henceforth classify anti-Semitic activity as un-American. As a Protestant and a German American, he emphasized, "I feel that I have the right and duty to speak out on this issue."

The historical context of that episode is worth noting. In Germany, the land from which Haller's family had come, high school principals in Nazi Germany openly encouraged anti-Semitism. Here in the United States, levels of anti-Semitism had reached their historic high, with the support of groups such as the German-American Bund. Just a few years earlier, more than 20,000 Bund supporters had filled Madison Square Garden for a pro-Hitler rally. Yet Ralph Haller stood apart—and stood up for what is right. The example he set offers a valuable guide for dealing with anti-Semitic vandals in our own time.

CELEBRITY ANTI-SEMITISM

While violent anti-Semitism may not be hard to recognize, celebrity anti-Semitism is somewhat more complicated. The problem is not so much that it is disputed, but that the perpetrator's friends and fans cloud the debate with rationalizations based on personal sentiments, not reason or logic.

A case in point is the anti-Semitic outburst by the actor and director Mel Gibson, who upon his arrest for drunk driving in 2006 ranted about "f___ing Jews" who "are responsible for all the wars in the world." An array of Hollywood stars and moguls rose to his defense. The actor Patrick Swayze, for example, called Gibson "a wonderful human being" and insisted that "people say stupid things when they happen to have a few [drinks]." Swayze had no comment when evidence subsequently emerged that Gibson has a track record, since the 1980s, of asso-

ciating with Holocaust deniers, something that does not appear
to be connected to his drinking problem.

The actress and director Jodie Foster called Gibson "kind"
and "honest," and "absolutely not anti-Semitic." There was, of
course, considerable irony in her statements, since just the previous year, Foster also publicly defended the propaganda filmmaker Leni Riefenstahl, whose films glorified Hitler. No matter
how much she admires Gibson or Riefenstahl, Ms. Foster should
judge them according to their actual statements and actions, not
according to her fantasy image of them.

Whether Gibson is permanently tarnished by his anti-
Semitic remarks or will bounce back remains to be seen. Recent
history offers examples of public figures who have made hostile
statements about Jews or other minorities and managed to
withstand the ensuing criticism, as well as celebrity bigots who
were less successful at weathering the storm.

Jesse Jackson at first denied, in 1984, that he had referred to
New York City as "Hymie town." But the *Washington Post* reporter who heard Jackson's anti-Semitic slur was sufficiently
convincing for the public, and Jackson soon admitted his guilt
and apologized. Some critics may have doubted the sincerity of
that apology, but because Jackson enjoyed significant sympathy,
both among his political constituents and a segment of the
media, he was able to continue his public career more or less
unscathed.

At the other end of the political spectrum, Pat Buchanan
never apologized for blaming American Jews for U.S. involvement in the first Gulf War. Nor has he recanted his praise of
Adolf Hitler, his defense of various Nazi war criminals, or his
claim that the gassing facilities in the Nazis' Treblinka death
camp "did not emit enough carbon monoxide to kill anybody."
Yet Buchanan to this day appears regularly on national television. How many public figures or pundits have refused, on principle, to appear with him on TV? It seems that the perception
that Buchanan represents a significant constituency has blunted
some of the opposition to his bigotry.

But others have fared differently. Trent Lott was compelled to resign as Senate Majority Leader after praising the segregationist Strom Thurmond. The New Jersey State Legislature eliminated the position of poet laureate after its occupant, Amiri Baraka, authored a poem accusing Jews of having advance knowledge of the 9/11 attacks. Major League Baseball forced Marge Schott to sell the Cincinnati Reds after she praised Hitler and degraded African Americans. Radio show host Michael Savage was fired after making derisive comments about gays. CBS television dismissed sports analyst Jimmy "the Greek" Snyder for his remarks about African American athletes.

The first appropriate response to Gibson came from ABC television, when it quickly canceled its contract with Gibson's film production company to make a miniseries about the Holocaust. But ABC promptly fumbled what would have been the perfect opportunity to demonstrate that bigotry has consequences. Its spokeswoman, Hope Hartman, said the cancellation was because Gibson's company had not yet produced a draft of the script even though nearly two years had passed since the contract was signed. ABC should have said clearly that it would be totally inappropriate to have an anti-Semite produce a Holocaust series—and, moreover, that as a matter of principle ABC will not do business with anti-Semites.

A star at NBC television recently faced his own dilemma over how to respond to anti-Semitism. On Donald Trump's show, *The Apprentice,* contestant Clay Lee asserted that a fellow contestant was stingy because he was "a tight Jewish boy." The slur came up in that episode's boardroom meeting, where Trump decides which contestant should be fired each week. With tens of millions of Americans watching, Trump had a golden opportunity to send a message that bigotry is unacceptable in American society and that people who make bigoted remarks cannot work for him. Instead, Trump declared: "Clay, I really believe that you are not anti-Semitic. . . . Because you've gone through a lot, being gay. And you've gone through your own form of discrimination."

A contestant the previous season who made an anti-Jewish remark likewise suffered no consequences from Trump (although
she was, appropriately, fired by her real-life employer after her
anti-Semitic statement was aired). That's a pity, because when
such remarks are excused on national television, that affects the
process by which American society determines the threshold for
tolerating bigotry.

ISRAEL-RELATED ANTI-SEMITISM

Anti-Semitism that is masked as criticism of Israel is the most
complicated type of anti-Semitism to discern, and consequently
the hardest to combat. The difficulty lies in the fact that people
who hate both Jews and the Jewish state can easily hide the former by focusing their hostility on the latter. Anti-Semites who
are sophisticated understand that open disparagement of Jews is
frowned upon in Western society. Thus they need to be careful
if they want their message to be considered legitimate and
thereby reach audiences beyond the fringe.

Sometimes it is clear that the line has been crossed. One example is the phenomenon of attributing to Israel classic stereotypes about Jews, such as greediness, clannishness, or control of
the media or governments. Another is attacking Israel by making derisive reference to Judaism or Jewish religious practices.

A third telltale sign is the practice of comparing Israel to
Nazi Germany, an analogy so hideous that it cannot be consid-
ered a part of reasonable discourse. Significantly, the U.S. State
Department, in its 2005 report on global anti-Semitism, stated:
"The demonization or vilification of Israeli leaders, sometimes
through comparisons with Nazi leaders . . . indicates an anti-
Semitic bias rather than a valid criticism of policy concerning a
controversial issue."

The 2006 Israeli conflict with Hezbollah generated a pre-
dictable round of such outbursts. At an anti-Israel rally in
Michigan, Arab-American militants carried signs equating the
Star of David with the swastika and proclaiming "Israel/Nazi

Are the Same Thing." Jihad Al-Khazen, former editor of the London Arab newspaper *Al-Hayat,* asserted that Israeli Prime Minister Ehud Olmert and other Israeli leaders are the grandchildren of Nazi war criminals who disguised themselves as Jews and fled to Palestine after World War II to escape prosecution. "I cannot find any other logical reason for Israel's Nazi-like practices," Al-Khazen wrote. British Member of Parliament Peter Tapsell, for his part, declared that Israeli behavior in Lebanon is reminiscent of the Germans' annihilation of the Warsaw Ghetto.

Yet it was interesting to note that the battle with Hezbollah also led to some Nazi analogies of a very different sort. R. Emmett Tyrrell, Jr., editor of *The American Spectator,* saw the United Nations' response to Hezbollah as comparable to, and even worse than, that of "the international community of appeasers in the 1930s." Jonathan Mark of the *New York Jewish Week,* criticizing CNN's emphasis on Lebanese casualties, remarked: "Somehow, when Edward R. Murrow went from the rooftops of bombed-out London to bombed-out Berlin he didn't look for little German children to turn into martyrs."

Similarly, the accusation that Israel's action against Hezbollah was "disproportionate" also elicited World War II comparisons. "Did Britain respond to the blitz and V–1 and V–2 rockets with 'proportionate' aerial bombardment of Germany?" Charles Krauthammer asked. "Imagine if we had been concerned about a proportional response at the beginning of World War II," wrote Cal Thomas. "Instead, America nuked Japan and firebombed Germany."

Of course, if the pundits were looking for historical analogies to the phenomenon of Iran and Syria using Lebanon-based terrorists as their proxies to harass Israel, they should have recalled the Sudeten German Freikorps. That legion of Nazi-armed "freedom fighters" was used by Hitler to put violent pressure on the Czech government to surrender the Sudetenland region, the buffer zone that helped protect Czechoslovakia from Germany. Some things never change.

Dual loyalty accusations are another example of old-fashioned anti-Semitism wrapped in seemingly legitimate criticism of Israel and its supporters. Pat Buchanan tried to rally opposition to the Gulf War of 1991 by claiming that four prominent hawks with Jewish-sounding names were part of "the Israeli Defense Ministry's amen corner in the United States" and were planning to send "kids with names like McAllister, Murphy, Gonzales and Leroy Brown" to do the fighting. A similar accusation was made by U.S. Congressman Jim Moran, an opponent of the more recent Iraq war; he claimed that the United States would never have gone to war if not for the influence of the American Jewish community.

For some, "neocons"—that is, neoconservatives who are seen as influential in the Bush administration—has become a convenient substitute for "Jews." Opponents of Bush's foreign policy have warned darkly that these Jewish advisers, who were often depicted as being secretly loyal to the Israeli Likud Party, were exercising disproportionate influence on U.S. policy. Even as (formerly) respectable a figure as ex–U.S. Senator Gary Hart asserted that the neocons are "ideologues" who are unable to distinguish between their loyalty "to their original homelands" (which ones could he have in mind?) and loyalty to "America and its national interests." No wonder New York Times columnist David Brooks commented that "con is short for 'conservative' and 'neo' is short for 'Jewish.'"

Some say there is an additional area of anti-Israel criticism that crosses the line into anti-Semitism: the use of extreme double standards. Norman Podhoretz crafted the definitive explanation of this phenomenon in his famous essay, "J'Accuse," in Commentary in 1982. Writing in response to the wave of anti-Israel invective that greeted that year's Israeli war against PLO terrorists in Lebanon, Podhoretz argued: "Criticisms of Israel based on a double standard deserve to be called anti-Semitic." As illustrations, he cited the view that "all other people are entitled to national self-determination, but when the Jews exercise this right they are committing the crimes of racism and imperialism. . . . [A]ll other nations have a right to insure the security of their borders; when Israel exercises this right, it is committing the crime of aggression. . . . [O]nly Israel of all the states in the world is required to prove that its very existence— not merely its interests or the security of its borders, but its very existence—is in immediate peril before it can justify the resort to force."

At the Berlin conference on anti-Semitism in 2004, the members of the U.S. delegation, which I (Ed Koch) chaired, emphasized both in our public remarks and our private meetings with other delegates that Israel should be judged by the same standards applied to all nations, instead of the double standard currently used. What other nations do with impunity and without criticism, Israel is condemned and demonized for. Making Israel the whipping boy in this way is really an attempt to disguise anti-Semitism as opposition to Israel's policies.

The best-known recent controversy over criticism of Israel that some see as anti-Semitic centered on a report by Professors John Mearsheimer and Stephen Walt, published by the Harvard School of Government in early 2006. Titled "The Israel Lobby and U.S. Foreign Policy," the report contended, in eighty-one overheated pages, that pro-Israel Jews in effect control America's media, elected officials, and foreign policy. Mearsheimer and Walt cleverly couched their arguments in terms that enable them to claim that they are challenging only Israeli policies, not Israel's existence; and only some American Jews, not all of them. But the truth is that the underlying message of their paper appears to be no more than the old canard that Jews are disloyal and dangerous.

As a matter of fact, many of the ideas in the Mearsheimer-Walt report bear a striking resemblance to an Egyptian text that most people would instantly recognize as anti-Semitic. The book, *Zionism and Its Fosterchild Israel,* is used in the Egyptian Military Academy. A typical passage asserts: "The domination of American policy by World Zionism and the dominant Jewish financial and political influence on American circles, on states-

men, press and publicity . . . have led to the subordination of the
U.S. administration to Zionist aims."

Professor Eliot Cohen of Johns Hopkins University explained it deftly in the *Washington Post*: "If by anti-Semitism one
means obsessive and irrationally hostile beliefs about Jews; if
one accuses them of disloyalty, subversion or treachery, of having
occult powers and of participating in secret combinations that
manipulate institutions and governments; if one systematically
selects everything unfair, ugly or wrong about Jews as individuals
or a group and equally systematically suppresses any exculpatory
information—why, yes, this paper [by Mearsheimer and Walt] is
anti-Semitic."

GOVERNMENT-SPONSORED ANTI-SEMITISM

No type of anti-Semitism is more dangerous than that which
enjoys the imprimatur of the government and is promoted with
the assistance of governmental resources. When it is circulated
through a nation's schools and news media, anti-Jewish bigotry
is able to penetrate the hearts and minds of the masses and, especially, of young people.

Arab and Muslim regimes that promote anti-Semitism occasionally claim that their invective is a response to Israeli policies, but their blatant use of vicious anti-Jewish stereotypes goes
so far beyond any rational discussion of Israeli behavior that no
reasonable person can see it as anything less than brutal bigotry.
An Egyptian television program that portrays Jews murdering
gentile children in order to obtain their blood is not a response
to Israeli policies. An Iranian leader calling the Holocaust a hoax
has nothing to do with the Arab-Israeli conflict. A Palestinian
Authority religious preacher quoting Hitler's favorite book, *The
Protocols of the Elders of Zion,* is not making a point about negotiations or borders. These people are engaged in anti-Semitism.

The same may be said for terrorist groups such as Hezbollah
and Hamas. Their spokesmen have become sufficiently savvy to
tell Western journalists that they are "against Israeli oppression,

not Jews" or "against Zionism, not Judaism." A case could be made that since these groups' raison d'être is to murder Israeli Jews, they are anti-Semitic in function, if not in theory. Even when they claim that they are responding to Israeli "occupation," they single out Jews, not "Israelis," for death. They do not attempt to murder Israeli Arabs or other Israeli non-Jews. If a group of Israeli Arabs decided to establish a settlement in the disputed territories, would Hamas try to kill them? Not likely.

The idea that a policy can be anti-Semitic in function regardless of its practitioner's declared motives has been raised, in the context of the Holocaust, by Prof. Henry Feingold, author of *The Politics of Rescue,* a book about America's response to the Nazi genocide. Assessing the British government's policy of restricting Jewish immigration and land purchases in Palestine during the 1930s and 1940s, Feingold wrote: "Is it conceivable that a policy that severely curtailed Jewish immigration and land sales in Palestine, in the teeth of the crisis, was not at least partly motivated by anti-Semitism? Palestine was such a logical haven for at least a portion of the refugees that to deny its availability meant that death was almost certainly the alternative."[1]

In the case of Hezbollah and Hamas, however, if one wants to prove their anti-Semitism, it is not necessary to rely solely on the fact that their actions harm Israeli Jews. Both groups have made it easier than that to determine their motives. Hezbollah is most notorious for blowing up the Jewish Community Center in Buenos Aires in 1994, killing eighty-five Jews and others, and wounding more than three hundred. It's hard to portray a massacre of Jews in Argentina as "resistance" to "Israeli occupation." Meanwhile, Hezbollah's television station, Al-Manar, has repeatedly broadcast anti-Semitic programs to such an extent that the French government, in 2004, revoked Al-Manar's license to broadcast in France. As for Hamas, the fact that its founding charter quotes from *The Protocols of the Elders of Zion,* the world's most notorious anti-Semitic tract, demonstrates unquestionably that hatred of Jews, not hatred of Israeli settlements, guides it.

Is there anything that can be done to combat government-sponsored anti-Semitism?

When an anti-Semitic French Muslim hoodlum stabs a Jew in Paris, or a Russian fascist writes an anti-Semitic article in a Moscow newspaper, there is little that Americans can do in response. But when a government engages in anti-Semitism, that opens up a wide range of possible avenues for U.S. intervention. Every government in the world wants something from the United States—trade, tourism, economic aid, weapons, diplomatic support. This creates the opportunity for our government to become a force in the battle against international anti-Semitism.

That's why it was so important that the United States sent a high-level delegation (headed by Ed Koch) to the 2004 Berlin conference on anti-Semitism. In his speech at the conference, Secretary of State Colin Powell broke new ground by going beyond general condemnations of anti-Semitism and declaring that comparing Israel to the Nazis crosses the line between legitimate dissent and crude anti-Semitism.

White House adviser Dr. Tevi Troy, another member of the delegation to Berlin, remarked in a subsequent speech that there was an important connection between the strong U.S. stance in Berlin and our nation's memories of "what the United States did—and, especially, what it did not do, during the Holocaust." He got it exactly right. It is precisely because the State Department failed to respond adequately to Nazi anti-Semitism in the 1930s and 1940s that U.S. officials must learn from those mistakes and strongly confront anti-Jewish bigotry today. Secretary Powell's speech was a good example of the kind of thing the State Department could and should have been doing seventy years ago.

It is crucial that the strong words spoken in Berlin be followed by determined action. As a result of legislation introduced by Rep. Tom Lantos, the only Holocaust survivor in Congress, the State Department was required to issue a report in 2005 on anti-Semitism around the world.

In some respects, the report was a major step forward. As noted earlier, it put the U.S. on record, for the first time, stating that comparing Israel to the Nazis "indicates an anti-Semitic bias rather than a valid criticism of policy." Equally important was that the report specifically included instances of Holocaust-denial in various countries as examples of anti-Semitism. There was no pretending that denying the Holocaust is just another interpretation of history.

Disappointingly, however, the State Department's report seemed to go soft when it came to certain Arab regimes. The report's section on Saudi Arabia, a major promoter of anti-Semitism, was just 182 words long. By contrast, Iceland was given 387 words, even though there were very few reports of anti-Semitism there. Only 86 words were devoted to the Palestinian Authority, despite the frequency of anti-Semitism in the P.A.'s newspapers and on its television and radio programs. Armenia (194 words), Brazil (149), and Azerbaijan (142), where there is no evidence of government-sponsored anti-Semitism, were given more space in the report than the Palestinian Authority.

Last year's annual U.S. report on human rights around the world was not much better. For example, regarding Egypt, the report stated that "anti-Semitism is found in both the pro-government and opposition press." There was no acknowledgment that government-controlled newspapers are overflowing with anti-Semitism. An anti-Jewish series that was broadcast on a private Egyptian television station was mentioned; the anti-Semitic programs on the government-controlled television station were not.

The report's section on Saudi Arabia noted that "there was substantial societal prejudice based on ethnic or national origin." No hint that part of the reason for anti-Jewish prejudice in Saudi society is the constant torrent of anti-Semitism in the Saudi government—controlled media and schools. Similarly, regarding the Palestinian Authority, the State Department report stated only that during the past year, the P.A. regime "prohibited calls for violence, displays of arms, and racist slogans, although this rarely was enforced." No mention of the proliferation of "racist slogans"—that is, anti-Semitism—in the P.A.'s media, schoolbooks, and elsewhere.

The good news, however, concerns the other requirement of the Lantos legislation, which was the appointment of a special U.S. envoy to monitor and combat anti-Semitism around the world. After an unexplained delay of some eighteen months, the administration chose Dr. Gregg Rickman, a scholar and an activist, who played a central role in the battle with Swiss banks to win restitution for Holocaust survivors.

The new envoy will certainly have his work cut out for him, because anti-Semitism, in all its varieties and guises, is unquestionably on the rise throughout the world and will only get worse unless decent people everywhere do their utmost to combat it. Has the international community finally recognized the mistake it made of ignoring anti-Semitism in the 1930s? The answer will ultimately play a decisive role in the future not only of the Jewish people, but of the entire free world.

POSTSCRIPT

As this book was going to press, a new public opinion survey found shockingly high levels of anti-Semitism in American society. According the poll, which was conducted by the Anti-Defamation League, 31 percent of Americans "believe that Jews are more loyal to Israel than to America."

I suspect that many of those 31 percent are not Jew-haters, but simply have not given any thought as to why Jews, who love America so deeply, worry so much about the security of the State of Israel. We know that every night when we go to sleep so easily and safely, there are communities of Jews in other countries who fear for their lives because of anti-Semitism. And we know that Israel is there to give them sanctuary and, if need be, send its troops to rescue them as it did at Entebbe in 1976. As for us, we are fortunate to live in a country which has given us so much and has permitted us, based on merit, to rise to the highest positions in this country. Everyone, whatever their race, religion, or ethnicity, owes this great country everlasting gratitude, and we should be willing to die for it if need be to protect it.

NOTES

CHAPTER 1

The Problem of Black Anti-Semitism

1. COFO, the Council of Federated Organizations, was a civil rights group established in 1962. It initiated the Mississippi Freedom Summer Project of 1964, which helped blacks register to vote.
2. Shirley Chisholm (1924–2005) was the first African American woman elected to the U.S. Congress. She represented New York's Twelfth District from 1969 to 1983. Chisholm campaigned unsuccessfully for the Democratic nomination for president in 1972.
3. Mohammed Mehdi was an Arab American activist well known in New York City for his frequent media appearances, in which he advocated the dismantling of the State of Israel.
4. LeRoi Jones, today known as Amiri Baraka, is a black nationalist activist and author who stirred controversy in the late 1960s with a series of anti-white and anti-Semitic poems and articles. He was named poet laureate of the state of New Jersey in 2002, but the position was abolished by the New Jersey State Legislature after Baraka wrote a poem claiming that Israeli workers knew in advance about the planned attack on the World Trade Center.
5. Anthony Imperiale (1931–1999) was a Newark City councilman whose tough law-and-order stance and occasional use of racial epithets made him a symbol of white backlash during periods of black-white tension in New Jersey in the 1960s and 1970s.
6. Richard Hatcher was elected mayor of Gary, Indiana, in 1967, the first African American to hold that position.

Taking Black Anti-Semitism Seriously

1. Longtime Anti-Defamation League officials Arnold Forster and Benjamin Epstein, in their 1974 book *The New Anti-Semitism* (New York: McGraw Hill), describe (pp. 59–62) how the African-American Teachers Association, of which Albert Vann was president, promoted anti-Semitism during the late 1960s. They note that the association's publication, *Forum,* was a "vehicle for anti-Jewish messages," and a second publication, *Black News,* which was "closely linked to ATA," was "also packed, issue, after issue, with anti-Jewish invective." Forster and Epstein also recall an episode in December 1968, when the ATA's Brooklyn coordinator, Leslie Campbell, read a poem on

WBAI-FM radio that which addressed Jewish union leader Albert Shanker in these terms: "Hey, Jew Boy, with that yarmulke on your head / You pale-faced Jew boy—I wish you were dead." After Mayor John Lindsay called for an investigation of Campbell, Vann responded at a press conference on January 19, 1969, at which he accused the mayor of trying "to appease the powerful Jewish financiers of the city."

Inviting Farrakhan

1. William B. Shockley (1910–1989), co-inventor of the transistor, was awarded the Nobel Prize in physics in 1956. His work led to the creation of the Silicon Valley scientific industry in northern California. Later he stirred controversy with his claims that blacks were genetically inferior to white, and his proposal that people with IQs under one hundred should be encouraged to undergo sterilization.

The Leonard Jeffries Case

1. This correspondence was a prelude to the lawsuit *Weinbaum v. Cuomo,* which charged New York state officials with racial bias in the funding of New York's two university systems, CUNY and SUNY. It was the subject of the lead article in the Metro section of the *New York Times* on February 29, 1992.

CHAPTER 2

A Message for All Time

1. Kurt Waldheim (1918–2007), a veteran Austrian diplomat, was elected secretary-general of the United Nations in 1971 and re-elected in 1976. His campaign for the Austrian presidency in 1985 and 1986 became embroiled in controversy when journalists revealed that Waldheim falsified sections of his autobiography to hide his service as a Nazi officer and his possible involvement in war crimes. Despite these revelations, he was elected president of Austria.

Baker and the Jews

1. An editorial in the *New York Post* on March 10, 1992, stated in part: "We don't have to wonder whether Secretary of State Baker really did say, about American Jews, 'F____ 'em. They didn't vote for us anyway.' We are in a position to know the genesis of the Ed Koch column in which Baker's comment was first reported. We also know that the secretary's re-

mark was reported immediately after he made it to more than one journalist. In short, the quotation can be taken at face value. . . . Unfortunately, this is not a new departure for Baker. Last week, the Israeli newspaper *Ma'ariv* quoted an even more hostile utterance made by the secretary of state some two years ago." According to a news article in the *New York Post* on March 6, 1992, David Bar-Ilan, executive editor of the *Jerusalem Post,* writing in *Ma'ariv* on March 5, 1992, reported that when a "Republican operative" said to Baker in 1990 that the administration's Mideast stand would alienate Jews from the GOP, Baker replied, "Don't worry, Jews remember the Holocaust, but they forget insults as soon as they smell cash."

A news article in *The Forward* on March 13, 1992, stated in part: "White House officials and GOP activists here tended to discount the specific report, which indicated the comment had come at a meeting within the past three weeks. 'Baker chooses his words very carefully,' one senior White House official said. But the *Forward* has learned that on at least one other occasion in the past year, Mr. Baker replied, 'F____ the Jews' when an interlocutor maintained that, if nothing else, domestic political considerations argued for a less-hostile-to-Israel policy. This account has been corroborated by several people who heard the story from Mr. Baker's interlocutor."

A news article in the *London Observer* on November 10, 1991, reported, in part: "In Madrid, the US held the Israelis firmly in check on procedures. But when the Palestinian delegate, Dr. Haidar Abdel-Shafi, mentioned Arafat and the PLO during his address, the Israelis sent a note to the U.S. delegation demanding to leave.

"According to Saudi sources at the conference, Baker sent a note to Prince Bandar Bin Sultan, Saudi Arabia's ambassador to Washington, and a close personal crony of the U.S. Secretary of State: 'The f____king Israelis want to withdraw.' Bandar wrote back: 'Let the f____king Israelis go. The good Americans will stay.' Baker, winking at Bandar, sent a note to Israel. Israel did not budge."

CHAPTER 3

An Obligation to Remember

1.   Hitler wrote in *Mein Kampf:* "If at the beginning of the [First World] War and during the War, twelve or fifteen thousand of these Hebrew corrupters of the people had been held under poison gas, as happened to hundreds of thousands of our very best German workers in the field, the sacrifice of millions at the front would not have been in vain."

2. The Intergovernmental Committee on Refugees was established as a result of the Evian conference, a thirty-two-nation gathering in France, organized by the Roosevelt administration for the ostensible purpose of addressing the Jewish refugee problem. Since none of the countries attending the conference was willing to take in more than a relative handful of refugees, however, Evian produced no concrete results. In *Paper Walls: America and the Refugee Crisis 1938–1941*, Prof. David S. Wyman writes: "True to the inauspicious circumstances of its birth at the Evian Conference, the Intergovernmental Committee on Refugees (ICR) did not accomplish much in its nine-year career. Recipient of little real authority, and for years no funds except a minimum for administration, the performance of the ICR failed to extend far beyond talk and paperwork." Wyman notes that even Roosevelt's Undersecretary of State, Sumner Welles, later admitted: "The committee could have been responsible for an outstanding humanitarian achievement prior to and during the war years, but . . . the final results amounted to little more than zero. The Government of the United States itself permitted the committee to become a nullity" (p. 51).

3. Irving Abella and Harold Troper, *None Is Too Many: Canada and the Jews of Europe 1933–1948* (New York: Random House, 1982).

What the Flames Could Not Consume

1. Linnas, Sixty-seven, a resident of Long Island, was stripped of his U.S. citizenship in 1981, after it was found that he lied on his immigration application to cover up his role as a commander of a Nazi death camp in Tartu, Estonia, from 1941 to 1943. He was ordered deported to Estonia (then part of the U.S.S.R.). After waging an unsuccessful legal struggle in which he was defended by the controversial Ramsey Clark, Linnas was sent to Estonia in 1987. Three months later, he died of heart failure while in a Soviet prison, awaiting trial.

Kristallnacht: The Beginning of the End

1. The Germans used the shooting of a German diplomat in Paris by the distraught son of Polish Jewish refugees as their pretext to launch the Kristallnacht pogrom, which had already been carefully planned long before.

2. The peace treaty brokered at Versailles to end World War I imposed penalties on Germany for having started the war. Many Germans blamed the Versailles treaty for their country's economic problems in the 1920s, which helped bring Adolf Hitler to power.

The Lesson of Kristallnacht

1. Recent research has established that a majority of the passengers managed to survive the Holocaust. But that does not change the tragic fact that they were sent back to Europe despite the obvious danger to them.

A Man Who Accomplished Miracles

1. Also known as the Vrba-Wetzler Report. In April 1944, two Slovakian Jews, Rudolf Vrba (Walter Rosenberg) and Alfred Wetzler escaped from Auschwitz and prepared detailed descriptions, with diagrams, of the mass murder process in the camp. They gave copies of their report to Jewish leaders and Western diplomats. Although the Allies had previously received information about the mass killings, the Auschwitz Protocols provided the most detailed description yet.

Heroes Who Understand History

1. Trifa, seventy, was an archbishop who headed the Romanian Orthodox Episcopate of America from 1958 until 1984, when he was deported from the United States. Trifa was found to have lied on his U.S. immigration forms to conceal his role in the Iron Guard, a Romanian fascist militia that carried out massacres of Jews in the 1940s. Trifa's war crimes became a matter of public knowledge thanks to the reporting of investigative journalists and protests by Jewish activists, led by Rabbi Weiss.

America and the Holocaust

1. After the Allies gained control of the Foggia air base in Italy in December 1943, Auschwitz was for the first time within striking distance of Allied planes. By 1944, the Roosevelt administration had detailed aerial reconnaissance photographs of Auschwitz, taken because the War Department was interested in bombing the German oil factories in the region. They carried out many such bombing raids on the oil sites in that region during the autumn of 1944 and the winter of 1944–1945. George McGovern, the former U.S. senator and 1972 Democratic presidential nominee, piloted a B-24 Liberator in the 455th Bomb Group and took part in one of those raids. The administration rejected Jewish groups' requests to bomb Auschwitz on the grounds that it could not "divert" military resources for other purposes. In a 2004 interview with Israel Television and The David S. Wyman Institute for Holocaust Studies, Senator McGovern said that the

administration's argument was just "a rationalization"; how much of a "diversion" would it have been, when he and other U.S. pilots were already flying over the area?

2. In a dramatic reversal of America's traditional open-doors immigration policy, the Johnson Immigration Act, passed in 1921 and tightened in 1924, stipulated that the number of immigrants from any one country during a given year could not exceed 2 percent of the number of immigrants from that country who had been living in the United States at the time of the 1890 national census. It was aimed especially at immigrants from Eastern and Southern Europe (Jews and Italians, primarily), since most of them had reached America after 1890.

    The annual quota for Germany and Austria was 27,370, and for Poland, just 6,542. Even those meager quota allotments were almost always underfilled, as zealous consular officials implemented the bureaucratic method proposed by senior State Department official Breckinridge Long—in his words, to "postpone and postpone and postpone the granting of the visas." A deliberately designed bureaucratic maze—a series of "paper walls," to borrow the title of Prof. David S. Wyman's 1968 book—ensured most Jewish refugees would remain far from America's shores. Thus during the period of the Nazi genocide, from late 1941 and until early 1945, only 10 percent of the already minuscule quotas from Axis-controlled European countries were actually used. That means almost 190,000 quota places were unused—almost 190,000 lives that could have been saved even under the existing immigration restrictions.

3. Hecht was the best-known Hollywood screenwriter in the 1930s, famous for his work on such blockbuster films as *Gone With the Wind, Scarface,* and *Wuthering Heights.* In the early 1940s, he became a leading activist in the Bergson group, a maverick political action committee that vigorously protested the Allies' failure to aid European Jewish refugees. Hecht authored a number of hard-hitting newspaper advertisements for the group, as well as a major theatrical production, *We Will Never Die,* that raised public awareness of the Holocaust. In the autumn of 1943, the Bergson group's campaign of newspaper ads, rallies, and Capitol Hill lobbying culminated in the introduction of a congressional resolution urging creation of a U.S. government agency to rescue Jews. At about the same time, several senior aides to Treasury Secretary Henry Morgenthau, Jr., discovered that State Department officials had been secretly obstructing rescue opportunities and blocking transmission of Holocaust-related information to the United States. Morgenthau's appeal to the president, combined with the pressure generated in Congress by the Bergson group, convinced FDR, in early 1944, to establish the War Refugee Board, a U.S. government agency to res-

cue refugees from Hitler. It played a major role in the rescue of some 200,000 Jews and 20,000 non-Jews.

CONCLUSION

1.   Henry L. Feingold, *Bearing Witness: How America and Its Jews Responded to the Holocaust* (New York: Syracuse University Press, 1995), p. 64.

ABOUT THE AUTHORS

EDWARD I. KOCH has devoted his life to public service. He has served as a New York City councilman (1967–1968), as a member of the U.S. House of Representatives (1969–1977), and as mayor of New York City (1978–1989). During the years since the conclusion of his mayoralty, Koch has been a television talk show host, national radio commentator, and syndicated columnist. In 2004, he was chosen to lead the United States delegation to the Berlin conference on anti-Semitism, and in 2005, he was named by the president to the U. S. Holocaust Memorial Council, the agency that governs the U.S. Holocaust Memorial Museum in Washington, D.C. His many books include *Mayor* (1984), Politics (1985), *Citizen Koch* (1992), and *I'm Not Done Yet!* (2000).

DR. RAFAEL MEDOFF is director of The David S. Wyman Institute for Holocaust Studies, which focuses on issues related to America's response to the Holocaust (www.Wyman-Institute.org). He has served as associate editor of the scholarly journal *American Jewish History* and is the author of seven books about the Holocaust, Zionism, and the history of American Jewry. His textbook, *Jewish Americans and Political Participation,* was named an "Outstanding Academic Title of 2003" by the American Library Association's *Choice Magazine.* Dr. Medoff has taught Jewish history at Ohio State University, Purchase College of the State University of New York, and elsewhere.

INDEX